P9-EKH-205

THE
MOST DANGEROUS MAN
IN THE WORLD

THE
MOST DANGEROUS MAN
IN THE WORLD

How One Hacker Ended Corporate and
Government Secrecy Forever

ANDREW FOWLER

Skyhorse Publishing

Skyhorse Publishing books may be purchased in bulk at special discounts for sales promotion, corporate gifts, fund-raising, or educational purposes. Special editions can also be created to specifications. For details, contact the Special Sales Department, Skyhorse Publishing, 307 West 36th Street, 11th Floor, New York, NY 10018 or info@skyhorsepublishing.com.

Skyhorse® and Skyhorse Publishing® are registered trademarks of Skyhorse Publishing, Inc.®, a Delaware corporation.

www.skyhorsepublishing.com

Every attempt has been made to locate the copyright holders for material quoted in this book. Any person or organization that may have been overlooked or misattributed may contact the publisher.

Text design by Megan Ellis
Cover design by Phil Campbell
Typeset by Megan Ellis

10 9 8 7 6 5 4 3 2 1

Library of Congress Cataloging-in-Publication Data is available on file.
ISBN: 978-1-61608-489-9

Printed in the United States of America

CONTENTS

INTRODUCTION

The first snow arrived early in London in 2010, dusting Westminster with a white blanket on the morning of 7 December, the sun had broken through grey cloud cover, making life a little more bearable for those who had begun queuing in the street since well before dawn.

Outside the drab, 1970s City of Westminster Magistrates Court the first television crews were setting up behind steel barricades, separated from the passersby who were already hurrying to work. Back home that night, viewers around the world would be entertained and intrigued by the goings-on that would take place there later in the day. A couple of centuries ago, not far from where the courts now stand in Horseferry Road, there were public floggings to keep the crowds amused. Now they gawped at a new kind of entertainment: 24-hour news, and its bottomless appetite for sensation and celebrity.

In Julian Assange they had both. His WikiLeaks organisation had stunned the world with its sensational exposés of leaked material, culminating in 'Cablegate'—thousands of classified diplomatic dispatches from US embassies around the world that gave an extraordinary insight into American foreign policy: from spying on the UN to how Arab nations wanted Washington to bomb Iran. It was the biggest single leak in history.

In the furore that followed there were calls for Assange to be hunted down and even assassinated; in the United States, Vice President Joe Biden had called him a 'high-tech terrorist'. Adding to the clamour, Assange was wanted in Sweden to answer allegations of 'suspected rape and sexual molestation' by two women—resulting in an Interpol arrest warrant for him to be extradited to answer the accusations.

Earlier that morning, Assange's lawyers had phoned to say that he would be handing himself in, at North London's Kentish Town Police Station, an event somewhat quaintly known as 'arrest by appointment'. It was close to the journalists' Frontline Club, where Assange had stayed in Paddington. The club name might suggest it's only for foreign correspondents but its well-stocked bar and convivial atmosphere attract a wide range of members. It says much about the powers of investigative journalism that, despite Assange's appearance at the club to announce one of WikiLeaks' biggest secret document drops, no one thought to look for him there when he was supposedly 'in hiding'.

Understandably concerned about his safety, WikiLeaks had played games with the media, putting out false stories about his whereabouts. One newspaper reported he might be in Abu Dhabi; his media assistant's mobile said she was out of the country. By 9.25 a.m. that same day the games were over and Julian Assange was on his way to a less glamorous location to fight attempts by Sweden to extradite him on the sex allegations.

Though clearly eager to defend himself against the sexual allegations, they weren't Assange and his legal team's principal concern. He was more worried about possible extradition from Sweden to the United States, where the Obama administration was investigating the possibility of prosecuting him for espionage. In raising the likelihood that, charged with spying, Assange could face the death penalty in the United States, his lawyers were pushing his case to the limits.

The journey to court took Assange on a tour past some of WikiLeaks' most powerful targets, down Whitehall and past the Downing Street, once home of former British Prime Minister Tony Blair, who was forced to defend the disclosure that his government had promised to protect US interests during an inquiry into the Iraq war. On the opposite side of the road stood the massive Ministry of Defence headquarters, with its bluff, off-white exterior.

Assange had posted the Ministry of Defence's Manual for Security on the WikiLeaks site. It put journalists in the same category as foreign intelligence services, criminals, terrorist groups and disaffected staff when it came to posing threats to the security of the country. In his present predicament it was hardly a comforting thought. Further south came the imperial neoclassical splendour of Thames House, the home of Britain's counterintelligence organisation MI5. Assange had given them a diplomatic headache by upsetting Britain's oldest ally, the United States, and exposing deception in its prosecution of war. He'd revealed the grim truth about America's invasion of Iraq, exposing potential war crimes, the torturing of Iraqi prisoners and revealing the true number of civilian casualities Washington had so carefully kept from the public. As the MI5 building disappeared in the rear window, the car turned into the court's underground car park. The seven and a half kilometre journey had taken just nineteen minutes. For the next five hours, Assange sat in the bowels of the building in one of the twenty-nine 'holding cells' used for male prisoners about to appear before the court.

At a little after 2 p.m., following a hectic morning dealing with Tube fare-dodgers and traffic infringements, the court was ready for Julian Assange. The man in the neatly pressed dark suit and off-white shirt looked strangely out of place. His pasty face, synonymous with his challenge to authority, had made him one of the most recognisable people in the world. Yet here he was, as far from the freedoms he claimed for others as it was possible to get. In an area looking more like a terrorist's top security pen than a court, Assange stood confined behind the reinforced transparent bars of a small cage in the far corner of the room, whispering through the gaps to talk to his lawyer.

The maximum number of journalists allowed in the court is twenty-five. By the time Julian Assange entered nearly fifty had shoehorned themselves in. Like rival football crowds, the journalists had separated themselves: the reserved dowdy British on one side, the comparatively excitable blond Swedes a good distance away. They'd sparred outside in the corridor about the various rights and wrongs of the Swedish case—neither side letting the facts get in the way of a good argument. The French sat in the middle, clearly delighted by the story of politics, power and sex unfolding in the courtroom.

Assange's legal representative Mark Stephens, in a grey pin-striped suit and dark patterned tie, listened intently as Judge Howard Riddle began Assange's bail hearing for an extradition case not scheduled to start until February 2011. Stephens is known in the trade as a media lawyer. It is not a kind description. There were questions about whether he was wearing more make-up than his sharp-minded and telegenic offsider, Jennifer Robinson, an Australian lawyer who made up for what Stephens lacked in finesse. Behind them sat the supporters, including a solicitor and a high-ranking academic. Never one to miss a good campaign, John Pilger, the Australian journalist whose exposés of government wrongdoing are legendary, listened intently, having earlier given the judge the benefit of his legal assessment. Pilger who, like Assange's other high-profile supporters offered £20 000 (AUD\$31 600) bail, told Judge Riddle in a cadence normally reserved for well-rehearsed TV pieces to camera: 'These charges against him in Sweden are absurd and were judged absurd by a senior Swedish prosecutor.' This was true, but another prosecutor had found that there was a case to answer—which was why Interpol had issued a warrant for his arrest.

Julian Assange, the once obscure Australian computer hacker, had become—through design or default—the biggest cause célèbre of the decade.

So who was this extraordinary individual who now threatened the political and military establishment of the world's most powerful nation? He had no fixed address, often dressed himself in worn-out, second-hand clothes, and travelled the world economy class with just a backpack and a computer. Like a beggar from the Buddhist philosophy he apparently once embraced, Assange repeatedly relies on the WikiLeaks community for sustenance. He developed the unusual habit of turning up at friends' places unannounced and staying for sometimes days on end. 'He'd just come out of nowhere and flop for a few days … then he'd be gone', according to one acquaintance. He'd been known to eat discarded takeaway food, fast going cold, with the question: 'Has everyone finished with this?' On any particular night he would stay with friends who he said loved and cared for him.

Yet he had marshalled hundreds of people around the world to work for WikiLeaks for free—supporting the organisation and its banks of secret computer servers that hosted some of the most sensitive, highly classified information in the world. And he'd done it very quickly. It would be wrong to think that WikiLeaks has been an overnight sensation—it has been a long time in the making. But it is also true that in just four years, WikiLeaks had produced an impressive strike record. At the start, however, its releases had been revelatory, rather than revolutionary.

In its short history, WikiLeaks had attracted serious attention and admiration, in particular from one of the world's most celebrated whistleblowers, Daniel Ellsberg. It was Ellsberg whose dump of classified material in the early 1970s, known as the Pentagon Papers, revealed how repeated US administrations had lied about their conduct of the Vietnam War. Ellsberg had paid a high price for being so outspoken—he was the first person in the US ever to be prosecuted for leaking to the media. And, he points out, the first person to be accused of espionage for 'revealing information to the American public'.

Ellsberg was called The Most Dangerous Man in America by President Nixon's national security advisor, Henry Kissinger. Now Ellsberg, an articulate and energetic seventy-nine years old, was passing on the baton to Assange—and going one step further. He agreed that Assange was a 'good candidate for being the most dangerous man in the world' and he should be 'quite proud of that'. He also had some advice for Assange. He was 'not safe physically wherever he is'.

Ellsberg knew first-hand how unsafe it is to make enemies in high places in Washington. At the height of the Pentagon Papers drama, the Nixon White House sent a CIA-sanctioned hit squad to 'permanently incapacitate' him. There were reports that the Pentagon had drawn together a group of operatives to track Assange down, using the vast array of America's intelligence-gathering and surveillance machinery in an attempt to trap him.

Assange's WikiLeaks' message was simple yet unsettling for his political opponents, and particularly for those who saw his WikiLeaks website as anti-American. The enigmatic Assange strongly believed in the US Constitution's First Amendment that enshrined freedom of speech. 'We are, if you like, enforcing the First Amendment around the world,' he said. The Most Dangerous Man in the World would be campaigning on a platform of free speech for all—a noble, but dangerous course. But then Assange has seldom shied away from danger. His two biggest qualities are 'He stands up for what he believes in' and, as one of his friends confided, 'He enjoys taking risks'.

The problem, in Assange's view, was the veil of secrecy surrounding government: 'The citizenry have a right to scrutinise the state.' But the question of what to publish and what not to publish would be an issue that would return time and again to haunt WikiLeaks as it fought to define itself in the unchartered waters of whistleblowing in cyberspace and journalism.

INTRODUCTION

Much of the debate would settle around WikiLeaks' legitimacy as a media organisation deserving the same privileges as any other, including newspapers, in the way it operates with respect to leaked material and the protection of sources. It's a grey and slippery area for newcomers.

The way WikiLeaks arrived on the world stage in early 2010 proved it was no ordinary media organisation. It posted a leaked video of a US military helicopter killing unarmed civilians in a Baghdad street and provocatively called it 'Collateral Murder'. When we tracked Assange down in Melbourne for an interview for ABC TV's Foreign Correspondent program, he was keen to lay out his views about the old media, much of which he described as 'stillborn'—in other words, dead. He wanted to build a more open relationship with the public where they too, not just the journalists, could see the raw data and make their own decisions.

The gunship video, showing US troops killing unarmed civilians, had been part of that, but the title 'Collateral Murder' drew fierce criticism that WikiLeaks had a hidden agenda. Assange was making steadfast enemies, particularly in the US military. He seemed well aware of that, and moved around and slept in a different house almost every night.

Seven months later he wasn't hiding out anymore, but living in a friend's English country mansion in Norfolk—confined and under surveillance and curfew as part of his bail conditions while he waited for the Swedish extradition hearings to start. As we sat eating quiche and drinking tea in the kitchen of the rambling manor, the editor-in-chief of WikiLeaks had the air of an exiled country squire. A few hours earlier, outside the local police station Assange attended as part of his bail conditions, he had been asked whether he thought his life would ever return to normal. 'I hope not,' he replied. Julian Assange wasn't embracing the trappings of wealthy living, but relishing the difference he believed he had already made to the world and to journalism.

It was shaping up to be an extraordinary struggle that would determine the parameters of freedom of speech in the years and decades to come.

1

FATAL ATTRACTION

Magnetic Island, off the north-east Queensland coast, is about as far away from Melbourne as you can get without leaving the country. Named by Captain Cook, who believed the island distorted his ship's compass readings, it now has another kind of attraction: it's where people go to retire, as well as a popular destination for holiday-makers looking to escape the blistering heat of Australia's summers. It also attracts artists and travellers who revel in its beauty and tranquillity.

It was to Magnetic Island that Christine Assange, an artist, made her way in 1971. She'd just given birth to her son Julian at the local hospital in Townsville back on the mainland. Known as the capital of northern Queensland, it is in fact a big country town. Its biggest claim to fame is that for many years it was home to Australian golfing legend, Greg Norman. As Christine made her way on to the ferry wharf, she must have wondered what life had in store for her and her newborn boy. There was no husband in tow. The two of them were on their own.

As a nonconformist Christine was used to coping by herself. She'd had a tempestuous relationship with her father, and has been described as 'very strong-willed'. At one time in an act of defiance she burned her school books—which, considering she was the daughter of a college principal, was clearly designed to have maximum impact.

By all accounts Christine's father, Warren Hawkins, was a strict disciplinarian at the college and was probably not much different with his family. He is remembered by one person who worked with him as a 'staunch traditionalist'. In the early 1970s, when she was seventeen, Christine ran away from home, having bought a motorcycle and a tent with the profits she made from selling her paintings. In Sydney, she joined a thriving counterculture community where she fell in love with a 'rebellious young man' she met at an anti-Vietnam War demonstration. His name was John Shipton. But the relationship didn't last long and a few months later she was heading back north, pregnant and single. Shipton would re-enter Julian Assange's life much later as a supporter.

Now as the ferry turned north-east and headed out into the seven-kilometre channel that separates Magnetic Island from mainland Australia, Christine prepared for their first night on the idyllic island. She'd managed to rent a cottage for $12 a week at Picnic Point, on the island's southern shore, just metres from the water.

Not much has changed along the palm-lined bay where Julian spent his first few months. It's like a time capsule of a bygone era of Australia: quiet, open roads and quarter-acre blocks. It's always been this way. Such is the pace of life on Magnetic Island that it's still a matter of heated debate there whether or not Christine Assange shot a taipan snake as it nestled on Julian's bed.

Even in his first months of life, Christine saw there was something special about Julian. She would hang intricately woven scarves across his pram so he could look at them, and Christine says he was fascinated by the patterns—he seemed to be unpicking them in his brain. Not far from where Julian and his mother lived, it's possible to gain a glimpse into their past, in the visitor book of the local cultural centre and museum. Christine left a note in there in a firm, elegant hand. She wrote that she lived 'in a bikini' and was 'going native with my baby and other mums on the island'.

Luckily, their nearby house had been built to withstand the massive tropical storms that intermittently hammer the coastline of northern Queensland. On Christmas Eve 1971, Cyclone Althea roared in from the Pacific, producing winds in excess of 200 kilometres an hour. The house survived the battering, which damaged or demolished 90 per cent of other homes on the island.

Five years later, Christine and her young son returned to Magnetic Island with someone she describes as a 'new husband' of three years, Brett Assange—a fellow artist. Together they had travelled around Australia with Christine's puppetry company, spending much of their time 'in Lismore and the Adelaide Hills'. Julian attended many schools—thirty-seven he says. His mother says that although he's super smart, he does get muddled at times—the number of schools was in fact thirteen. At one point they rented a house on an abandoned pineapple farm in Horseshoe Bay at the northern end of Magnetic Island, where they had to 'slash [their] way to the front door with a machete.'

For the rebellious Christine, Julian's upbringing was consistent with her view that formal education could instil an unhealthy respect for authority. Julian seemed to thrive. For a boy his age he showed an extraordinary interest in mathematics and even philosophy—remarkable for an eight-year-old. He devoured dozens of books on the subjects. One of his distant relatives in Lismore is quoted as saying, apparently without a sense of the obvious: 'He was a geeky, smart kid.' Even at such a young age Julian gave an early indication of what lay ahead for him. His stepfather, Brett Assange, remembers, 'He always stood up for the underdog'. He had a very good sense of equality and equity and was 'very angry about people ganging up on other people'.

Julian Assange says he was happy with the peripatetic life. 'We were travelling and touring around many different places, so this was quite a rich environment.' He particularly enjoyed the country: 'I was living like a Tom Sawyer.' He built his own raft, 'had other boys steal it and reclaim it'. He also had his own horse. 'I have no complaints at all about this part of my childhood,' he told me.

The principal of the Lismore school Assange attended said he is not surprised that Julian Assange was a former pupil. 'We try to develop free thinkers and people of independent thought here and Julian would be the ultimate example of that,' he said.

In 1979, Christine and Brett Assange separated. She moved to Lismore and met up with a musician, Keith Hamilton. They had a son, but by 1982 the relationship had broken down.

Christine became involved in a ferocious custody battle and fled to her old haunt, Magnetic Island, with her two boys. Seeking safe sanctuary in Picnic Bay, she rented an apartment on The Esplanade overlooking the flat, sandy beach and remarkably clear azure sea. But the sanctuary didn't last long.

Julian says he remembers 'having to move very suddenly' to avoid detection by Hamilton. For the next five years, Christine and her two sons played a tormented game of hide and seek across Australia. The old days of moving around the countryside began again, but this journey had a very different flavour from the earlier happy-go-lucky odyssey. Just who Keith Hamilton was is still not clear. Julian says he understood during their days in hiding that he was the son of a notorious cult leader, Anne Hamilton-Byrne.

* * *

Anne Hamilton-Byrne led a secretive sect that called itself The Family, or The Great White Brotherhood. At one time she had twenty-eight children. Some of them were hers but most had been adopted, a number of them through false papers. From what has been learned about the sect it would be safe to say that what it did was as close to evil as it's possible to be.

Hamilton-Byrne was certainly delusional. Not content with being the 'reincarnation of Jesus Christ' she suggested she was related to French aristocracy. Her elegant clothes and long flowing hair meant she may have looked the part but, like a great deal of her life, it was built on fantasy.

Anne Hamilton-Byrne was in fact Evelyn Edwards, one of seven children born to a railway engine cleaner in Sale, Victoria. It appears her family had a history of mental illness. Her mother was known for setting fire to her hair and talking to the dead. Other relatives were institutionalised and her aunt suffered from psychiatric problems, too.

In the 1960s Anne Hamilton-Byrne developed an interest in Hatha Yoga, and for a while she taught it in Melbourne. By all accounts the business worked well. Exactly how she started The Family isn't clear, but like many sects this one had a benign beginning. Its first meetings were held on a property near Ferntree Gully west of Melbourne, owned by the then head of Queen's College at Melbourne University, Dr Raynor Johnson.

Perhaps Johnson chose the area to settle because it reminded him of his north of England birthplace. Ferntree Gully, with its European-style gardens, is famous for its lack of native vegetation. At between 400 and 500 metres above sea level, it is also one of the wettest suburbs of Melbourne. However, the house had one major benefit— its remoteness from prying eyes.

After retiring from Melbourne University, Johnson began giving lectures to discuss the problems of human spirituality. How he got the crowds in is difficult to imagine, with lectures called 'The Macrocosm and the Microcosm', but he did. It was said Dr Johnson's goal was to 'understand the meaning of life' and that 'he was always ready to help others in their quest'. These lectures are possibly where Hamilton-Byrne got to hear about him, or it might have been because Hamilton-Byrne's second husband worked for Johnson as a gardener. According to one of Hamilton-Byrne's 'children', she apparently turned up on Johnson's doorstep one Sunday and soon after, the Family was born.

Its recruits came from a broad section of the community: lawyers, teachers, nurses and doctors swelled the ranks. A particularly strong recruiting ground turned out to be Newhaven private psychiatric hospital in the Melbourne suburb of Kew. The owner was a member of the cult and Anne Hamilton-Byrne was given a place on the board. Patients, often at their most vulnerable, were given experimental treatment as they struggled with their psychiatric illnesses. The treatment included heavy doses of LSD—a drug much favoured by Hamilton-Byrne. The hospital proved to be a highly successful recruitment for the Family.

Hamilton-Byrne bought land next door, naming it after the Johnson's property Sentiniken Park—Hindu for 'Peaceful Abode'. She also splashed out a sizeable sum of money for a home on the shores of Lake Eildon. The drive there, along winding roads and through kilometres of rocky and forested countryside, takes about three and a half hours. But every year thousands of holidaymakers believe it's worth the trip, as they head out of Melbourne eager to enjoy the camping grounds and the fresh mountain air of the Dandenong Ranges. Set in acres of wooded bushland the house would have made a perfect holiday retreat. But the double-storey, wood-panelled home with panoramic views of the lake would instead be used for hiding children, and much worse.

In Hamilton-Byrne's mind they were a happy family. The children were dressed alike and had their hair dyed blonde, reinforcing the impression that they were all related. As Victorian police officer Lex De Man (who later investigated the sect) told the Australian *Sixty Minutes* program: 'Bleached blonde hair, singing like the Von Trapp family, living out Anne's fantasy of—in her thoughts, I'm sure—it was something like an Aryan race. Horrific.'

As holiday-makers just a few hundred metres away enjoyed life on the lake, there was no joy for the children. Instead, they were subjected to sadistic attacks. For wetting their beds they were beaten unmercifully with a collection of instruments—pieces of wood with nails and canes specially designed to cut the skin. Sometimes the children were hit in front of the others as a warning. In her book *Unseen, Unheard, Unknown* (the sect's motto) Sarah Hamilton-Byrne, taken from her mother at birth, says: 'We watched them trying to stifle their sobs, trying to be brave. And then, almost inevitably, we watched them break down, howling and screaming for mercy.' For failing to do a menial task, or for too much weight gain, they were starved; forced to 'miss' several meals at a time. A word out of place could mean being sent outside to sleep on the ground in sometimes freezing temperatures.

Yet what the children feared most was something that many cultures celebrate—puberty. They knew that they would be subjected to horrific experiments. Locked in a dark room they were forced to take LSD while Hamilton-Byrne and psychiatrists or doctors who were members of the sect looked on. There they humiliated the children as they struggled to deal with the effects of the hallucinogenic drug, which Anne Hamilton-Byrne said would 'cleanse their spirit'.

Sometimes Hamilton-Byrne targeted 'special qualities' which she called 'blocks' to enlightenment. The children were supposed to 'look at' these and 'work on' them while under the influence of the drug. The effect was terrifying for a fourteen-year-old. Sarah remembers examining her hands in the dimness of the room. 'They were shining and then the skin seemed to writhe and crawl off my hands like it had become maggots feeding on a corpse.' Through this drug-induced haze, 'Anne appeared God-like' and even 'said she was Jesus Christ'.

In her twisted logic, Hamilton-Byrne told them the discipline would make them into better human beings. Instead it turned them into tragic and terrified individuals fearful of the world—and psychologically damaged. Only in the past few years have some of the children, now adults, managed to speak about what happened. Little wonder it's taken them so much time. When they went to the police all those years ago no one believed their stories. They were returned to the Eildon Lake house, and severely beaten. In 1987 police raided the house, but by then Hamilton-Byrne and her husband had fled. For the next six years they stayed one step ahead of the law as agencies from Australia, the United States and Great Britain tried to track them down. Eventually they were arrested by the FBI, hiding out in a Midwest American town, traced after making phone calls to Australia. Extradited to Melbourne they were charged with conspiracy to defraud, perjury and falsely registering the births of unrelated children as their own triplets. The Hamilton-Byrnes pleaded guilty to the lesser charges and were fined a paltry $5000. They were never charged with child abuse, according to Lex De Man, because the victims were 'so damaged they would never have been able to withstand cross-examination in the witness box'.

The Assange family escaped the devastating impact of The Family. Assange said neither he, nor his mother or half-brother, had ever been involved in the cult. Christine said she could not be completely sure Hamilton was a member of The Family, but he behaved very oddly at times, dyed his hair blond and bore a striking resemblance to Anne Hamilton-Byrne before 'she had her face lift'. Keith Hamilton had also used the surname Meynel—the same name as Hamilton-Byrne's supposed favourite poet, Alice Meynel. For Christine, that was more than enough evidence.

During the period they hid, Assange said he was told Hamilton used several different identities. They were forced to change their hiding place, sometimes very suddenly. He says he believed The Family had a large network of people and they 'always managed to find out where we were'. But the Assange family managed to stay ahead in the chase.

One of many houses Christine rented while they were on the run happened to be across the road from an electronics shop. At just eleven years old, Assange was already showing extraordinary mathematical capabilities. He would go to the shop and write programs on its Commodore 64. One of the first mass-produced computers, the Commodore 64 was the model T Ford of its day. He sharpened his skills, unravelling well-known programs and discovering how they were written. Encouraging her son's extraordinary capabilities, Christine bought the computer for him. The price of nearly $600 might not be much in today's money, but back then it was several weeks' wages. Such was the cost of this computer that Christine had to move the family to cheaper accommodation to pay for it. It was a sacrifice that would have far-reaching effects, something they never could have envisaged as the single mother and her two boys continued their nomadic existence.

Assange had a searing intellect that set him apart from most children. He gave an insight into that life on his blog IQ.org (an eclectic collection of political musings and aphorisms), citing findings that 'children with IQs up to 150 get along in the ordinary course of school life quite well, achieving excellent marks without serious effort'. But children who rose above an IQ of 170 were liable to regard school with indifference or with positive dislike. Assange had an IQ 'in excess of 170' according to a friend. Christine said she understood very well the problems Julian faced as a child with a 'high level of genius'. He got easily bored and when he suffered from an illness similar to glandular fever she took the opportunity of taking him out of school. For eighteen months he was home-schooled by specialist teachers. His academic life took off. By the time he returned to school he had taught himself machine code—a computer programming language.

Over the next few years after high school Assange became more closely drawn to the subterranean culture spawned by the dawn of the computer age. It allowed him to interact with the outside world, without having to personally engage with those he contacted. It was reminiscent of his high school days where Assange's bookishness earned him the title 'The Prof' among his contemporaries. He said he liked learning 'and telling people what I learnt' so The Prof was 'a kind of natural label to use'. Assange wrote of himself and a teenage friend: 'We were bright sensitive kids who didn't fit into the dominant subculture and fiercely castigated those who did as irredeemable boneheads.'

In 1987 Assange added the equivalent of mag wheels and a hotted-up engine to his computer. A modem transformed it from a machine that mainly played games to a supercharged device that could link directly to other computers. The World Wide Web, and the Internet didn't exist then—but computer networks and telecom systems were already connected in a little known subterranean system. And Assange desperately wanted to find the key that would let him in. By the age of sixteen, Julian, his mother and half-brother were living on the outskirts of Melbourne. The town of Emerald, forty kilometres south-east of Melbourne, was a perfect place for an artist like Christine. Famed for its steam train, Puffing Billy, which carries thousands of tourists on a gentle journey along the twisting tracks from Emerald, over picturesque bridges spanning idyllic valleys to Belgrave, it is also home to a vibrant theatre community.

While Christine continued her artistic work, Julian would head to his room—and his computer. He had teamed up with two other teenagers just as obsessed by the exciting new world of computerisation, and more importantly, with hacking. They sent simple messages to each other's computers and talked about expanding their knowledge. Back then hackers were seen as oddities in society, certainly not the major threat they are today. Not wanting the world to mistake them for wimpy nerds they would call themselves The International Subversives.

Though they didn't realise it at the time, Melbourne would provide just what The International Subversives needed. It wasn't just, as Assange half-jokingly pointed out to me, 'The weather and the beaches were bad and that's what kept people indoors'. There were other more serious reasons. Melbourne is seen as the intellectual capital of Australia, as well as the centre of a collectivist culture and politically active community. But there was something else far more prosaic that made this group of Australians among world leaders in the art of computer hacking.

Back in those days, high-speed cables and wireless were still twenty years away. The hackers connected to each other in the same way Graham Bell did when he made his first phone call, by a pair of copper wires. What set Australia apart from many other nations was the fact that local phone calls were cheap. And better than that, the price was fixed. For just a few cents you could have the connection between several computers open for days on end. It didn't matter if they were in different cities or even different states—the cost would still be the price of a local call.

As Assange points out, people using computers in other countries were 'paying [for] every second'. In Australia, the cheap local calls provided the perfect environment for The International Subversives 'to develop their skills and training without paying for it'.

They didn't just talk to each other; they picked the brains of the best and brightest to help them better understand the fast-developing electronic world around them. They used what were known as BBS—bulletin boards to post messages for anyone to read. The BBS was likened to a community information board outside the local town hall, where passersby could read what was posted, or add their own comments.

For the group, the title 'International' caused its biggest challenge. It's relatively easy to be a local subversive, but if they were going to be true to their name they would have to make it overseas—which effectively meant in the United States. Assange remembers: 'Back then there was no Internet. [It] was just in an embryonic pre-Internet stage. There was Internet in the United States but [it was] not connected to Australia.'

First they had to find a way to add a considerable amount of grunt to their still somewhat puny computer systems. The easiest way to get more power back then was to piggyback on another computer. There were a couple of easy options: one was just down the road— the Royal Melbourne Institute of Technology (RMIT). An imposing institution, it had been among the first to embrace the beginnings of computerisation. Students were given their own accounts and access codes, which enabled them to hack into the RMIT mainframe. The International Subversives didn't do any damage, they just wandered around to see what was there. But then they started using their RMIT accounts to attack other institutions.

Four hundred kilometres north of Melbourne, Canberra is home to the Australian National University (ANU). Set amid sprawling grounds, it was established to provide Australia's federal administration and government with a local intellectual hub to draw on. As a university heavily driven by research, it demanded and got some of the best computers at the dawn of the Internet age that could crunch numbers and information faster than anything else on earth. Naturally enough, Assange and the International Subversives were keen on getting inside, and not just to look around.

In Melbourne the Australian Federal Police (AFP) had been tipped off about the activities of The International Subversives. They had no idea who they were but they knew what these hackers were after. They wanted processing power to further their ability of getting into other computer systems. And that is exactly what the ANU computer could give them. Ken Day understood the problem only too well. He'd been commissioned to set up the Australian Federal Police Computer Crime Investigation Unit. Under-resourced at the start, he'd resorted to using superseded computers that a local bank had destined for the rubbish tip. 'We just had to make do with what we could get our hands on,' he says. 'Computer crime back then wasn't seen as being sexy or worth spending money on.'

FATAL ATTRACTION

When Assange and the others broke into the ANU computer system, their elation at having cracked the code must have been tempered by the discovery that, despite its lack of resources, the AFP was on their tail. As Day put it: 'We were watching them watching us.'

Assange was now nineteen years old and had moved out of home to live with his girlfriend. They soon had a son, Daniel, but Assange still found time for The International Subversives. The group started a magazine under the same name, which was solely distributed to contributors.

* * *

The Lonsdale Telephone Exchange in the centre of Melbourne, with its black marbled façade, is an eye-catching building. In the late 1980s it was a gateway to other telephone exchanges and organisations linked to super computers around the world. One of the hackers who knew Assange describes breaking into the network as being like a shipwrecked man washed ashore on a Tahitian island populated by 11 000 virgins just ripe for the picking. But first they had to do it. And, of course, not get caught. They were motivated by the desire to gain knowledge and prove themselves against the best systems in the world. But The International Subversives were also bound by a code of ethics: nothing was to be altered in any of the data they saw and everything had to be put back exactly the way they found it. The International Subversives called it ethical hacking.

In the underground world of hackers everyone has a nom de guerre. Assange called himself Mendax. The *New Yorker* claims Assange took the name from the Roman poet Horace's 'splendide mendax', or 'nobly untruthful'. But it's just as likely he named himself after the 1920s Australian science-fiction writer Erle Cox's Major Mendax, an eccentric inventor. Mendax experimented with 'matter transmission', 'invisibility' and 'extracting gold from seawater'—an alchemy that might have delighted the teenage Assange. For Major Mendax the experiments never quite worked out. For Julian Assange it was just the opposite.

Just how Mendax broke into the Lonsdale Exchange is covered in the book *Underground* by Suelette Dreyfus and its co-author and researcher, Julian Assange, published in 1997. It required a lot of guile and intelligence, as well as a huge amount of nerve. When Assange, thinly disguised as 'Mendax', tried to dial in to the Exchange on a phone line with his computer, the Exchange at first refused to accept his connection. Assange was confronted by a blank screen. He tried again, but still no response. After several minutes he made it to the next stage, but he was unable to log in. To trick it, he entered the command 'log out'. The Lonsdale Exchange failed to accept his command. 'Not logged in,' it said. So Assange deduced: 'I have to type in log *in*, not log on.' He was right. In he went.

It asked for a username and password. Again Assange's deductive reasoning gave him a head start over the computer he was trying to outwit. Assange knew that Telecom was dealing with the giant Canadian telecommunications provider Nortel. It stood to reason that their technicians would have to have access—and the username and password would have to be straightforward and easy to remember.

Nortel?

Nortel.

He was in.

The problem was that the telephone switch had a strange language, and without an interpreter Assange was like a man in a foreign bar trying to order a complicated cocktail. Drefyus tells us what happened next:

> [Assange] wanted something innocuous, which wouldn't screw up the 1000 lines permanently. It was almost 7 a.m. and he needed to wrap things up before Telecom employees began coming into work. 'RING' seemed harmless enough. He typed the command in. Nothing happened. Then a few full stops began to slowly spread across his screen: …'RUNG'.

The system had just rung all 1000 numbers at the same time. One thousand phones ringing all at once. Assange decided he'd had enough. He'd got in to the Exchange and in to its mainframe computer. He unplugged the computer and relaxed.

But it wasn't long before Julian Assange and another member of The International Subversives were back. Once in, they headed straight for Nortel. Inside there were more than 11 000 computers all linked to each other around the world. The computer system had been heavily firewalled against Internet intrusion, but inside there was virtually no security. By coming in the 'back door' via a Telecom phone line, The International Subversives were free to roam around one of the biggest and most powerful networks in the world. And that's exactly what they did, from the Nortel site in Melbourne's St Kilda Road, to the company's headquarters in Toronto.

As the AFP team tried to keep track, Day knew how significant the break-ins were becoming: 'They were into the core systems, the heart of our comms, and so if you ever wanted to pick a pivotal place where we're vulnerable, back then that was it.'

What Nortel gave the Melbourne hackers was the key to the world they didn't particularly like. The late 1980s was a time when the two Superpowers—the USSR and the United States—faced off in a game of nuclear high noon. Every Easter millions of people around the world marched in the streets to demonstrate their opposition to nuclear weapons. Melbourne always guaranteed a big turnout. The hackers were developing another way of demonstrating their opposition; as Assange told me, it was an 'extremely educational experience that you were able to do a little bit about the things that were pissing you off'.

Using a program written by Assange, they hacked into dozens of top-secret US military installations through Nortel, including the US Air Force, the aerospace company Lockheed Martin, the US Naval Undersea Warfare Engineering Station, and TRW Redondo Beach California, the top satellite communications organisation where Christopher Boyce had worked. He was jailed for selling classified documents to the Soviet Union and claimed he had seen evidence of CIA covert operations against the Whitlam Labor Government in the 1970s.

But what seemed to drive the hackers most was the fear of nuclear war, and they wanted to get their message across. While living on the outskirts of Melbourne, Assange vividly recalls the siren from the local fire brigade sounding like 'the start of World War Three'. In his sleep he would 'be dreaming that everything was going, going to be ash'.

FATAL ATTRACTION

Assange managed to make his way deep inside the computer system of the Los Alamos nuclear research site in the US state of New Mexico—one of the most highly secure places on earth—without being detected, again through Nortel. He says they were moving through the installation 'at high speed', which he describes as being like 'trophy hunting'; the fact it gave you bragging rights was important. He dismisses that he did anything dangerous by breaking in because the computers were 'air gapped', which means the ones that were linked to very sensitive nuclear operations could not be accessed from the outside. 'We were not blind fools on the keyboard.' He claimed that they were bound by 'ethical codes and ethical standards', ideologies they pushed strongly in the Melbourne hacker community—the most important thing was to do no harm.

As they trawled through the most secret and sensitive sites in the US, what amazed Assange was the discovery of 'a backdoor' to the US military national security coordination centre—an area that is supposed to keep US computer systems and installations secure. 'We had total control,' he says. He could scroll through the list of reports about 'a suspected break-in' from anywhere, 'a US base in Greece or any country'. All the attacks 'would be reported back to this machine'. What Assange found most disturbing was that the 'US military had its own computer hackers' who were using the national coordination centre for 'target practice'. Assange believed hackers should be anarchists, not working for the military.

What happened in October 1989 would be an act of anarchy that was hard to beat. It gave the US a fright and it thumped home hard an anti-nuclear message with a distinctly Australian flavour.

* * *

The weather at the Kennedy Space Centre in Florida had been unsettled for some days, with squalling rain and high winds. Still smarting from the destruction of the Challenger mission a few years earlier with the loss of all on board, NASA didn't want a repeat performance when it launched its Galileo probe. There had been several delays, but now the weather was clear. As hundreds of NASA staff across the United States turned up for work and turned on their computers, all was not well. Instead of the normal screen saver with the NASA logo, a rude sign popped up across their terminals: Your Computer Has Been Wanked.

The US workers apparently had no idea what the word wanked meant. If they had they might have suspected where the message came from. If they'd looked at the bottom of their screens they may have read: 'You talk of times of peace for all, and then prepare for war.' Followed by the word: 'oilz'. But just as they hadn't known what wanked meant, they were equally oblivious to the Australian rock band Midnight Oil, nicknamed 'The Oilz', and its anti-nuclear and anti-military lyrics.

The computers were telling their users—who were, by now, nearly hysterical—that all their confidential and top-secret files were being deleted. Each time the operator pushed the command button to retake control of the computer, the message 'Delete, Delete, Delete' showed up instead. Ron Tencati, head of NASA cyber security, wrestled to deal with the flood of panicked staff. The Galileo probe was heading for a mission to Saturn, powered by a plutonium engine—not the first time that nuclear fuel had been used to give missions extra reach. As well as going further than any other probe to the outer edge of the solar system, it would also pass very close to the earth before it started its journey.

'We had a shuttle on the launch pad about to launch that had plutonium energy canisters for its power source. If this blew up like the Challenger did, all of this plutonium was going to kill everybody in Florida,' he pointed out. You didn't have to be a genius to work out what Worms Against Nuclear Killers meant.

Eventually, the launch took place, with great applause and even more relief at mission control. As the NASA staff returned to their desks they discovered none of their files had been deleted. It had been a hoax. Even so, Tencati says he's not exaggerating when he describes the attack at the time as feeling like 'an electronic Pearl Harbour'.

NASA began trying to unpick the course the worm had taken and the provenance of the attack. After days of analysis they had the country: France. But French intelligence officials working feverishly on the case at the headquarters of the Directorate Securite Territoire (DST), were not convinced. Sure it had passed through France on its way to NASA. But exactly where had it originated? Days later, they had the answer: Nortel, the very company that provided the hardware and infrastructure for Telecom Australia.

Although nobody was ever charged with the Wank Worm attack, Assange admits it came from the Melbourne hacker group. But he is coy about the involvement of The International Subversives. No one knows who wrote the program for the worm, he maintains.

Meanwhile, the challenge of trying to balance his life as an international hacker and a father took a big toll on Assange. By 1991 his world was coming apart. His wife walked out on him, taking their son with her. Their break-up was acrimonious and it devastated Assange. He had trouble coping. By all accounts, Assange fell into a deep depression. He'd even stopped using his prized computer. And, just as importantly, he'd started to become careless, leaving his hacker's library of computer disks, containing user-lists, encrypted passwords, and telephone numbers, scattered on the floor. By now he knew that the Federal Police were tracking The International Subversives' every move. He'd read an email to that effect while he was rifling through the computers at the ANU. There was no evidence that Assange wanted to be found out, but he was certainly acting as though he did. On 29 October 1991 there was a loud knock at the door. It was the AFP's Ken Day, flanked by several police officers.

'I'm Ken Day. I believe you've been expecting me.' Day says he can't remember what Assange said in reply, but Assange says it was something like: 'Aren't you too short to be a cop?'

Assange was wrestling with the classic dichotomy of a hacker's personality. He needed to be anonymous, to 'fly below the radar' as Day described it. But at the same time Assange sought recognition within the hacking community of 'being the best' to feed his own ego. Aware that the AFP was closing in, he still couldn't resist talking on the phone to other hackers about his exploits—and the AFP had been listening to every word.

It was a strong indicator of the way Assange would behave in the years to come.

2

CYPHERPUNKS

Having the federal police burst in the door and discover enough criminal evidence to lock you away for ten years would have a big impact on most people, but not on Julian Assange. If anyone believed Assange was going to slip back into a quiet life after being arrested, they were gravely mistaken. Even with the AFP still digging into many of his underground hacking ventures, Assange continued to live life on the edge.

Among fellow hackers, his tangle with the authorities had turned him into a minor star. He signed his communications as 'The Prof' and such was Assange's recognised ability, he'd managed to position himself at the forefront of the struggle over the direction of the Internet. Some saw only its commercial opportunities—that millions of dollars could be made. Many others, including Assange, stood for an open and free system, where collective action and community benefit always came before cash.

From his home in suburban Melbourne, Julian Assange linked up with kindred spirits around the world. They called themselves the Cypherpunks, a pun on the words cipher, the art of encryption, and punk. The name was created by a computer programmer who had been a member of what she described as 'a lefto-revolutionist programming commune' in Berkley, California, which built the first public online computer system in the 1970s. The Cypherpunks were an elite club of hackers, mathematicians, nonconformists and activists. Their manifesto firmly wedded them to the notion that an individual's right to 'privacy is necessary for an open society in the electronic age'. They believed they could not 'expect governments, corporations, or other large, faceless organisations to grant us privacy'.

The Cypherpunks were among the first to use a new system of communication that would later be acclaimed as the precursor of ideas like Facebook and other social networking sites. Instead of having to post individual messages on a noticeboard, a system called Usernet allowed its users to 'talk' to many people at the same time.

Assange operated one of the Usernet first chat rooms. 'Suburbia' which became famous as an open forum for new ideas, a place where anyone from anywhere in the world could speak their mind. The recurring topics focused on attempts by the government to control free speech, the possibility of nuclear war, the role of US military bases overseas, and how to crack computer encryption codes.

But of greatest interest to Assange at this time were plans by the underground computer community to target the controversial Church of Scientology, which teaches its members that human beings are immortal aliens trapped on earth in a human body. Scientology had recently clocked up a victory over Melbourne radio station 3RRR, forcing it to make an on-air apology for 'gratuitously vilifying' it. Around the world it was the same story: the Church of Scientology was taking legal action against everyone—from former members who revealed its inner workings and beliefs, to journalists and news organisations.

For Assange and the other Melbourne hackers, Scientology embodied everything they stood against: a rigidly conformist and opaque organisation that exercised great power over what its members said, thought and did. It had recruited powerful and influential people to its ranks, particularly the rich and famous who might attract others. The Church seemed perfect for the 'me' generation; it not only guaranteed immortal spiritual life and made you feel good, for a price it taught you how to have power over others. Assange aired his views to his friends, and anyone else who was plugged in to his bulletin board. 'What you have then is a Church based on brainwashing yuppies and other people with more money than sense,' Assange wrote. 'If Nicole Kidman, Kate Ceberano, John Travolta, Bruce Willis, Demi Moore and Tom Cruise want to spend their fortunes on learning that the earth is in reality the destroyed prison colony of aliens from out of space then so be it. However, money brings power and attracts the corrupt.'

He soon received a call. When the phone rang on Assange's silent number he might have expected an intelligence agency to be on the other end. Instead the voice he heard belonged to a private investigator working on behalf of the Church of Scientology. The Church was particularly interested in David Gerard, one of Assange's friends. Gerard ran his own chat room, encouraging open debate about alternative religions. When an ex-Scientologist confirmed during one discussion that it was part of 'secret Scientology scripture' to try to communicate with plants, the Church took him to court bizarrely for 'copyright violation'. His house was raided and his computer taken away.

The private investigator asked Assange how long Gerard had had an account with 'Suburbia'? Assange refused to hand over any information. Instead he tipped off Gerard—and posted a call to arms. 'The fight against the Church is far more than the Net vs a bunch of wackos with too much money. It is about corporate suppression of the Internet and free speech,' Assange posted on his site. The Internet, he argued posed the greatest threat to Scientology in that it was, by its very nature, 'a censorship-free zone'. He wrote that 'censorship, concealment and revelation (for a fee) is the Church's raison d'etre'.

How Assange tackled Scientology provided an insight into his ability to transfer his mathematical logic to a political cause. He warned that 'the precedents the Church sets today' would become the 'weapons of corporate tyranny tomorrow'. If ever there was a cause célèbre for underground hackers, the Church of Scientology provided the perfect target. Its former four-storey building, worth millions, fronted on to Russell Street, one of Melbourne's tree-lined boulevards. Assange saw it in stark terms. 'It is about ... the big and rich versus the small and smart.' He called up his Cypherpunk mates for a demonstration on the following weekend, outside the building in the centre of the city.

Saturday 16 March 1996 produced a near perfect day. Overnight rain had given way to a few showers, leaving the city's buildings bathed in the watery glow of the autumn sun. Only eleven people turned up, carrying placards that read 'Hands Off the Internet' and Scientology 'Suppresses Free Speech'. The fact that Scientology's officers—on guard outside the building, watching and filming—almost outnumbered the demonstrators was an indicator that the battles over freedom of speech had already shifted ground.

In future they wouldn't be played out on the streets. They would be fought on the disputed territory itself—in the electronic world of cyberspace. It would certainly give the underground activists the home team advantage. But they knew if they weren't smart they stood a good chance of getting caught. The Church had already won several court cases by what Assange called 'its manipulation of the legal system'. Computer networks had been 'seized' and operators 'forced to reveal their users' personal details'. In the end the Church managed to silence the Cypherpunks by their aggressive legal actions, as they had with other opponents.

Meanwhile, the Cypherpunks started building up an armoury. Assange began creating free software to make the now emerging Internet more accessible for all, and developed systems to wage cyber warfare against his enemies. Just a few months earlier, he had created an extraordinary device capable of scanning hundreds of thousands of computers at any one time to find their weaknesses. It was called a Strobe port scanner, and once a connection point or 'port' was discovered without sufficient protection to stop intruders, it was like an open door—anyone could walk in. Once inside, a skilled hacker could read emails, bank statements, passwords and keys to other computers. All the most sophisticated defences of governments and big companies were vulnerable to one weak entry point. Millions of dollars spent on securing computers and ensuring high-level encrypted passwords would be useless if a 'port' was poorly guarded. It was just like a huge mansion equipped with the most sophisticated security—everything double-locked and barred—but the bathroom window left open. Strobe could also be used by a company to test its own defences against its vulnerability to attack, but no one took that as a serious reason for its creation.

Assange and the Cypherpunks prepared to target governments around the world—communist or capitalist, it made no difference. The big advance in technology at the time involved low earth-orbiting satellites, known as Leos. Governments like China, which strictly controlled everything its population heard and saw, were particularly vulnerable. As Assange pointed out, it was very difficult to 'build a firewall against satellites'. But there were other systems of control that China wasn't alone in using. Both the United States and Australia banned reception from satellites on 'non-government-approved frequencies'. In the last few years, he told the other Cypherpunks that 'oppressive governments' had controlled the possession of everything, from short-wave receivers to computer printers. Even typewriters in Iraq had to be registered, and the government had to be supplied with an example of how the machine printed, creating a kind of mechanical fingerprint. It wasn't difficult to imagine that governments would try to register and regulate the possession of modems, the electronic gateway that connected early computers to the emerging Internet.

* * *

June 1996 was a particularly humid and unsettled month in Washington. The US capital had recently been hit by floods, thunderstorms and power blackouts. As Phil Zimmerman, a genial, bearded computer programmer, made his way towards the Capitol for a special Senate committee hearing investigating the use of encryption, it wasn't just the weather that was depressing him. The FBI was investigating Zimmerman because he'd developed a public version of a system that would allow all text sent by email to be heavily encrypted. It was doubtful even the biggest code-breakers in the world, just up the road from Washington at the National Security Agency (NSA), could read this kind of encrypted material. Zimmerman called his encryption system Pretty Good Privacy, or PGP. For the underground activists it was more than that—it was a fantastic tool to protect civil liberties against the state and corporations.

For nearly a decade they'd been suspicious that the NSA, which was responsible for the collection and analysis of foreign communications, was standing in the way of what they saw as the right to privacy. They argued there was no contradiction between the individual's right to a private life and demands that the state and large corporations should be more transparent. For them, it was the issue of the state having too much power by collecting individual data and using the knowledge as a weapon to control and intimidate. Against that, they argued, the individual should be protected. It came as no surprise that the NSA supported a level of encryption that was woefully weak. One estimate said it would be possible to crack the 56-bit Data Encryption Standard (DES) being proposed for all US computers in just two minutes. Zimmerman thought that with its budget the NSA would be able to 'do it in seconds'. Few doubted that Pretty Good Privacy, with its 1024-bit key, was going to be difficult and time-consuming for any intelligence agency to decipher.

Back in 1991, the US government had called on manufacturers of secure communications equipment to insert special 'trapdoors' in their products, so that the government could read anyone's encrypted messages. The US National Security Council had been told three years earlier that the FBI, the NSA and the Department of Justice were demanding tough laws that would mandate the public to use only 'government-approved encryption products' or adhere to 'government encryption criteria'. For the Cypherpunks, it was the equivalent of a rule outlawing the use of letters sealed in envelopes and forcing everyone to use postcards for their personal mail.

Fearing the net tightening, Zimmerman acted first, releasing his new system because he 'wanted cryptography to be made available to the American public before it became illegal to use it'. Zimmerman became so worried he gave it away for free to increase the uptake. The result was beyond his wildest dreams. His encryption program 'spread like a prairie fire', and within months it wasn't just the Cypherpunks like Julian Assange who were encrypting their inner thoughts. The biggest users, human rights groups, used it to encode evidence and protect the identities of witnesses.

As he walked into the air-conditioned room to speak to the Senate Committee on Communication, Science and Space, Zimmerman prepared to give them both barrels. 'The government has a track record that does not inspire confidence that they will never abuse our civil liberties,' he told the assembled senators. The FBI had a bad record with civil rights, and also with targeting groups merely because they opposed government policies, spying on the anti-war movement—even wire tapping Martin Luther King's telephone.

Zimmerman knew what it was like to have the FBI on his case. Four years earlier when he'd put his PGP encryption online, special agents had raided his home. It took until January 1996, just a few months before he fronted the senators, for the Justice Department to finally drop the possibility of prosecution. But even then, the export of encryption systems remained classified as dangerous to the security of the US as fighter-bomber aircraft, tanks and guns. Just why the Justice Department didn't proceed with a case against Zimmerman isn't clear. It's possible the US First Amendment—enshrining freedom of speech—put the prosecutors on shaky ground.

Whatever the reason, the Pretty Good Privacy encryption was now well and truly out of the bag. As he left the hearing, Zimmerman made one final observation: PGP was a force for democracy. 'I want to read you a quote from some email I got in October 1993, from someone in Latvia, on the day that Boris Yeltsin was shelling his own parliament building: "Phil, I wish you to know, let it never be, but if a dictatorship takes over Russia your PGP is widespread from the Baltic to Far East now and will help democratic people if necessary. Thanks."'

Few had embraced Pretty Good Privacy more enthusiastically than Julian Assange, who used it to encrypt his emails. His stand against authoritarianism and what he saw as the unnecessary intrusion of the state grew more robust as the date for his court appearance and sentencing loomed closer.

James Carter, who was involved in the same computer-hacking adventure as Assange, had received a relatively light sentence, requiring him to 'be of good behaviour' for three years and pay $2100 reparation to the Australian National University for breaking in to its powerful computer. Yet it had been a close call. The twenty-six charges he'd pleaded guilty to—involving breaches of the Crimes Act and fraudulent use of a telecommunications network—could have put him in jail for several years. The judge suggested to Carter that he get a copy of the judgment, 'put it in a frame and put it on your wall to remind you to be a good boy for the next three years, otherwise you will be in terrible trouble'. Carter demurred, but it would be a different story with Assange.

A little more than a year later, on 5 December 1996, Julian Assange made his way to the Melbourne County Court, marching briskly past the waiting TV crews, his hair tied in a ponytail, his fawn-coloured raincoat flapping in the breeze. Of his experience in court, Assange told me later: 'It's an unusual experience when the judge says "the prisoner will rise" and no one else stands up.'

As uncomfortable as Assange appeared, within a few seconds Judge Ross delivered the good news. He wouldn't be facing a jail sentence because it would have been unfair to treat him more harshly than his co-defendant, Carter. The judge also took into account that Assange hadn't made any money out of the operation. And—in a line which could have come out of the Cypherpunks manifesto itself—he said Assange had merely hacked into computers to access material that empowered him. His 'unstable personal background' during his formative years was also a factor in the judge's decision. In a judicial flourish, which Judge Ross mistakenly believed would be the end of the matter, he said that if Assange was the 'highly intelligent' person that had been described to the court 'it is very unlikely you will come back'.

Assange, however, was not pleased with the outcome. 'Your Honour, I believe the prosecution has made several misleading claims in terms of the charges, and therefore I elect to continue this defence if Your Honour would let me,' Assange said. The judge told Assange he 'would be well advised' to come forward and sit down behind his defence lawyer. Assange pressed on defiantly: 'I feel a great misjustice [sic] has been done and I would like to record the fact that you have been misled by the prosecution in terms of the charges ... and a number of other matters.' The judge suggested that the defence lawyer have a word with his client.

In the end, Assange decided not to go for a jury trial. He had already spent five years on the legal process and, as he told me, 'had other things to do with his life'. He signed the agreement and walked out of the court into a Melbourne summer's day. Assange still argues that the law he was 'supposedly' guilty of breaking was a bad law. What seems to annoy him most is that the charges suggest he broke not so much the law of Australia, but the ethical standards of The International Subversives. He says he was charged with 'inserting data into a computer without authority and later deleting data from a computer without authority'. While that was true, he points out that the program he'd deleted was the very program he'd inserted, his own program. Assange says he'd been abiding by the ethical code of The International Subversives, which was 'to leave things as you found them and not damage anything'. This clear sense of ethics in action was consistent with Assange's belief that nothing should stand in the way of knowledge. The startling simplicity in his thinking would later come under serious challenge in the murkier world of WikiLeaks.

* * *

In his cheap student digs, Assange slowly set about creating a clandestine form of communication every bit as brilliant as PGP. Any form of encryption is only as strong as the keys that protect it—no matter how strong the encryption, the weakest link is the person who holds the key. Assange and another computer programmer decided to create a system wherein important information could be made to 'disappear' on a computer.

There are two ways of cracking open an encrypted file. One is to use a mathematical system using a high-powered computer to run millions of combinations of possible passwords in the hope of unlocking the files. It requires a lot of effort and, some say, a bit of luck. The alternative is to try to persuade the owner of the files to give up the keys to unlock the encrypted material either by psychological pressure or an old-fashioned beating. In the shadowy world of espionage and counterespionage, getting the keys and unlocking the files in this way is known as rubber hose decryption. In other words, if you aren't smart enough to crack the code itself, you do your best to force the person who knows the code to crack under a beating with a rubber hose or any other weapon that comes to hand. The system Assange had developed was known as 'deniable encryption', a method of not only hiding the encrypted material, but, just as importantly, hiding the fact that it was encrypted.

Assange posted his invention on the underground Cypherpunks network, with the tongue-in-cheek name, 'Rubberhose'. Assange added a trap that, under duress, would hand over a key, supposedly to unlock the entire computer. This key would provide access to distracting information, but not the kind that was being searched for, leaving the other extremely sensitive material untouched and buried in the computer hard drive. Of course it wasn't just human rights workers who would benefit from 'Rubberhose' deniable encryption.

Around this time, a quietly spoken New York architect had begun setting up an organisation that would pose the biggest challenge yet to government secrecy. John Young, who would play a major role in the future of WikiLeaks, sharpened his radical politics in the 1960s as a student at Columbia University. Like many of his friends, when Young left university he went on to work for the big end of town, but unlike the great majority of them he maintained the libertarian leanings of his youth. Young had already signed up to the Cypherpunk mailing list, and made regular contact with Julian Assange.

In June 1996, Young celebrated his first year of membership with a present for the Cypherpunks. He set up a website called Cryptome with his wife, specifically dedicated to freedom of speech, exposing 'government impropriety' and hosting leaked government documents. The architect began building one of the most significant 'counter-culture' websites of the Internet age, cramming computers, scanners and servers into his Manhattan home. Young says he and his wife, registered the site because, as he told *Wired* magazine: 'We like to put up original documents so people can make up their own minds. We see it as a librarian service.' Young's home was a library like no other. Although it had panelled walls and exquisite rugs on its parquet floor, that's where the similarity ended. It became a repository for thousands of leaked documents—classified material as well as hefty texts which, while not top secret, were inaccessible to most people until they were scanned on the Cryptome website. This wealth of painstakingly sorted information wouldn't be possible, Young said, without the Internet and the Cypherpunks mailing list. 'It's the greatest thing since love.' John Young might not be wearing flowers in his hair anymore, but his anarchic spirit remains unchanged. Within the first three years, the site had accumulated thousands of documents and was receiving hundreds of hits a day. The juicier postings included a list of people who were working for the British overseas intelligence agency MI6. *Readers Digest* described the website as 'an invitation to terrorists'.

Perhaps not surprisingly, Cryptome was also attracting the interest of the NSA. Every day at 7 a.m., the spy agency would drop in on the site using an automatic information gatherer called a robot, download two copies of the latest files, and then leave.

But John Young says he was left scratching his head about what the spooks at the Korean Information and Security Agency (KISA) were up to. The South Koreans, like the NSA, had sent a robot, but instead of gathering the information and heading off home it kept on requesting access to the same three files—a little like asking the same question over and over again on the phone and driving the other person crazy. The requests tied up the line, causing a logjam in the system and threatening to crash part of the Cryptome server. Young called KISA's website, but the phone rang out. He tried blocking access by the robot to the Cryptome site, but that didn't work either. The west-side Manhattan apartment was taking on the look of Mission Control on a bad day. Even the webmaster who administers US internet traffic weighed in, telling the South Korean spooks that 'It would be unfortunate to have to block all traffic from KISA to the US to prevent the problem'. By the following day, KISA explained it had been having trouble with its robots and 'cordially apologise[d]' for 'an unintended attack' on Cryptome. The reason the agency hadn't been able to get back sooner was 'because we had Chu-Suk holidays, similar to Thanksgiving Day'. The official explanation was that the person in charge of robots had had the day off.

Watching from the sidelines in cyberspace, Julian Assange had been closely interested in Cryptome. The whistleblowing website perfectly fitted his campaign for more open government, accountability and the protection of free speech around the world. In October 1998, Assange decided to meet some of his Cypherpunk friends, who until then had mostly been just an email address. Gently ribbing his adopted home town, which often wins tourism awards, he posted his plans for a round-the-world trip on the Cypherpunks email list, saying he was 'about to escape from the perils of a summer in "the planet's most livable city" and go trekking about the worlderful [sic] world of snow, ice, slush, and imploding communism'. His trip would take him to the US and Europe, but also to countries where democracy was either in its infancy, or had not yet been born, and where the Internet, too, was only nascent.

He would be 'hopscotching' through Russia, Mongolia and China, and visiting Poland and Eastern Europe, he said. If anyone felt like 'getting together for beer, vodka, Siberian bear steak, or just a good yarn, please let me know'. On this trip he looked for both physical and intellectual support. Writing of San Francisco, the heart of technology and Internet innovation and the birthplace of the Cypherpunks, he said 'no hovel, couch or spare room is too small'.

It might have been the itinerary of any wandering young backpacker, but it also had all the hallmarks of someone on a mission who was looking for meetings with kindred spirits; a recruitment drive to build a team for what was to come. Assange signed off his Cypherpunks message quoting the French aviator and author, Antoine de Saint-Exupery: 'If you want to build a ship don't drum up people together to collect wood and don't assign them tasks and work, but rather teach them to long for the endless immensity of the sea.'

While Assange would shortly register Leaks.org as a domain name, the idea of exactly how an information whistleblowing site would operate was still forming in his mind. Clearly seduced by the politics of direct action, and influenced by the success of Cryptome on the Internet, he also understood that big battles were still to be fought on traditional territory. Just a few months earlier, an estimated 40 000 people had taken to the streets of Seattle to protest against a World Trade Organization meeting downtown. The year 2000 was shaping up to be a defining one, not only in the history of activism, but for the Internet too. There was a real fear of the 'Millennium Bug', the theory that when the world's computer clocks registered 000 they would trip all the world's major servers, crashing the Internet. The activists were pouring in to Melbourne—some to see if the world would end, others to prepare to change it with a demonstration in Melbourne against globalisation, partly organised by Assange. Yet another group was there for both reasons. They were the computer geeks, straddling the activist world between cyberspace and the streets.

At this time Assange was balancing his activism with regular employment, which provided a sizeable income. He insists that though he worked for large corporations, he only did consultancy work. And he was unimpressed with the culture of his fellow workers in Silicon Valley. 'They were all totally obsessed by their stock options,' he said. What's more, he felt that the 'heavy lifting' connecting

Australia to the emerging World Wide Web had been done and there were other challenges ahead. An insight into his thinking is revealed in the blog he wrote called IQ.Org, in which he spoke of establishing a 'foundation … which holds some of my copyrights'—computer software codes he had written. He would use income from it to fund his activities. 'Normally NGOs [non-government organizations] beg, but I'm no good at that sort of thing,' he said.

With enough funds to see him through, Assange had time to gather his intellectual resources. For all his acclaimed ability in writing computer programs, Assange had never completed university. Now at the age of thirty-two he took the plunge, taking up a full-time course in physics and mathematics at the University of Melbourne. The art of couch-surfing that Assange used so successfully to make his way across the world kept him in good stead when he arrived back in Melbourne. By some accounts, the place he stayed in resembled a squat, but it seems someone was paying the rent. He spent restless nights wrestling with the mathematical complexities of computer algorithms. Much to the amazement of the other occupants of the house, Assange would sleep with a red light permanently on because he said the colour it cast across the room made it easier for him to think when he woke in the night, something that often happened. Unable to find any paper, he would scribble the code for his latest programming idea on the nearest thing that had a writing surface. He covered the doors and the walls with hundreds of concepts and ideas, the list of characters stretching sometimes up to a metre long.

He seemed to revel in the experience. In 2004 he turned up at a maths camp at the University of NSW. The campus may have been a long stretch from the centre of Sydney, but it was close to open parkland and the gentrified suburbs that butt onto the ocean. Run by the Australian Mathematical Science Institute, it allowed students to mix the discipline of numeracy with the delights of a Sydney summer. Assange fitted in well. Unlike the stereotypical computer whiz, he chatted as easily face-to-face as he did over the Internet. He stayed in touch with the friends he made there the following year when the camp moved to the Australian National University in Canberra. He formed a particularly close relationship with one woman student, Lisa*.

Like Assange, she studied at Melbourne University and attended the course with the idea of getting extra marks for the honours degree she was completing in physics. Assange made himself irresistible, according to Lisa: he was intriguing, a gifted storyteller, and intelligent. The relationship blossomed as she got to know him better. 'He can put the charms on when he's interested.' One time he courted her with an unusual present. 'It sounds corny now saying it but he wrote poetry on a Styrofoam cup and put it outside the door at the maths camp.' She doesn't remember what the poetry said, but she was flattered: 'He was special to know. He was different from people, unique, and that's the sort of person you want to know. Initially.'

They went on bike rides together and fed the swans in the creek that ebbs and flows through the ANU campus. As the relationship developed it provided a rather unusual insight into not only his romantic view of the world, but his version of crisis management, at least in his personal life. He and Lisa revelled in their travels together. 'He's very good at going on adventures, because his whole life is an adventure,' she said. Lisa also learned that Assange had another startling quality: 'He doesn't plan ahead', a trait that in the

* not her real name

future would create friction inside the WikiLeaks camp and at the same time baffle his opponents in the outside world. On the spur of the moment, Assange and Lisa decided to go to a concert by former Australian Idol contestant Chanel Cole. As they travelled down through the twisting roads from the highlands that separate Canberra from the New South Wales coast, Lisa remembered she'd forgotten to bring any blankets to sleep in. Unperturbed, Assange said: 'Why don't we just knock on doors and see if there are any blankets we can have?' Assange's ability to get help from strangers was both charmingly naïve and mildly exploitative. It would become a constant theme of his nomadic days as the head of WikiLeaks. 'He has the confidence,' she said. 'You become more confident when you're around him.'

When the camp ended, Lisa and Assange headed back to Melbourne. Lisa moved in with him, a simple terrace in Grattan Street, Carlton, just across the road from the main Melbourne University buildings. Its ornate extravagance born of goldrush money was in stark contrast to Assange's home, furnished with the austerity of an impoverished student. As Lisa pointed out: 'Half his house was salvaged from the dumpsters of Melbourne Uni.' One day in the second half of 2005, she recalls coming home, swinging open the wrought-iron gate, and opening the front door. She walked up the stairs and into Julian's room where he had installed a huge whiteboard on which he had written just one word: WikiLeaks. Assange had been secretly working on the concept for months. Lisa took it all in her stride: 'He was always telling me about ideas.' He explained to her that the concept of WikiLeaks would be a place where 'anyone in the world can post documents, anonymously'. Lisa said she quite liked the name, but challenged Assange, pointing out it might be better to drop the 's'. She said: 'Wouldn't it be better to be Wikileak?'

'No,' said Assange. 'W-i-k-i-l-e-a-k-s.'

In a tiny terraced home in the middle of Melbourne was born the concept of an Internet whistleblower site which would challenge the mainstream media and put governments and major corporations on notice.

* * *

By early the following year 2006, Assange was reaching out to one of his old Cypherpunk friends, John Young, who founded Cryptome a decade earlier. Though they'd never met, Assange was about to entrust him with one of his greatest secrets, and to ask for his help. 'Dear John, you knew me under another name from Cypherpunk days,' he said. He told him he was 'involved in a project that you may have a feeling for'. He said he would 'not mention its name yet' in case Young did not feel able to take part. Assange described his plan as 'a mass document-leaking project' that required someone 'with backbone' to hold the .org domain registration. But even Young, if he accepted, would not be told where the master servers would be housed. Their location would remain secret, 'obscured by technical means'. Assange warned Young he expected his new enterprise 'to come under the usual political and legal pressure'. In asking Young to register the name, Assange made it clear he would 'not need to claim any other knowledge or involvement'. In other words, Julian Assange was asking the founder of Cryptome, an organisation whose idea it could be argued he was now in part appropriating, to be the silent partner in his venture.

Young replied by encrypted email saying he had registered the WikiLeaks.org site in California for Assange, but contained in the message was the hint that he was less than happy. He'd obviously been flattered that Assange had come to him for help but Young understood the type of people who are drawn to the world of covert activity, including himself. He quoted Machiavelli that a conspirator could not act alone, and that 'those he works with will likewise be malcontents'. The trouble is, Machiavelli pointed out: 'As soon as you have opened your mind to a malcontent you have given him the material with which to content himself.' If Assange didn't take that as a warning, perhaps he should have done.

3

LIFT-OFF

The long sliver of sparkling water that snakes inland from the north-west is known as Puget Sound. It carries the clear currents of the Pacific Ocean south to the bustling city of Seattle on America's north-west coast. With Puget Sound on one side and Lake Washington on the other, Seattle nestles in a sea of tranquillity. From the front deck of Microsoft founder Bill Gates' lakeside home, a remarkable city skyline is revealed at dusk. Other high-tech moguls have flocked to Seattle's shores, some to innovate new products, others to serve the insatiable demands of Boeing and the computerised aircraft it makes just down the road.

As well as being one of the best paid and highly educated communities in the United States, Seattle is also one of the most liberal. The vast majority of the population favour strong anti-gun laws and support same sex marriages. They were among the first to rail against the prevailing economic wisdom of free markets—during a World Trade Organization meeting in 1999, an estimated 40 000 took to the streets.

Seattle's thriving counterculture extends to Riseup, a secretive organisation dedicated to opposing 'capitalism and other forms of oppression'. Riseup's registered address is an office in a rather stark brick building. It's from here that Riseup promises to provide 'secure communication' for people involved in 'struggles for liberation' who don't want governments snooping on what they say. In the second half of 2006, Riseup delivered to Julian Assange what he was looking for: a secure network to help his nascent WikiLeaks organisation communicate with its supporters around the world. Secrecy was of paramount importance for Assange, not just for those already working for the organisation, but also for those yet to be recruited. WikiLeaks began running a covert operation to muster support, warning those it contacted not to refer to the organisation by its full name but to use the initials WL instead. Part of its recruitment drive assured supporters in emails that Riseup had an established lawyer and 'plenty of backbone'.

WikiLeaks had not even been launched yet, but it was already evolving at breakneck speed. Eager for help, it revealed to Riseup that it had developed the technology for 'untraceable, unstoppable mass document leaking ...' The primary targets would be 'highly oppressive regimes in China, Russia and Central Eurasia' but WikiLeaks would also cater for those in the West 'who wish to reveal illegal or immoral behaviour in their own governments and corporations'.

WikiLeaks aimed for 'maximum political impact', using technology that was fast and usable by people who weren't tech-savvy. In a line that could have come straight from Harvard Business School,

WikiLeaks pointed out the efficiency of its new whistleblowing system: per hour spent provided the greatest 'positive impact' on the world. It was also, they declared, 'within our means to achieve'.

WikiLeaks wanted Riseup to be one of the 'stable and trustworthy' locations for document drop-offs in different countries. And in the language of underground activism, WikiLeaks explained how it would handle leaked material. A 'deniable drop-off' would most protect those receiving leaked material; any person in possession of a leaked CD/DVD or thumb-drive with encrypted information on it could legitimately deny knowing what it contained and protest their innocence. A 'regular drop' was far more dangerous because the receiver became a go-between, passing on unencrypted media and printed documents to WikiLeaks. Anyone caught with that material would have to be a fast talker, unable to argue that they weren't in the know. WikiLeaks already had drop-off points in New York and California and was looking for one in Seattle. Whether or not Riseup officially took up the offer to become involved in WikiLeaks' clandestine activities is not clear, but what is known is that one of Seattle's most famous cyber secrecy advocates Jacob Appelbaum, became a WikiLeaks supporter—and a huge admirer of Julian Assange. It was something he would pay for dearly later as he became drawn in to a ferocious battle over the future of WikiLeaks.

By being so open with Riseup and his supporters, Assange had taken a gamble and risked compromising his plans. But with the organisation growing at a phenomenal pace, Assange felt he had little choice but to widen his circle. WikiLeaks had by now expanded beyond the initial group of Chinese dissidents, mathematicians and those who WikiLeaks refers to as start-up techies from the United States, Taiwan, South Africa and Australia. Assange quickly put together an advisory board of cryptographers, reporters, representatives from Russian and Tibetan refugee communities, and one former US intelligence analyst. CJ Hinke, the founder of Freedom Against Censorship Thailand (FACT), confirmed he had regularly been consulted by WikiLeaks 'on such issues as credibility and importance of leaked materials'. He admitted to *Wired* that he was initially concerned by 'WikiLeaks' Secret Squirrel approach'; its determination to keep not only it sources secret, but also many of the activities of the organisation itself. But he has since developed 'great regard and trust for their mission'.

Like much of Assange's business practices, the advisory board was very big picture and it didn't care much for detail. When contacted by US magazine *Mother Jones* in 2010, several of the supposed advisory board members said they had been listed without their consent. Even John Laurie, one of the Internet's early proponents and a big supporter of Assange's work, found it hard to explain why he'd been included on the advisory board list. Australian broadcaster and public intellectual Phillip Adams was also on the list but Adams says he resigned early on because of health issues and workload. Some of the others had never even been contacted.

WikiLeaks had already captured the activists by recruiting John Young, the head of the similar organisation, Cryptome, to its board of advisors. What WikiLeaks needed was credibility with a broader part of the population. Assange reached out to Daniel Ellsberg, a skilled military analyst and famed whistleblower. He wasn't a typical dissenter: Harvard-educated, he had served two years in Vietnam as a civilian in the State Department and earlier worked for the Pentagon on nuclear weapons policy. Commissioned by Defense Secretary Robert McNamara, Ellsberg contributed to a review of Vietnam War history and discovered what successive administrations really thought of the conflict. Unable to remain silent about the White House's belief that the war was 'unwinnable', in 1971 he leaked the Vietnam history, known as the Pentagon Papers, to the *New York Times* and other US newspapers, defending his actions as upholding the highest principles of the US Constitution. Amid the clamour for his prosecution from the White House, Ellsberg handed himself over to US law enforcement agencies, saying he was prepared to accept the consequences of his actions and face charges under the Espionage Act of 1917. In the end, the case against Ellsberg was thrown out of court, not because—as is popularly believed—he was protected by the Constitutional First Amendment which guarantees free speech, but because the White House illegally wiretapped Ellsberg's phone and broke into his doctor's office. In a major victory for Ellsberg's campaign, however, the US Supreme Court ruled that only a free and unrestrained press could effectively expose deception in government.

Ellsberg says that he wasn't particularly surprised to receive an encrypted email from WikiLeaks at his home near San Francisco. He might have been seventy-five years old, but he still had the old fire. Just a few years earlier he'd been arrested during a demonstration against the Iraq invasion. Though Assange had always been a great admirer, what really put Ellsberg on the radar for WikiLeaks was a piece he wrote in *Harper's Magazine* in September 2006, expressing hope that someone would leak information about the US

Government's plans to invade Iran as a way to stop what he saw as an imminent US attack.

The email to Ellsberg, which was full of Assange's trademark rhetorical flourish, said Ellsberg's recent statements on leaking had been followed with 'interest and delight'. Assange informed Ellsberg that WikiLeaks had crossed over from 'prospective' to 'projective', the basic technology had been 'prototyped' and now the organisation had to 'move and inspire people'.

Assange was pitching to one of the greatest strategic minds in America, a man who'd had a system of decision-making called the Ellsberg Paradox named after him. It was a theory that demonstrated how people are naturally risk-adverse and prone to making decisions based on a hazard that doesn't exist.

Assange was, without a doubt, proposing risky business to Ellsberg: 'We'd like your advice and we'd like you to form part of our political armour,' he wrote. 'The more armour we have, particularly in the form of men and women sanctified by age, history and class, the more we can act like brazen young men and get away with it.'

So desperately did WikiLeaks want Ellsberg on board, it proposed erecting the equivalent of a statue to him in cyberspace. It would be called The Ellsberg Prize for Courageous Action, a worldwide competition every year to recognise a particularly fearless whistleblower, plus a special prize to recognise a US leaker—a gesture which WikiLeaks hoped other countries might follow. Awarding an anonymous whistleblower without revealing their identity was a novel idea and required a great amount of creativity.

Sitting talking in his home in Kensington, overlooking the San Francisco Bay, Ellsberg told me that at the time he was approached, he was sceptical of what WikiLeaks might achieve. Ellsberg had said to himself: 'Who's this coming out of the blue?' It all looked very strange to him.

Ellsberg believed that the whole idea was possibly naïve, but more likely to have been an 'entrapment', a cover for an intelligence operation in which all the whistleblowers were 'hoovered up' in one go, believing they were sending information to a legitimate site catering for leakers. Even so, Ellsberg remembers making a couple of telephone calls to the numbers on the emails and recollects possibly leaving a message. 'I didn't get anything back and then I just put it out of my mind; I just didn't think it would come to much,' he said. 'I get a lot of nutty things, you know, in the mail, one way or another.' This failure to follow through and make contact with Ellsberg at such a crucial time in the development of WikiLeaks was a critical oversight. For all his claims to have admired Ellsberg's stand as a whistleblower since he was a young man, Assange and his supporters had missed an important opportunity.

In the years to come, Ellsberg's support would play a significant role as Assange came under sustained attack, but it's reasonable to believe that if Ellsberg had been on board earlier, the trouble the group—and particularly Assange—faced later could well have been averted. Ellsberg would have provided a much-needed guiding hand as the WikiLeaks activists struggled to define the organisation and its 'new kind of journalism'. Ellsberg had significant experience dealing with the media. He believed it had its failings, but he was not as overwhelmingly critical as Assange at times turned out to be.

The problem with journalism, as Assange saw it, was the power imbalance between the journalist and reader. The journalist had access to information and could use it to manipulate the 'ignorant' reader. There was no easy way for the reader to check 'whether they are being lied to by the journalists'. The WikiLeaks model would solve that problem by wherever possible releasing 'full primary source material' to give readers and other journalists the opportunity to check the veracity of the reported information.

But the WikiLeaks model went further than giving readers a better chance of noticing the elisions and particular biases of journalists. The leaked documents WikiLeaks planned to publish could also alert arms of government to the failings of others in the administration—and create better governance as a result. Assange cited the invasion of Iraq as an example where tightly held secrecy about the government's plans to attack reduced the chances of the war's success. Assange said that one of the documents secured by WikiLeaks showed that although planning for the war was well underway in 2002, the UK was telling the UN Security council and the press that no war was being planned at all. The UK had set up a small, tightly controlled planning committee to prevent the truth leaking out. What is astonishing is that many of those who were not informed were in the Ministry of Defence. They were the very people who would have to make Iraq function efficiently after the invasion, those who would be involved in policing and reconstruction.

Assange said that many organisations involved in the reconstruction only had 'three or four days' to make their plans to get all their equipment together before heading off to Iraq, an impossibility. There is strong evidence that the result of those failures of policing and reconstruction led directly to the civil war that engulfed the country. The bedrock of Assange's 'new journalism' was accountability and verification, and these ideas would garner support among the public who wanted a game-changer after the debacle of the Iraq War reporting. But the high ideals that had given birth to WikiLeaks soon came up against the oldest obstacle faced by publishers and reporters alike—the looming deadline.

In late 2006, Assange knew they had to get something online quickly to keep the momentum building, but it wasn't easy. They had one document they thought might make a splash. It had been handed to the Chinese government and secretly given to WikiLeaks by an informant. If the document, supposedly written by one of the most important leaders in Somalia, Sheik Hassan Dahir Aweys, was authentic, it revealed a secret plan to assassinate the Somali government and impose sharia law on the country. What the document gives us is not so much an insight into the machinations of Somali politics, but an understanding of how WikiLeaks worked in its very early days. Instead of handing the document over to an outside journalist, Assange and his small team did the work themselves. Though scornful of much of the mainstream media and its rush to churn out material without proper scrutiny, he now found himself under the pressure of a red-hot story about to go cold if they didn't act quickly. The action was unfolding in a remote, yet strategic, part of Somalia, midway between the Indian Ocean coast and the Ethiopian border. Two hundred and fifty kilometres north-west of the capital, Mogadishu, Awey's fighters in the Islamic Courts Union were giving the government troops a caning around the town of Baidoa. With the US-backed Ethiopian army racing to the rescue, it was a perfect 'peg' for the story. But there was uncertainty about some of the translated words in the Somalian document. WikiLeaks already had one translation, but the team was still not absolutely sure—they need verification. A translator's fee of $300 for 1000 words was too expensive, so they appealed for Somali speakers to help out.

In a lesson learned from mainstream journalism, Assange understood the need to balance his obsession with accuracy with an ability to successfully appeal to a broad audience. One missive, revealed to the WikiLeaks team and almost certainly from Assange, says that complex subjects need not necessarily be boring, that in particular, the introduction needs some early colour to give it a lift. So, from the beginning, WikiLeaks was editorialising around its leaked documents, as one description of Awey's corruption attests: 'There he is, flame on his chin, holy book in his hand and anti-aircraft cannon between his legs.'

What emerges from the WikiLeaks discussions headed by Assange is the power of the collective process then at work inside the fledgling organisation, and the forensic attention to detail. Using the same technology that revealed how the Iraq War intelligence reports were changed and 'sexed up' by the British government to justify the war, WikiLeaks unpicked the pedigree and provenance of the Somalian document: when it was first written, when it was changed, even the name of the person who changed it. They were particularly careful not to name one of the authors of the draft document, in case he was the whistleblower. WikiLeaks had established a system whereby its sources of information remained anonymous even to Assange. But the major question about whether the document is a fake remains unanswered.

John Young makes the point that spooks treat forging and forgeries as 'high art'. In the end, the WikiLeaks team still can't be certain whether the document is authentic or not. But instead of discarding it, they dealt with both possibilities, positing the proposition that it is authentic and a forgery, and turning out a highly readable, analytical story that examines whether the CIA are up to their old tricks, or whether radical Islam is about to turn Somalia into another Iran.

Assange was unsure where to publish the document. He'd had 'junk' published in the London *Independent*, the Melbourne *Age*, the *Sydney Morning Herald* and *The Australian*. He favored *Counterpunch*, a US magazine described by its editors as 'muckraking with a radical attitude'. Though Assange would have been in the company of contributors such as British journalist Robert Fisk and US intellectual Noam Chomsky, he was concerned about the readership, which, though large, 'tends to pal up on one pew and sometimes even sings and claps'.

In the end, the Somalian report stayed with WikiLeaks. Assange decided that WikiLeaks would become a kind of online newspaper, and wouldn't rely on the editorial judgement of others to decide what was published. It was a big step to take for an organisation still trying to define its role in the world of journalism. Assange believed that if he couldn't find an outlet he liked or trusted, he would publish himself. It was an indication of the kind of belief that drives others to self-publish books and magazines, an enterprise often the preserve of the deluded or the desperate. Julian Assange was neither, but he did have a firm belief that only he would decide what would be published and what would not. It was a decision that would define Julian Assange and WikiLeaks.

In the early days there appeared to be an indication that Assange was not interested in the smaller stories that might emerge from the documents being regularly leaked to WikiLeaks. Some of the WikiLeaks workers argued strongly that people who risked their jobs to get information out should be treated equally, whether or not their stories were of international significance. But while Assange could see the merit in broadening the WikiLeaks support base to include the less sexy material, Assange continued to focus on what he hoped would be headline news. As well as wanting to score big hits, Assange kept developing what he called his brand of 'scientific journalism', by publishing stories and including the original documents, thereby allowing readers to not only make up their own minds about whether the report and its analysis was right or wrong, but to add their comments online too. This was the 'Wiki' in WikiLeaks—the ability of readers to add their comments, and make alterations to the text of the original story if they could prove that the facts or the analysis were wrong.

Assange was drawing on the emerging success of the online encyclopaedia Wikipedia, which made its name by allowing anyone in the world to contribute content. Assange seemed to relish the moment that WikiLeaks would be subjected to critical feedback, describing it as 'an act of creation and correction'. The Somalian document and others would face the scrutiny of readers cutting, cutting, cutting apart their pages 'until all is dancing confetti and the truth'. It may have sounded like a theatrical flourish, but it underpinned the philosophy of WikiLeaks, an organisation that went beyond its journalistic mandate and aimed to become the most powerful intelligence agency on earth; an intelligence agency of the people—open sourced, democratic and 'far more principled' than any government intelligence agency. It would have no national or commercial interests at heart; its only interests would be truth and freedom of information.

Unlike the covert activities of national intelligence agencies, Assange wanted WikiLeaks to rely on the power of what he called 'open fact' to inform citizens about the truths of their world. He believes that there is a direct correlation between closed and unjust organisations and their ability to handle the truth. Assange argues on IQ.org that leaks produce the most fear and paranoia within an organisation the more secretive and unjust it is.

In a world where leaking was easy through organisations such as WikiLeaks, the secretive or unjust systems were more likely to be hit than the open or just systems, Assange says. He points out that, since unjust systems by their nature induce opponents, and in many places barely have the upper hand, mass-leaking leaves them 'exquisitely vulnerable' to those who seek to replace them with more open forms of governance. As Assange eloquently wrote, close to the time of WikiLeaks' launch: 'Only revealed injustice can be answered; for man to do anything intelligent he has to know what's actually going on.'

WikiLeaks would not resonate to the sound of money or guns or the flow of oil, but to the 'grievances of oppressed' and exploited people around the world. It would be the outlet for every government official, every bureaucrat, every corporate worker, who became privy to embarrassing information that the institution wanted to hide but which the public needed to know. What conscience could not contain, and institutional secrecy unjustly concealed, WikiLeaks could broadcast to the world. If it sounded naïve, altruistic or, depending on your point of view, a grave breach of confidentiality to try to create such an organisation, it wouldn't be long before the theory was challenged. When that happened, it would be an experience that would leave Assange and the others battered and uncomprehending.

* * *

Just upstairs from the Penache restaurant in an unprepossessing building barely a kilometre from the White House is the headquarters of the Federation of American Scientists (FAS). The organisation was founded by a scientist from the Manhattan nuclear bomb project after he saw the devastation his work had caused at Hiroshima. It's been probing government secrets ever since, and demanding public disclosure of even the most sensitive issues. Such are its credentials and standing among freedom of information activists, one of its senior researchers, Steven Aftergood, was invited to join WikiLeaks' advisory board.

In early January 2007, Aftergood responded to Assange's request in the form of a story he wrote in his online newsletter, *Secrecy News*. Reporting that the WikiLeaks website was not yet 'fully live', he revealed that an initial offering purportedly authored by Sheik Hassan Dahir Aweys of Somalia's radical Islamic Courts Union would soon be posted on the Wikileaks website with a zipped file, accompanied by an analysis of the document's authenticity and implications.

The article turned into a savage attack on the organisation. 'We do not favour automated or indiscriminate publication of confidential records,' it said. In the absence of accountable editorial oversight, publication could easily become an act of aggression or an 'incitement to violence' or even an 'invasion of privacy'. Aftergood expressed concern that WikiLeaks might cause an 'offence against good taste'— a remarkable complaint from the founder of an organisation such as FAS which supposedly championed more open government.

It was as though WikiLeaks had asked its favourite uncle for a bit of friendly advice, and been told very publicly and in no uncertain terms to sod off. But Assange should have heard a warning in Aftergood's message. Aftergood predicted the changing mood in a nation that has freedom of speech enshrined in its constitution. While WikiLeaks sought to make 'unauthorised disclosures' technologically immune to government control, Aftergood wrote that an opposing school of thought, which he did not directly identify, proposed expanding US government authority, even seizing control of information that was already in the public domain if its continued availability was deemed unacceptably dangerous.

The article quoted a lawyer who suggested that even the Constitution might be used to restrict what he called the possession and dissemination of 'catastrophically dangerous' information. WikiLeaks was being warned off before it had been officially launched.

Within hours of Aftergood's attack in *Secrecy News*, John Young, the first person to accept an advisory board position, logged on to the WikiLeaks private online discussion site from his Manhattan home and began writing an extraordinary message. Young warned that WikiLeaks should expect smears, lies, forgeries, betrayals, bribes, and what he called the host of common tools used to suppress dissent. He said the organisation should beware that releasing information about WikiLeaks' founders and supporters would be grist for the 'truth twisters'. It was necessary to remain as anonymous as possible, otherwise WikiLeaks was doomed.

While he was critical of Aftergood for trying to make his organisa-tion, FAS, appear more respectable and honourable than WikiLeaks, Young was also miffed that he had been left out of the critical plan-ning stage of WikiLeaks' development, the launch of its first online document drop—the Somalian exposé. The significance of one line buried in Young's text probably went unnoticed at the time. He warned that the WikiLeaks online discussion list was in danger of being leaked by hackers.

It was certainly lost on whoever responded from the WikiLeaks camp—most likely Assange—pointing out that despite Young's fears, WikiLeaks' opponents so far had essentially been uncoordinated. The attacks they had experienced had been unmotivated, limp-wristed and lacked precision and common direction. The organisation should use the time before any concerted assault came to get its message out and define itself. WikiLeaks, it was claimed, had time to 'set the key in which future bars of our song are to be played by the public orchestra'. Critically, Assange asserted that he did not believe in unquestioning obedience to authority, but favoured ethical behaviour in all circum-stances. There was a place for principled civil disobedience, where an act of distributing information may embarrass authoritarian power structures or expose oppression or major crimes. Assange recognised leaking often involved major personal risk but there was a duty to act. 'Every person is the ultimate arbiter of justice in their own conscience,' he wrote. Assange was exploring dangerous territory here. Relying on individuals to set their own moral compass is only one step away from recommending that people take the law into their own hands.

Young, for one, seemed unimpressed, describing the WikiLeaks 'ethical statement' as defying credulity in a similar way to what he called the professional peddlers of 'responsible' leaks, organisations like the FAS and Aftergood's *Secrecy News*. Sensing that WikiLeaks might be in trouble from unidentified external forces he asked if any advisory board members had jumped ship yet. WikiLeaks assured Young no one had left, but it said that Aftergood's criticism had stung and 'they wanted him fed to the sharks'.

Reflecting the growing sense of hubris among the WikiLeaks team, they announced they were about to become even bigger than Wikipedia one of the most successful information sites the Internet age had ever produced. WikiLeaks said it had been inundated with leaked material—1.1 million documents ready to be processed. What it needed now was more staff, and more money.

Three days later, on 7 January 2007 at 6.46 p.m., WikiLeaks posted an email which would forever change its relationship with Young. Though it was an internal document sent to only a few selected supporters, it sounded like a pitch from a desperate spruiker trying to raise money for dodgy investments. As a brazen demand for cash, it took some beating:

> 'How much will YOU pledge to WikiLeaks for its next six months of activities?'

WikiLeaks said the organisation could operate at a slow pace with under $50 000 a year, but its goal was to raise pledges of five million dollars by July. They weren't quite throwing in the steak knives too, but it wasn't far off it. Smaller pledges could be used in ways that would generate larger ones. WikiLeaks was thinking big. It had acquired a secret list of attendees at the World Economic Forum shortly to be held in Davos, Switzerland, and would be urging them to contribute. Top of the hit list was George Soros, who was famous for being a multi-billionaire and well known for acts of philanthropy, but who was also suspected of secretly funding dissident groups who received money from the CIA. It was dangerous territory for WikiLeaks to be entering.

Twelve minutes later John Young fired off a blistering attack warning that a five million dollar funding goal by July would kill WikiLeaks. It made WikiLeaks look like a Wall Street scam. Five million dollars could not be needed so soon, except for suspect purposes. Even Soros would kick them out of the office for such 'over-reaching'. Foundations were flooded with big talkers making big requests, flaunting famous names, and promising spectacular results.

Young was scathing about WikiLeaks' claims to have more than one million documents ready for leaking—far too many to be believable without evidence. WikiLeaks hadn't even officially been launched yet. It had only leaked one document, which outlined a possible plan to assassinate members of the Somali Government—and even that was of 'highly suspect provenance'. Young recommended a more cautious approach: firstly, by explaining what the funds were needed for and how they would be managed, and secondly, how the money would be protected against fraud and theft. He said WikiLeaks would be better off establishing its bona fides first by publishing a credible batch of documents, testing feedback and criticism.

He argued that WikiLeaks should show it could handle the 'heat of doubt' and condemnation and use that to support fundraising. Young said the biggest crooks bragged overmuch of how ethical their operations were; WikiLeaks should avoid ethical promises, period. They'd been used too often before to fleece victims. He advised WikiLeaks to demonstrate sustained ethical behaviour, not to preach it. He also raised the prospect that WikiLeaks had a secret funding agenda. If fleecing the CIA was the real purpose of the five million dollar target, he suggested a much higher funding goal, in the $100 million range. The US intelligence agencies were awash in funds they could not spend fast enough. Academics, dissidents, spy contractors, whole countries were falling over themselves to tap into that bountiful flood.

Young signed off: 'In solidarity to fuck em all'.

A few hours later, WikiLeaks responded: 'Advice taken, we'll polish up our shears for cutting fleeces golden.'

Young sent another blistering message. He may not have been Nostradamus but he proved to be very good at making his own prophecies come true. With no explanation he announced that his organisation, Cryptome, would be publishing the contents of the WikiLeaks membership list and 'how I was induced to serve as US person for registration'. To underline his displeasure, he added: 'WikiLeaks is a fraud: fuck your cute hustle and disinformation campaign against legitimate dissent. Same old shit, working for the enemy.'

The effect on WikiLeaks was one of stunned disbelief. Young had been involved with the organisation right from the start, had registered the organisation in the United States, and put his name to it. He had an enviable record of disclosing information and though he was known to be eccentric and at times a little erratic, nothing prepared Assange and the WikiLeaks team for this. They had been careful even encoding the word WikiLeaks to make life harder for intelligence agencies if they began investigating. They hadn't used their real names; every communication had been sent by encoded emails. It had given them a sense of security and comfort. Now the organisation had been penetrated not by the enemies it had repeatedly identified as likely aggressors—powerful state authorities, or huge companies—their internal operations were about to be exposed by one of their own. WikiLeaks was about to leak.

The formal request to Young belied the angst: 'John, please do not do that.' Assange tried to placate Young, saying that he understood he may have felt out of the loop when *Secrecy News* broke the story of the organisation's first leak, but even if Young believed that some at WikiLeaks were CIA stooges, he couldn't treat everyone on the list that way and publish their names.

Young took little notice of the special pleadings and dumped hundreds of emails on his website, although he did redact many of the names and email addresses of both active WikiLeaks' workers and its dozens of supporters.

Assange wrote to Young saying that he did not understand Young's sudden change of heart. He wanted to know why Young had decided to pull his support for WikiLeaks and publish the emails.

Young said he thought he'd been played for a sucker. WikiLeaks had failed to introduce the much-vaunted public discussion forum to allow critiques of its work to be posted online, but the five million dollar goal had been the last straw, a sure-fire indication of a scam. Young threatened to name everyone involved in WikiLeaks and their affiliations if they didn't reveal themselves in an open forum. It turned out to be an idle threat but Assange didn't know that at the time. WikiLeaks had just been given a healthy dose of its own medicine.

It was a difficult argument to make that WikiLeaks should demand absolute secrecy about its own activities, but openness in others, and this was a contradiction that would continue to dog the organisation, providing ammunition for its growing band of opponents. It wasn't just governments, big corporations, the military and intelligence organisations that didn't like what WikiLeaks was doing. Many journalists, activists and hackers were either envious or sceptical of the information-age newcomer. They were formidable opponents for a fledgling organisation that was already under attack from within, and struggling to find its feet.

4

SAVE THE WORLD

It was early 2007, and Julian Assange's daughter, whom he'd had with his partner, Lisa, had recently celebrated her first birthday. But the relationship had hit turbulent times and Assange was no longer living with them. Lisa believed Assange was desperate for a stable family but he was 'haunted by demons' which revealed themselves by the fact he had 'massive trouble sleeping'. As WikiLeaks struggled to get off the ground, he turned to the son he had from his earlier marriage for help in getting the organisation started. Having fought and lost a bitter custody battle for Daniel sixteen years earlier, to be reunited in such a labour of love now would make up for all the time they had spent apart.

According to Assange's mother, Christine, one reason why he was so focused on forcing governments to be more open stemmed from that custody battle. Freedom of Information requests they carried out later unearthed a trail of decisions made by 'radical feminists', both in the Family Court and Legal Aid, whom she said opposed men having custody of children. Both Julian Assange and his mother were so concerned they set up the Parent Inquiry into Child Protection to investigate abuses and possible changes to the law. Assange even provided direct help to the Victorian Police Child Exploitation Unit in another area. His 'technical advice' and support assisted in the 'prosecution of persons suspected of publishing and distributing child pornography on the Internet'. What's never been revealed before is that as well as tracking down pornographers, according to Christine her son also put his technical expertise to use helping Victorian police 'remove a book on the Internet about how to build a bomb'.

Assange and Daniel shared many interests, and Daniel was well aware how stimulating the venture would be. While he was growing up he had learned a lot from his father, who treated him as an equal. And he had no reason to think things would be any different if he joined him in WikiLeaks. They would be a good team: Daniel understood his father well and he had had similar troubles as Assange had growing up, problems that are often associated with high intelligence.

But after lengthy consideration Daniel, who had a gift for science like his father, decided not to take up Assange's offer. He had too many serious doubts that the WikiLeaks project would ever work, later telling the online publication *Crikey* that at the time he thought the idea of leaking government documents 'to the entire world' was a 'ridiculous concept'. Though Daniel was wrong about the impact that WikiLeaks would have, he did possess a deep understanding of what drove his father.

Assange had always been interested in political activism and had a huge interest in science, philosophy and mathematics. But he turned away from what he saw as the function of science in feeding the war machine, and put individual activity at the centre of his philosophy instead. The application of state power to silence and control the individual would be repeatedly resisted by Assange, as it had been from the beginning of his travels through the underground network of the Cypherpunks, to the birth of WikiLeaks. It was a journey that had driven him into the arms of anarchic liberalism.

But how to 'save the world' and put theory into practice was an altogether different issue. Writing in June 2007, just after WikiLeaks had gone live, he said that the world could be perceived as so vast that the individual could not envisage their actions making a meaningful difference. People tried to fool themselves into believing that one could 'think globally and act locally'; however, to anyone with a sense of proportion, acting locally was a marginal activity. It was not setting the world right. The task was to create ideas or interventions that had a global impact. He hinted that maybe WikiLeaks was the answer. 'Perhaps I have found one [an idea],' he wrote. 'I support similarly minded people, not because they are moral agents, but because they have common cause with my own feelings and dreams.'

Few others knew Assange's weaknesses better than his son, Daniel. 'He gets easily frustrated with people who aren't capable of working up to his level and seeing ideas that he grasps very intuitively.' They were attributes that would attract the best and brightest to work alongside Assange, but those qualities would eventually drive some of those same people away, turning them into enemies at a time when he would need all the friends he could get.

But 2007 was a time for embracing not only new friends but new ideas. If WikiLeaks was to raise its profile on the world stage it would have to do better than the Somalian document which, although having achieved a creditable mention in the *New York Times*, had hardly raised a blip elsewhere, apart from the savaging it received from *Secrecy News*. To give WikiLeaks a world presence, Assange needed an international stage. He found it at the World Social Forum, a gathering of activists and alternative thinkers, which was about to hold its annual conference in Nairobi. Scheduled to be held at the same time as the World Economic Forum in Davos, it was designed to draw attention to the gulf between rich and poor nations. More importantly it was expected to draw a crowd of more than 50 000. On the spur of the moment, Assange sent out an email to WikiLeaks supporters asking if anyone fancied a trip to Kenya. As the crowds made their way to the conference opening ceremony in the centre of Nairobi, they could not have been aware that they were about to witness the emergence of an organisation that would have a huge impact on human rights around the world, revealing acts of tyranny and oppression in Kenya which had been conceived just a few hundred metres from where they were standing at Parliament House. The motto, boldly emblazoned over the main entrance, read: 'For a Just Society and the Fair Government of Men.' WikiLeaks would reveal that nothing could have been further from the truth.

Within a few weeks, Assange's appearance at the forum in Kenya bore fruit for WikiLeaks, taking the organisation from being a maverick online publisher to being entangled with mainstream journalism. Assange knew that while the purity of his WikiLeaks model gave readers the chance to view original documents, the editorial reach of their online publication was severely limited. Assange was moving inexorably towards collaboration with mainstream newspapers, beginning with the UK's *Guardian*. This would be a benefit to both parties, giving the newspaper scoops and providing WikiLeaks with a huge platform to reach a wider and more influential audience— something the Internet itself could not deliver.

In August 2007, the *Guardian* published an exposé, based on a WikiLeaks document, revealing that the former Kenyan President Daniel arap Moi had siphoned off more than a billion dollars of government money and shifted it overseas into nearly thirty countries. The *Guardian* reported that it had seen a 110-page report by the international risk consultancy company Kroll, which revealed that Moi had illegally acquired multi-million pound properties in London, New York and South Africa, as well as a 10000-hectare ranch in Australia and bank accounts containing hundreds of millions of pounds. The *Guardian* said Moi's associates colluded with Italian drug barons and printed counterfeit money; his clique owned a bank in Belgium, and their fear of losing wealth prompted threats of violence between Moi's family and his political aides.

The Kroll investigation into the former regime was commissioned by President Mwai Kibaki shortly after he came to power on an anti-corruption platform in 2003, supposedly the first step towards recovering some of the money stolen during Moi's 24-year rule, which earned Kenya the reputation as one of the most corrupt countries in the world. Political pressure forced Kibaki not to act on the report, which was believed to have been leaked to WikiLeaks by a senior government official upset about Kibaki's weakness.

The Kenyan leak established a partnership between WikiLeaks and the *Guardian* and produced a model for how it planned to do business with other mainstream media organisations. It would be a difficult journey for an organisation that was contemptuous of how lacklustre many of the world's newspapers were in holding those in power accountable. WikiLeaks would choose who it did business with carefully. The UK's *Guardian* newspaper, with its liberal-Left reporting history, was an obvious choice, and others with a similar political pedigree would follow, such as *Der Spiegel*, *Le Monde* and *El Pais*. The arrangement would involve a great degree of trust on the part of WikiLeaks that the newspaper would not 'steal' the story and publish without attribution. For its part, the newspaper had to trust that WikiLeaks wouldn't give the story to someone else after all the hard legwork had been done. Whatever the flaws with this system of operation it was far superior to another arrangement WikiLeaks also tried: the auctioning of its documents to the highest bidder as a way of funding the group's operations. That had been a spectacular failure with few takers. It was also an odd fit for an organisation whose stated goal was to hold the rich and powerful accountable for the deeds they would prefer weren't made public.

In November 2007, WikiLeaks published the first document that directly related to US foreign policy: an instruction manual, Standard Operating Procedures for Camp Delta, one of the detention camps used to hold prisoners in the United State's Cuban enclave at Guantánamo Bay.

The document focused heavily on how best to restrict and control access of the International Committee for the Red Cross (ICRC) to those often being held in solitary confinement. The degree of nervousness expressed by the US Government in its dealing with the ICRC can best be understood by the fact that the organisation received 148 mentions in the document. US soldiers at Camp Delta were warned repeatedly to be guarded when dealing with the ICRC. They were given directions that ICRC officials were not allowed to ask long questions of detainees and that if an inmate's mail was censored the ICRC would be told, but they would not be allowed to see the contents. More importantly, the ICRC would not be allowed to visit a prisoner for the first thirty days of their confinement at Camp Delta. The US military had always denied that certain prisoners were off-limits to the Red Cross until the WikiLeaks document exposed the lie. More followed, including a report that revealed instructions on how to use military dogs to intimidate prisoners. 'MWD (Military Working Dogs) will walk "Main Street" in Camp Delta during shifts to demonstrate physical presence to detainees,' according to a directive in the 'Psychological Deterrence' section.

The document was signed by Major General Geoffrey Miller. According to media reports, Miller introduced harsh interrogation methods to Guantánamo, such as shackling detainees into stress positions and using guard dogs to exploit what the former head commander in Iraq, Lieutenant General Ricardo Sanchez, referred to as 'Arab fear of dogs'. The story had been posted on WikiLeaks and written by Julian Assange and others. This time, there appeared to have been no relationship with the existing media organisation. It seemed that WikiLeaks was feeling its way—exploring the parameters for what was to come. In the anarchy of the editorial process and the eventual direction of WikiLeaks it was a kind of trailer for the main events to follow. No one knew what was going to happen next, including, it seems, WikiLeaks itself. In February 2008, WikiLeaks delivered a bombshell of a story. It had its epicentre just 300 kilometres south of Guantánamo Bay.

* * *

Long sandy beaches and aqua seas attract hundreds of thousands of tourists every year to the Cayman Islands. They arrive by huge ocean liners the size of apartment blocks, in motorboats and yachts, all drawn to the beauty of this coral island paradise. As the tour boats arrive and weigh anchor in Cayman Bay, the first view for those on board is the palm-fringed beauty of Seven Mile Beach and the colonial style, low-rise buildings gleaming white in the brilliant sun.

The Caymans have much to offer, but some of the visitors are drawn here by what's not so apparent. The people who live and work on the Caymans pay no tax. Among the boat tour operators and travel agencies that jostle for space along the waterfront are the pick of the world's banks, including HSBC and Barclays. They provide a service that has made the Caymans one of the most significant financial centres in the world.

It's a long way from the mountains of Switzerland, but the Julius Bäer bank headquartered in Zurich occupies one of the best pieces of real estate on this island haven. Since 1994, Rudolf Elmer, one of the bank's senior accountants, had headed up the Cayman branch. He had a well-appointed office with sweeping views of the azure Caribbean Sea. But whether it was the stress of dealing with billions of dollars of other people's money, the office politics or a personal issue, something snapped in Elmer. When a number of the bank's documents went missing, the bank subjected staff to a lie detector test. Heavily medicated with painkillers for a bad hip, Elmer failed to complete the test. When the bank fired him, Elmer decided to blow the whistle on its activities.

As an accountant, Elmer knew the power of documentary evidence. So when he left the bank he took with him a full inventory of the bank's server, containing thousands of account details, names, addresses and transaction information. Elmer claimed he had it with him because during the hurricane season he had to leave the island, taking a copy of the server with him. The bank didn't believe him. They called it theft. It wasn't long before Elmer began using the ammunition to attack his old employer. He said he had witnessed 'practices used by the Julius Bäer bank to evade or reduce its own tax payments'. Elmer accused the bank of 'double bookkeeping' practices. He said the bank administered billions of dollars worth of investments in the Caymans, yet reaped the profits tax-free in Switzerland. The bankers 'pretend that management in the Cayman Islands makes the decisions' while the main bank in Zurich actually controls all the transactions.

Elmer pointed out that an 'in-house pseudo insurance company' in the Caribbean sent out exorbitant premium invoices 'that reduce the amount of taxes owed in Switzerland and other countries'. He also alleged faked loans to customers were used to reduce tax bills by deducting bogus interest expenses. Elmer used his data as a lever in the bitter dispute with his former employer. He had sent anonymous emails to Bäer customers, threatening to disclose that their accounts contained unreported taxable income. 'I did it to protect myself and my family,' he said.

The conflict dramatically escalated when a Swiss financial newspaper anonymously received a computer disk with customer records dating from 1997 to 2002. The US Internal Revenue Service also got a copy just in case they missed another huge tranche of records uploaded from Elmer's hard drive on to a far more public area—the WikiLeaks' website.

Rocked by the exposure, the bank's lawyers demanded that WikiLeaks take down what they called the offending documents. When WikiLeaks refused, the bank launched a court challenge—not in the Caymans, but thousands of kilometres away in San Francisco, where the WikiLeaks domain name had been registered two years earlier by John Young.

There, in the towering glass building on Golden Gate Avenue that houses the US District Court, Julius Bäer's lawyers successfully persuaded Judge Jeffrey White that WikiLeaks had published confidential documents that violated their client's right to privacy. Judge White's decision had immediate effect. Three kilometres away, Dynadot, a California-based Internet company, was ordered to pull the plug on WikiLeaks.org's domain name server (DNS). Angry Internet activists had already set up mirror sites, allowing access through other domain name servers. And WikiLeaks itself had gone to great lengths to decentralise its website operations so opponents could not easily shut them down. More than half a dozen domain names, including WikiLeaks.org, WikiLeaks.be and WikiLeaks.cx, all led to the same site, providing alternatives if one of them was disabled. In the future WikiLeaks would have to take more extreme security precautions using a disused underground bunker built in central Stockholm during the Cold

War. The facility, owned by Swedish broadband provider Bahnhoff, offered the ultimate in protection: its own fibre optic cables had not been tapped into by the Swedish intelligence agencies at the time, according to the company. Bahnhoff boasted that the facility, cut out of solid rock thirty metres underground and protected by a half-metre-thick door, was bomb-proof. As if that wasn't enough protection, several old diesel engines from German submarines were on standby to supply backup power.

As Judge White made his way home that night, he probably had no idea of the fury that was about to be unleashed against his decision to shut WikiLeaks down. The American Civil Liberties Union and the Electronic Frontier Foundation, a strongly committed and heavily organised group dedicated to the defence of freedom of speech, filed a motion to the court protesting against what it called the censorship of WikiLeaks. They were joined by the Reporters Committee for Freedom of the Press (RCFP), bringing together an extraordinary array of opposition to what they saw was a clear case of a First Amendment argument in favour of free speech. The RCFP understood only too well what was at stake. Established in 1970 to provide legal support to reporters needing help, one of the founding members of the committee that established RCFP was Ben Bradlee, the *Washington Post* editor who also published the Pentagon Papers and what was at the time the world's greatest journalistic scoop, Watergate.

The RCFP drew together representatives from almost all the major US newspaper publishers, including the American Society of Newspaper Editors, the Associated Press, the Hearst Corporation, the *Los Angeles Times*, the National Newspaper Association, the

Newspaper Association of America, the Radio-Television News Directors Association and the Society of Professional Journalists. On the grounds that WikiLeaks had not appeared in court to defend itself and no First Amendment issues had yet been raised, the media coalition requested to be heard as a friend of the court to call attention to relevant points of law that the court had apparently overlooked.

They argued that it was unlawful to dramatically curtail access to WikiLeaks simply because of a complaint involving a few documents. It violated the bedrock principle that an injunction involving one set of documents could not be extended to all others. More significantly, the RCFP cited the case of the Pentagon Papers in which the Nixon Administration had tried to prevent publication. In that case, it had been argued that the First Amendment prohibited preventing publication even when national security may be at risk, and the press' source was alleged to have obtained the documents unlawfully. The privacy and commercial interests cited by Julius Bäer's lawyers were simply not important enough to have their publication prevented.

Faced with such concerted and well-argued opposition from this highly regarded expert group, Judge White not only dissolved the injunction requiring Dynadot to suppress Wikileaks' DNS entries, but also denied the bank's request for an order prohibiting the website's publication of the bank's documents. As RCFP Executive Director Lucy Dalglish said, 'It's not very often a federal judge does a 180-degree turn in a case and dissolves an order'. On 17 January 2011, Rudolf Elmer appeared at London's Frontline Club, alongside Julian Assange who was making his first public appearance since being bailed on allegations of sex crimes in Sweden. In a staged ceremony, Elmer handed Assange some computer disks which he said contained details of tax avoidance by 2000 very wealthy individuals. He said he had tried to interest the Swiss police but they had taken no action, except to try to extradite him to face charges of breaking Swiss banking secrecy laws. His last chance, he said, was WikiLeaks.

If WikiLeaks hadn't been on the US military's radar as a possible threat before, the court decision seemed to galvanise its intelligence arm into action. Three weeks after Judge White handed down his decision, the US Army's Counter Intelligence Centre issued a special report focused entirely on WikiLeaks, which Assange got his hands on and leaked.

Classified 'Secret', it also carried the restriction 'Nofor'—no foreigners were to be given access to it. Without a hint of irony the document pointed out that the governments of China, Israel, Russia, Thailand and Zimbabwe had all blocked access to WikiLeaks. The document came to the conclusion that WikiLeaks posed what it called an information security threat to the US army. Without specifying what the threats were, it stated that the WikiLeaks site had provided foreign terrorist groups, insurgents and other potential adversaries with potentially actionable information for targeting US forces. It said the possibility that current employees or moles within the Department of Defense, or elsewhere in the US government, were providing sensitive or classified information to Wikileaks.org could not be ruled out.

Ominously, the US military even provided a blueprint to shut WikiLeaks down. It pointed out that the organisation used trust as a centre of gravity by assuring insiders, leakers and whistleblowers who pass information to its personnel or post information to the website that they will remain anonymous, adding pointedly, 'The identification, exposure, or termination of employment of or legal actions against current or former insiders, leakers or whistleblowers could damage or destroy this centre of gravity and deter others from using Wikileaks.org to make such information public'. It amounted to a declaration of covert war on WikiLeaks. The organisation wouldn't find out about the military's plans until much later but Julian Assange was already preparing for an assault.

In the wake of the court victory he began carefully examining what lessons WikiLeaks could learn from the adversary it had just beaten. As he told me: 'We looked at banks that we had been exposing in the Cayman Islands and those offshore jurisdictions, and tried to understand what it is that these offshore jurisdictions are really doing.' Assange identified that offshore banking arrangements had a number of significant characteristics. They were mainly based on small islands with only a few thousand population and they were capable of producing a package of laws that were attractive to a particular type of investor. For Assange, the appeal was how the financial security of this kind of jurisdiction could be used for the benefit of journalism and his WikiLeaks venture. It was just a nascent idea forming in his mind, but in the not-too-distant future it would be part of a radical alternative to protect his journalism. Assange says he thought to himself: 'What if we can turn this on its head?' As he conceived it, the impregnable fortress that was often used to protect the assets of the rich could be subverted for Wikileaks' whistleblowing.

Before those elaborate arrangements were made, Assange had some old scores to settle first. He would take on Scientology, one of the most litigious organisations in the world. The organisation that all those years earlier had managed to silence criticism with threats of legal action was next in the firing line, and this time WikiLeaks had planned strong defences before it posted a host of Church of Scientology documents. They involved the work of a person identified as Frank Oliver who had signed what must be the most extraordinary employment contract the world has ever seen, with a branch of Scientology called the Sea Organisation, or SeaOrg. In it, he said he was of sound mind and agreed to contract himself to the organisation 'for the next billion years'. WikiLeaks' Scientology package contained memos and other documents Oliver received while working in the Office of Special Affairs, which performs public relations damage control for the Church. As the *Register* online newspaper pointed out: 'They read like a cross between Sun Tzu's *Art of War* and a Richard Nixon strategy memo on dealing with a hostile press.'

'Never treat a war like a skirmish,' the documents advise. 'Treat all skirmishes like wars.'

According to a 'Manual of Justice', purportedly written by Scientology founder, L Ron Hubbard, Church officials responding to negative magazine articles should 'hire a private detective of a national-type firm to investigate the writer, not the magazine, and get any criminal or communist background the man has'. The officials should then use the information to 'write a very tantalising letter' and ask the reporter to come in for a meeting. In what must be one of the most bizarre public relations directives ever, the manual suggests that if the reporter agrees to the meeting, ask them 'to sign a confession of collusion and slander—people at that level often will, just to commit suicide—and publish it in a paid ad in a paper if you get it'. The manual states: 'Chances are he won't arrive. But he'll sure shudder into silence.'

On a more practical level the documents suggest ways investigators could discover personal details about the movements of those opposed to them, getting airline frequent flyer numbers and then calling the airline to discover a person's itinerary. The documents also name 7000 organisations and individuals who are 'suppressive persons and suppressive groups'. The purpose of the Department of Special Affairs was to accomplish 'total acceptance of Scientology and its Founder', the documents say, and to take 'responsibility for cleaning up the rotten spots of society' in order to create a 'safer and saner environment for Scientology expansion and for all mankind'.

Within days of the documents being posted on the WikiLeaks site, Scientology's lawyers in Los Angeles ran the same argument their counterparts in Melbourne had used, accusing WikiLeaks of violating US copyright law. It was unlawful to 'reproduce or distribute someone else's copyrighted work without that person's authorisation', a letter from the attorneys read. It threatened that courts had entered 'numerous permanent injunctions and [been] awarded statutory damages' for infringing the copyright of Scientology's works. The documents were 'unpublished, copyrighted works. Please be advised that your customer's action in this regard violates United States copyright law. Accordingly, we ask for your help in removing these works immediately from your service'.

Instead of buckling, WikiLeaks continued the assault, saying that after reviewing documentation on Scientology's 'attacks, legal and illegal', on critics 'ranging from *Time* Magazine and CNN' (which it said had spent more than $3 million defending against just one of their suits), to investigative freelance journalists whose books had been pulped by publishers rather than face litigation costs, WikiLeaks had come to the conclusion that Scientology was 'not only an abusive cult, but that it aids and abets a general climate of western media self-censorship, due to the fear of litigation costs'. WikiLeaks added that if the West could not defend its cultural values of free speech and press freedoms against a money-making cult like Scientology, it could hardly lecture China and other state abusers of these same values.

In an attempt to discover who had leaked the material, the Scientology lawyers asked for the 'release of the logs of the uploader'. If it was designed to intimidate, it had just the opposite effect—WikiLeaks acted. 'In response to the attempted suppression, WikiLeaks will release several thousand additional pages of Scientology material next week.' And it did.

Nothing further was heard from the LA lawyers. One of the biggest and most vexatious litigants had been silenced and defeated. It was a sweet revenge for Julian Assange who had failed so spectacularly in Melbourne all those years ago to inflict any damage on the Church of Scientology, defeated by a legal muzzle which had silenced everyone else too, until now.

Exactly who leaked the Scientology documents has never been discovered, though the Church tried to find out. The system that WikiLeaks used to protect a whistleblower's identity had worked perfectly. The material simply arrived on the WikiLeaks server, posted by an anonymous whistleblower with access to the documents. But that safeguard could not extend to protecting whistleblowers from themselves. In the early hours of the morning on 16 September

2008, the private Yahoo email account of Sarah Palin was hacked into by a user calling themselves Rubico.

As John McCain, the Republican presidential candidate, and his deputy, Sarah Palin, crisscrossed the country in a final push in what was expected to be one of the closest elections ever, 20-year-old David Kernell thought he might make the difference and tilt the balance in favour of the Democrats. He was looking for something that would 'derail Palin's campaign'.

She had been accused of using her private email to shield government business from public scrutiny. All Kernell needed was the answer to her Yahoo email password question and her date of birth. When it came to breaking into her account, it's probably a good thing Palin didn't design the security codes to launch a nuclear strike. Her birthday appeared on her Facebook page, and the password was simply a name of one of her children. The problem was any frontal assault on the email would identify the person who had broken in. So Kernell used a computerised 'cut out'—an Internet host which provides a new identity to 'launder' his attempt to impersonate Sarah Palin. Once inside the account, Kernell copied Palin's list of emails, and posted it on the web where WikiLeaks picked it up. The hack also uncovered some unflattering family photos and the addresses of Palin's friends, the usual kind of material you'd expect to find on anyone's email account. But there was also evidence that Palin was using her personal email for state business.

Among the emails in Palin's account were several from government email addresses belonging to her aides, including a draft letter to California Governor Arnold Schwarzenegger, a discussion of nominations to the state Court of Appeals, and several bearing the acronym for the Alaska Department of Public Safety. Assange argued that the emails proved that Palin had used her private account to hide material concerning government business which should rightfully be in the public domain.

Palin brushed off the question of whether she'd done anything wrong and called in the FBI to find the hacker. They didn't have to look far, and the following Saturday night FBI officers swooped on Kernell's apartment where he lived with flatmates just a kilometre from Tennessee University, and photographed and logged everything in the place, including his computer. Though Kernell had carefully shielded his identity, he hadn't been careful enough. His Facebook email was linked to Anonymous—the anarchist website he'd used to attack Palin's account. When the FBI demanded to know from the organisation that provided the 'cut out' who had accessed Palin's account, they promptly handed over the email address. The curly haired, cherubic Kernell, who might have hoped to please his father, a local State Democrat Party leader, by embarrassing Palin, was eventually found guilty on two charges of obstructing justice and unauthorised entry of a computer. He received a one-year jail sentence and three years' 'supervised release'. The judge ordered Kernell to spend his sentence in a 'halfway house' and not a federal prison. John McCain's campaign described the hack as a 'shocking violation of law'. Barack Obama's office called it 'outrageous'.

Assange defended WikiLeaks' publication of the private photographs of Palin's children because they authenticated the email account. 'Everyone now knows the documents to be true,' he said. 'These previously unseen photos of Palin's children were selected to lend credibility to the politically important text—the list of emails containing governmental correspondence.'

While the United States was moving away from hard right Republicanism towards the political centre ground, on the other side of the Atlantic the political consensus was fracturing, and extreme racism had began to re-emerge in Britain. Like all extremist parties, the leaders of the Far Right British National Party (BNP) deny it is a racist organisation, but they know their members understand only too well what the party really stands for. Even so, the last thing many of them want is their names revealed to the public, least of all to their neighbours or workmates.

After it had briefly appeared on a blog, WikiLeaks posted the membership list of the British National Party. It contained the names, addresses, ages and occupations of many of the 13 500 BNP members. Among the members were schoolteachers, doctors, lawyers and police officers. It is illegal for anyone in the British police to be a member of BNP and at least one person lost their job.

WikiLeaks was fast emerging as a major force in the world of investigative journalism and human rights; a game changer in the way stories broke and were reported. Just a few months earlier, Julian Assange and WikiLeaks had received the prestigious Economist Index on Censorship award for journalism for the inroads they had made in New Media. The Index on Censorship presents annual awards to courageous journalists, writers, lawyers, campaigners, filmmakers and whistleblowers from around the world who have made a significant contribution to free expression over the previous year. Assange joined some of the most highly regarded journalists in the world for the awards ceremony in London.

While WikiLeaks had made headlines with its prize, it was having less luck getting anyone from traditional journalism interested in an extraordinary story it had published on its website. It involved the murder of hundreds of Kenyans suspected of being members of a notorious gang. Outlawed following a spate of slum violence, the quasi-religious group from the dominant Kikuyu tribe had become one of Kenya's largest crime and extortion rings.

Instead of arresting them and placing them before a court, a group of Kenyan Police carried out the systematic execution of anyone they suspected. As the bodies began to pile up in their hundreds in the Nairobi mortuary, police officers who disapproved of the killings tipped off the Kenyan Human Rights Commission. Their investigation revealed a pattern of execution: many had been shot at close range or strangled to death after being tortured, others set on fire after being doused in paraffin. The completed report, entitled 'Cry of Blood', was damning of the government. 'These acts were ordered, directed or coordinated by the top leadership of the Kenya police acting jointly with a common purpose,' it said. It also reported that the police had been complicit in the deaths of up to 500 young Kenyans in the past eighteen months.

President Mwai Kibaki ignored the call for a full inquiry. Like its victims, the report was buried. The Human Rights Commission found itself in a bind. As Assange told me the report was 'too dangerous to release' inside Kenya. Even posting a copy on an outside web page like WikiLeaks would be risky for those who leaked it in Kenya. But whoever it was decided to take the chance—and handed over a copy. WikiLeaks posted it on its site with great fanfare.

Assange was greatly disappointed that the report was mainly ignored by the established media. Only the UK's *Sunday Times* and its reporter Jon Swain gave the story any prominence. There would have to be changes to the way WikiLeaks did business in the future if Assange was to honour his pledge to its whistleblowers that the risks they took would be worthwhile and that their material would have maximum impact. Just six months after the report was filed on the WikiLeaks site, two human rights lawyers, Oscar Kingara and Paul Oulu, who had been providing evidence to the Kenyan Human Rights Commission and also trying to get the International Criminal Court involved, were gunned down. As Assange tells the story, he clearly understands the terrible significance of what happened: one car pulled up behind and another pulled up in front. Both men were shot through the windows and a student who tried to take the bodies back to the university 'to make sure there was a proper autopsy' was also shot.

Assange was proud of the award Amnesty International gave WikiLeaks for its work in exposing the police killings, but the WikiLeaks activists in Kenya also raised serious questions that the organisation had never faced before. As we sat talking in a Melbourne sanctuary provided by his friends in early 2010, Assange wrestled with the dilemma of the Kenya killings. 'They face many more risks than we do—as a sort of, as a white foreign national, I'm in a privileged position and these people cop it first,' he said. Then Assange used a curious phrase to describe what had happened to the dead men. 'For me personally, they are my canary in the coalmine,' he said. Assange may not have meant it, but his comments sounded callous.

Protecting the whisteblowers who risked their lives seemed easy to deal with compared to this new complexity, the unintended consequences of an exposé that had left two men dead and another shot at close range. The business of leaking had just got a whole lot more complicated and ethically fraught.

5

LONG REACH OF THE LAW

On 1 August 2009, Birgitta Jonsdottir settled down to watch the local 7 p.m. news in Reykjavik. Jonsdottir, a poet and anarchist, had exchanged her street demonstration skills for parliamentary process. Just four months earlier had been elected to the Icelandic Parliament as a member of The Movement, a political party that campaigns for democratic reform 'beyond the politics of left or right'. She'd risen to power on a wave of public concern about how Iceland had suffered so badly during the global financial crisis. It had been hit worse than most other countries and was left close to insolvent.

One of Iceland's major savings banks had been among the first to harness the power of the Internet and produce online banking. Called Icesave, it had attracted 350 000 investors in the UK and the Netherlands, with £4.5 billion of deposits, but the financial crash had destroyed its investments and now it was owned by the Icelandic government, who was keeping it afloat. With Iceland's population at just 320 000, the debts alone were enough to take the country to the brink of insolvency. As the short days of winter turned into the near, never-ending days of summer, it was estimated that the local population faced the dreadful likelihood that every man, woman and child in the nation would have to pay up US$50 000 each to bail out the bank. With unemployment increasing rapidly and the economy in freefall, one of the most advanced nations on earth stood teetering on the brink of the abyss. Other banks had been in trouble too. Iceland's largest bank, Kaupthing, received a €700 million loan from Iceland's Central Bank, announcing that it was 'committed to working with the government to ensure regular workings of the Icelandic financial system'. In other words, if Kaupthing went belly up, Iceland's finances would be in tatters. Birgitta Jonsdottir knew better than most how dire the situation had become. It's why she never strayed far from the TV evening news— the country's main bulletin.

At the local TV station, Kristinn Hrafnsson, an amiable yet highly focused investigative journalist, was unusually flustered. A few weeks earlier Hrafnsson had received a tip that a then little-known website, WikiLeaks, was about to publish a document which might interest him. It involved the Kaupthing bank, an organisation that had caused Hrafnsson problems before. A few months earlier he'd lost his job at a rival TV station after exposing a link between the bank and a shady Iranian businessman. What the WikiLeaks document revealed was shocking even by the standards of the global financial crisis, which had come close to destroying the world economy. It showed that borrowings of billions of dollars made by customers of the bank were backed by virtually no security at all.

The leaked documents revealed the bank had loaned billions of euros to its major shareholders, including a total of €2 billion to a company with large shareholdings in the bank and subsidiaries meaning it now owned nearly a quarter of the bank. 'The biggest borrowers had no collateral at all. Working swiftly, Hrafnsson put his scoop together for that evening's news broadcast. It was a classic story of insider trading, with the public being asked to bail out the bank because it was too big to fail. But just before the TV news titles rolled the bank's lawyers pounced, managing to secure an injunction to stop the broadcast of Hrafnsson's story. The message was simply relayed to Hrafnsson: 'We were supposedly breaching bank secrecy laws,' he said. Under legal pressure, the station pulled the story, and all its newsreader could do was point viewers to the WikiLeaks website. But it was enough: the story was out. The number of hits from Iceland on the WikiLeaks website was phenomenal that day.

At home, Jonsdottir sat on the sofa open-mouthed. Like many Icelanders she was furious. She wondered why it took so long for the information about the bank's practices to be revealed—and why it had come from a website she'd never heard of before. Whoever had done the leaking was well informed and courageous. Iceland was not an easy place to be a whistleblower. 'Those very few that dare to question this insanity, they will be just basically character assassinated,' she said. 'In Sicily, they shoot you; they character-assassinate you here … they kill your reputation and you can't get a job anywhere.'

There were other questions too about how it was possible for an Icelandic court to prevent the publication of information that had already been published on the Internet. For although the Kaupthing bank had managed to stop Kristinn Hrafnsson, there wasn't an

Icelander with even the vaguest interest in the future of their country who didn't know about the contents of the WikiLeaks dossier. In Aldous Huxley's *Brave New World*, those who opposed the all-powerful state were threatened with exile to Iceland. Though Huxley didn't mean it as a compliment, Icelanders have embraced it as a description of them as a proud and independent people.

Jonsdottir would be instrumental in hatching a truly revolutionary idea with Assange to make Iceland an international publishing centre, where journalists and writers could work free from the kind of fear of defamation laws which were silencing the media in the UK.

* * *

If Iceland was part of a brave new world then the United Kingdom was beginning to resemble *1984*—George Orwell's grim prediction of a world controlled by a totalitarian regime, where uncomfortable facts about the past can be rewritten or erased. In September 2009, the *Guardian* reported it had received a demand to delete the online historical records of its reporting of the Trafigura toxic oil disaster. Carter-Ruck, a high-profile defamation law firm based in London, said the reports were 'gravely defamatory' and 'untrue'. They said it was wrong to report that Trafigura's waste may have caused deaths and severe injury, even though, as the *Guardian* reported, Trafigura had agreed to pay compensation to its 31 000 West African victims.

A few days later Britain plunged even deeper in to an Orwellian world. In the legal equivalent of having a journalist eaten alive by rats, Carter-Ruck had managed to obtain what is known as a super-injunction. It prevented the *Guardian* from revealing any information covered by the injunction, including the fact that there was an injunction at all. Across the city in the *Guardian* offices, how to inform its readers about what was going on without breaking the terms of the injunction demanded more than a small amount of literary dexterity. David Leigh, the *Guardian's* at times acerbic head of investigations, wrote that it involved: 'Legal obstacles, which cannot be identified … proceedings, which cannot be mentioned, on behalf of a client who must remain secret. The only fact the *Guardian* can report is that the case involves the London solicitors Carter-Ruck.'

Carter-Ruck's claim to fame has been the large number of notable defamation and libel wins for its high-profile litigants. Its weapon of choice is the no-win no-fee system. Carter-Ruck's cut-price offers and the UK's libel laws, some of the worst in the world for journalists and publishers, produced an attractive package for anyone wanting to take court action. It can also encourage what Australian barrister Geoffrey Robertson QC is credited with describing it as 'libel tourism' where litigants go shopping around the world to find the jurisdiction where they are most likely to win. Though Robertson was more subtle than others about Carter-Ruck's legal business practices, he wasn't the only one who took exception to how the firm operated. The satirical magazine *Private Eye* had started referring to Carter-Ruck as 'Carter-Fuck'. Though they subsequently reached a rapprochement, when Carter-Ruck asked the magazine to stop misprinting the first letter of 'Ruck' as an 'F'. *Private Eye's* response was to print the first letter of 'Carter' with an 'F'.

Humour, though, didn't solve the problem. Labor MP for Newcastle-under-Lyme, Paul Farrelly, decided to raise a question in the House of Commons about Carter-Ruck and Trafigura—a tactic seen by many as a back-door way to get material on the record if gagged by the courts. As a former journalist, Farrelly understood only too well how the system worked, but the plan ran into problems. Carter-Ruck's injunction made the reporting of even the question a breach of the injunction. The *Guardian* revealed to its readers it had been forbidden from telling them.

It caused a furore. It was one thing to censor the press and quite another to silence Parliament. In the end, Carter-Ruck posted a statement on the company website saying that it had never been its intention to prevent the press reporting on Parliament and that it had since agreed on changes with the *Guardian* to the gagging order so that the newspaper could report on the issue.

While some celebrated what they saw as a victory for freedom of speech, Julian Assange launched a blistering attack on how free speech had not been saved in the UK. In a WikiLeaks online editorial, Assange argued that the secret gag order against the Trafigura report '*remains in effect*, and entirely prevents the reporting of the report's contents'. He argued it was not the only one. The previous month he said the *Guardian* revealed it had been served with ten secret gag orders—so-called 'super-injunctions'—since January. In 2008, the paper was served with six. In 2007, five. 'Haven't heard of these?' asked Assange. 'Of course not—these are *secret* gag orders; the UK press has given up counting regular injunctions.'

Assange said that because of the damaging threat of legal costs, UK newspapers had silently removed some of the original dumping investigations from their databases. 'For example, the *Independent*'s "Toxic shame: thousands injured in African city" no-longer "exists" except at *WikiLeaks*,' Assange wrote. 'Now is not the time to be distracted from this reality, or to see the unravelling of a grotesque attack on parliamentary reporting as a step forward; it is a return to last week. We are back at the UK censorship status quo, which may be described, without irony, as privatised feudalism.' Assange wanted no congratulatory mutual praise or celebrations of victory. In a call to arms reminiscent of his Melbourne days, Assange wrote: 'So take your hands from each other's backs, sharpen your (s)words—and get to work. The battle isn't over ...'

Assange was right about that. Several months later he confronted Professor Alasdair Mullis, an acclaimed expert on defamation law and the editor of the book *Carter-Ruck on Libel and Privacy*. At a debate sponsored by the European Union, Mullis pointed out that while he was not connected to Carter-Ruck, he did have an issue with the BBC. He'd live to regret taking on Julian Assange.

> MULLIS: A number of news organisations have got the facts wrong. The BBC for example suggested that, in fact, Trafigura had killed people. That's not true.
>
> ASSANGE: How do you know that it's not true?
>
> MULLIS: Because they paid damages. Why would they pay damages if they could prove it?
>
> ASSANGE: Because they settle that out of court for tactical reasons.

Assange asked again how Mullis knew the allegations weren't true, citing a UN report that 108 000 were taken to hospital to seek medical attention in Côte d'Ivoire after the oil dump by Trafigura.

> ASSANGE: Now I say to you: 108 000 people go to hospital, all different types—children, old women, et cetera— even just going to hospital, is it unreasonable that fourteen of them died, on the way, in Ivory Coast in Africa, in the middle of the night? Of course you expect fourteen people to die, if they are driven to hospital. And here you are saying that it is not true. What are your facts, sir?

> MULLIS: All that I'm saying is that the BBC chose not to defend it.

> ASSANGE: No, that's not what you said. Is it?

> MULLIS: I can't remember.

Mullis tried to regain ground, asking why, if the BBC had been so sure of its story, it had not chosen to defend the case?

> ASSANGE: Because they viewed it might take two million pounds in the UK system to defend it. In the UK the burden of proof is on the publisher. Have you stopped beating your wife yet? Prove it to me. See you in court.

Assange stared straight at Mullis and the audience tittered.

This exchange reflects much of Assange's fearlessness and the sort of bravura he has to stare down anyone no matter how qualified they appear to be or how expert in their subject. For Assange, the arguments revolved around logic. He was driven by the belief that sound judgements could be made by being armed with the facts. Doggedly, he would follow a line of argument to its endpoint.

In the final weeks before Christmas 2009, Assange headed for Iceland where he met up with Daniel Domscheit-Berg who'd left his job to join WikiLeaks. Domscheit-Berg, from Germany, had brought to the organisation a commodity almost as valuable as his expertise in computers. His life savings would help fund the organisation. As Assange headed along the seemingly endless road that weaved its way across the barren flat expanse between the airport and the capital, Reykjavik, to address a conference organised by a group calling themselves Digital Freedom, there was no doubt it would be a meeting of sympathetic minds; Iceland had developed a strong culture in favour of keeping the Internet free and open, part of WikiLeaks' basic creed.

Up on stage, Assange and Domscheit-Berg were an eye-catching double act. Assange with his resonant voice, dramatic gestures and flowing white locks alongside Domscheit-Berg, every bit the German anarchist, earnest and thoughtful with horn-rimmed glasses. Birgitta Jonsdottir was also on the bill that night, but she was still waiting her turn. In a Reykjavik café, she recalled how well Assange and Domscheit-Berg performed. 'They really worked well together,' she said.

Domscheit-Berg had joined up with Assange two years earlier. He'd been a leading member of the German Chaos Computer Club, which though it sounds like an anarchist cliché—is in fact a highly respected organisation that keeps a watchful eye to prevent state intrusion into people's personal lives. Domscheit-Berg told me he'd been approached by a friend who 'had a genuine interest in changing the world for something better' and asked if he wanted to join WikiLeaks. Originally, Domscheit-Berg had been concerned about the comments made by Cryptome's John Young that WikiLeaks was a fraud and could even be a CIA front, but he'd put those reservations to one side and taken the plunge. He'd jumped in so deep that he abandoned his job as a computer security officer and gathered up his life savings of more than 40 000 euros to fund what he knew would be an expensive exercise—buying servers and computers, and travelling. He was so committed to the idea he even changed his name from Daniel Domscheit-Berg to Daniel Schmitt. Not much of a difference, but enough, so he thought, to make life slightly more difficult for anyone who came looking for him. He had eventually spoken to Assange, not face-to-face, but through a chat room.

They hit it off immediately. At the conference Assange laid out his plans to protect WikiLeaks by using all the tricks the big companies and the wealthy used to protect their profits with offshore accounts. It was a blunt message: 'If you look at how multinational organisations move their tax structuring through offshore jurisdictions or just through trusts within countries like the UK, we have to do the same thing in order to protect our sources [from] malicious, vexatious lawsuits affecting our ability to continue.'

Donations needed to be anonymised through offshore bank accounts, so that security equipment such as encrypted telephones, Internet infrastructure and postal addresses could be rented, without the funds being traceable.

Assange argued that if you wanted to publish high level material like WikiLeaks without suffering vexatious lawsuits, there was no choice but to use trusts or international cross jurisdictional arrangements to protect the organisation. He said the issue was not about evading a judicial system but about preserving an organisation's ability to continue to publish while the judicial process played out. He said most big organisations would drop their cases before they got to final judgement. But they wanted to make publishers, like WikiLeaks, bleed in the meantime because that's how they worked.

Impressed by the ideas put forward by Assange and Domscheit-Berg, Jonsdottir, who made her speech on freedom of information and digital copyright, spoke briefly to Assange about meeting up later. She could see plenty of opportunities for WikiLeaks and her party to work together on the issue that united them both: whistleblowing and the protection of sources. Everyone was swept up in the important issues of the information age. Later that night, Jonsdottir mustered her Movement Party executive for a late night discussion, inviting along Assange, Domscheit-Berg and other Icelandic WikiLeaks volunteers.

Jonsdottir arranged a meeting at one of her local haunts, the Peace House, where they discussed many of the problems that both her party and WikiLeaks faced. WikiLeaks found itself fighting legal battles in many jurisdictions, and the Movement Party had problems at home. Iceland had been named by Reporters Without Borders as having the freest media in the world, but in the changing political climate the country had lost its title. As the evening wore on, the meeting adjourned to the only place left open that was still serving food. Over tapas at a local Spanish restaurant, Jonsdottir and the group discussed drawing together the best laws from tax havens and legal entities which protected freedom of speech, and adapting them to provide a safe haven, particularly for those involved in the legally hazardous business of investigative journalism.

'You might want to take that risk, but what a bummer if you take a risk and then the stuff is taken down,' she said. The new laws would guarantee 'the stuff is not going to be taken down no matter what'. Under the proposed laws, once material was placed on the server in Iceland it would be illegal to remove it from the public sphere. Her party would present a bill to the Icelandic Parliament to make the country, in effect, a journalistic paradise, where the right to free speech and the protection of whistleblower sources would be protected by the full weight of the law.

Jonsdottir remembers that both Assange and Domscheit-Berg got very excited. 'They were saying, "Yes, let's do this".' Jonsdottir, an intelligent woman, had a persuasive manner that would be important to win over the government. She had already won over Assange; he was attracted to her spirited attitude. They were close politically, but just how close they became emotionally Jonsdottir won't say. Even so, they were a formidable political duo.

As an opposition MP Jonsdottir needed to persuade the ruling parties to vote for her proposal. Assistance for the cause came from an unlikely source. She'd been invited to a cocktail party at the US Embassy and decided as a mild act of mischief to take either Domscheit-Berg or Assange as her guest. WikiLeaks wasn't high on Washington's radar at that time, though it had certainly achieved enough to make party-going at the US Embassy a fairly hairy pursuit. 'I said to them as a joke, "Why don't one of you come there with me.

We can just pretend that one of you is my boyfriend because you can't just go and bring friends".'

In the end it was decided Assange would be her partner. But Jonsdottir, working back at Parliament, missed meeting up with Assange and went off to look for him. 'I go to his guest house to get him and I can't find him and I do, like a couple of circles around town, at the places where they used to hang, and I go back to work,' she said. Finally, Assange made contact. He had gone on his own and according to Jonsdottir, he spent some time talking to the American Chargé d'Affaires, Sam Watson. Chatting with Watson was either a coincidence or a deft piece of political strategy by Assange.

In mid-January 2010, Sam Watson began writing a routine report on Iceland's financial problems. The government was particularly concerned about how it would be possible to fund the refinancing of Icesave, the bank that had attracted so many investors from the Netherlands and the UK, but which was now relying on support from the Icelandic Government. He described how representatives of the government had been in talks with the embassy and wanted the US to help settle what was turning into a bitter dispute with the Netherlands and the United Kingdom. He noted that the US had said it would be neutral on the matter, a position that was to be interpreted by the Icelandic delegation as condoning the bullying of Iceland by the more powerful countries who wanted the government to not only pay the debts, but also expected a premium on top. Watson noted that the Icelandic delegation believed that if the Icesave issue wasn't resolved soon and Iceland defaulted on its loans it would 'set Iceland back thirty years'.

When Watson pressed the send button on his embassy email, he thought that would be the last he would see of his succinct report as it winged its way electronically across the north Pacific and into the mainframe computer of the State Department in Washington. He also copied in high-ranking officials in the National Security Council and the US Department of Defense.

A few weeks later, Jonsdottir arrived at the prime minister's office ready for a meeting with the heads of government. They all trooped in to the main meeting room and prepared to sit down around the large table. On the agenda, among other matters of state, was the Icesave issue. As they waited for the final person to turn up, someone in the assembled group became very focused on their telephone. But it wasn't a phone call that had got their attention. They were listening to the news and with each passing second they became more and more alarmed. Eventually they turned and said to no one in particular: 'Oh I've never heard of such a thing. How is this possible?'

The news report had left nothing in doubt. Everything was there: the attempts to head off a referendum that might lead to Icelanders deciding not to pay for the debts incurred by Icesave. And the involvement of the Americans in a matter many in Iceland believed was none of their business, particularly as they appeared to be siding with the 'bullies'. Jonsdottir believed that if Iceland had accepted the settlement being pushed by the UK and the Netherlands—and indirectly backed by the Americans—the interest payments for the bail-out loan would have amounted to '70 per cent of the income taxes in Iceland'. The source, of course, was WikiLeaks.

The news story galvanised the Icelandic people behind both Jonsdottir and WikiLeaks, which was only too happy to be cited as the source. Though it helped build support for the changing media laws, these were only the first faltering steps of the campaign. It would be months before the law was changed but when that happened WikiLeaks would benefit profoundly with a new legal legitimacy in Iceland: Assange could register WikiLeaks' business name and set up servers to hold their secrets, instead of having them scattered across the world.

WikiLeaks would receive many more cables, in all nearly 260 000 pages of classified US State Department documents. The Iceland US embassy cable was just one of these. Releasing it in an attempt to garner favour with Iceland and Jonsdottir's media law reform plans had risked exposing the scale of the leaks to come. But Assange was confident the embassy party had created a big enough diversion to throw any investigation off the scent. The fact that he was seen talking with Sam Watson was designed possibly to implicate him in the leak—and kept any investigators away from the future cache of cables. It was a high-risk gamble.

In late March 2010, with the world watching the first eruptions of the Eyjafjallajökull volcano which would go on to paralyse air traffic in the months to come, WikiLeaks was planning an even bigger world-stopping event. Not far from the US Embassy, Jonsdottir had rented a tiny yellow painted cottage where Assange and his small team would work together. The WikiLeaks personnel, many of them local recruits, were already furnishing it with the equipment that was needed—video editing machines and banks of computers. For the following week, they would be handling an explosive piece of US military information that would guarantee that Julian Assange never got another invitation to a US Embassy party again.

6

OPEN FIRE

The house in Grettisgata Street, in the centre of Reykjavik, is tiny but has one big advantage: it's free-standing. There are no common walls and it's a difficult place to bug. When Birgitta Jonsdottir rented it she knew exactly what she was looking for: a place where the WikiLeaks team could carry out the biggest operation in the group's short history.

Just a few days earlier, Jonsdottir had met up with Assange in a café. As she sat down, he opened his laptop. What rolled across the screen was a classified video, shot from a US military helicopter showing it opening fire on a crowd of people in a Baghdad square in 2007. As the bodies fell, slaughtered by 30-millimetre cannon shell, Jonsdottir was moved to tears. But what happened next filled her, and Assange sitting next to her, with outrage: the gunship rounded on the rescuers and pounded their minivan, killing those on the ground, including a still-moving Reuters journalist and seriously wounding two children in the van. It was a horrific scene. Jonsdottir and Assange both believed that if it were released, public outrage might help end the war in Iraq sooner. But they needed to keep the fact that they had a copy of the video secret from the US military —until they were ready to go public with it.

Assange believed they were already under surveillance by America's National Security Agency, the NSA, whose key role is to spy on foreign countries but which had recently been caught spying on its own citizens. Assange said he and Jonsdottir had seen someone covertly filming them. This played on Assange and made him even more paranoid as he began recruiting locals to work on what he cryptically referred to as project B, the Iraqi video.

Gudmundur Ragnar Gudmundsson, an articulate and shrewd computer expert who used to run his own business, had been friends with Jonsdottir for years. Mixing on the fringe of politics in Iceland he's had some crazy requests, but nothing prepared him for the telephone conversation he had with his old friend in late March.

'Can you help us do some video editing ?' Jonsdottir asked. Ragnar said yes.

'Can you come over?' she asked.

'Ok,' he said.

'Now?'

'Yes. Where?' Ragnar asked

A simple question, but one that required a long explanation about where they might meet just to discuss the whereabouts of the WikiLeaks address. In the end it all became too hard and Jonsdottir simply gave him directions over the phone.

When Ragnar arrived at the house he was confronted by a spartan, white-walled workspace crammed with computers and editing equipment. Assange was there and they were introduced. Ragnar had been drafted to produce an online version of the video, ready to be broadcast on the Internet at precisely the same time as Assange and the WikiLeaks team launched the video at the National Press Club in Washington. Ragnar found the experience emotionally draining: 'I am in the helicopter, I am the member of the crew, this is like—[a] "we are shooting at them" kind of experience for me. Iceland actually joined the group of nations to carry the war on Iraq. I didn't get really mad, it's just so sad.'

In their determination to get to the bottom of the story, WikiLeaks had collaborated with their friend at Icelandic TV, Kristinn Hrafnsson, to check out what exactly it was that the gunship video showed. For while WikiLeaks had the video, they still didn't know what it meant, or exactly where it was shot. Assange concentrated on what he called the 'back story'. He wanted to know more about the people who had been killed. He also wanted to know why they had died. The more he looked at any material and the more research he did, the clearer the story always became. This was the case with the gunship video. 'We originally thought this was a video about Afghanistan,' Assange said. 'It was only once we decrypted it, which took a volunteer effort of many people donating their computers to help go through all the different passwords and find the one decryptor, it was only then that we started to see what was going on … and the more we looked, the worse it became.'

Both he and Hrafnsson wanted to get to the truth of what had happened in East Baghdad that day. It was agreed that Hrafnsson and an Icelandic TV team would travel to Iraq to track down the families of the victims. Hrafnsson was determined to put names and faces to the dead and injured, so often just expressed as numbers in the military reporting of casualties. For Hrafnsson, as it is for many journalists who witness the killing of innocents, it was the children that made him want to find out more. 'I could easily identify with those children because they are a similar age as my own,' he said.

Assange and Hrafnsson worked well together. Just as Assange and Domscheit-Berg had balanced each other's personalities and qualities, Hrafnsson was the calm foil to Assange's mercurial outbursts. But, Domscheit-Berg, who had appeared as the inseparable partner in a WikiLeaks double act, was to be shut out of the organisation's biggest operation. Assange and Domscheit-Berg had had a number of differences of opinion, but the biggest was over money and the funding of WikiLeaks. The organisation had taken itself offline for more than two months, citing a shortage of funds, and had only recently returned to normal service after raising hundreds of thousands of dollars in donations. When Domscheit-Berg joined the organisation he understood it would one day start paying its employees, but now, with money problems, Assange had seemingly changed his mind. Domscheit-Berg was astonished, telling Assange: 'I didn't give up my job under the premise that I would never earn any money. I need to pay for a roof over my head and need to be able to have food.'

Assange started to move against Domscheit-Berg 'because his presence was causing problems'. But he still wanted to keep him working for WikiLeaks because 'we didn't have many people volunteering full-time'. Assange admits that he 'engineered' a way that Domscheit-Berg 'would be kept away from more delicate things that we were doing'.

The two had already started falling out when the WikiLeaks group was cooped up in another building, an apartment, a few months earlier. Back then the days were even shorter—just two hours of sunlight. For those not used to it, the long nights gave them a permanent feeling of being jetlagged. As the WikiLeaks team worked hard to develop a framework for the new Icelandic media laws, personalities clashed. 'It was just too tense, and it just became more aggressive and aggressive every day,' Domscheit-Berg said. 'Then Julian started to tell me about how he's senior and I'm junior, that's why I am not allowed to criticise him.' Just before work started on the Iraq video, Domscheit-Berg left Iceland and went back to Germany. The relationship was quickly unravelling, and before the year was out both men would acrimoniously part for good.

As the small team worked long days on the Iraq video, Assange began finding himself increasingly isolated in the organisation he founded. He seemed to be turning against the very people who provided the stability he needed. The relationship with another steadying force, Jonsdottir, was also under strain. Apart from being heavily involved in writing the script for the video, Jonsdottir was also co-producer. Yet when she tried to discuss the issue of how to deal with YouTube if it attempted to take the video down because it was so violent, Assange ignored her. 'It was very tense and lots of arguments,' Jonsdottir said. 'It was very difficult; I walked out three times.' There is no doubt that Assange was under a lot of strain and he seemed to realise he needed help.

Assange reached out to Rop Gonggrijp, a Dutch activist and hacker, and a friend he'd known for many years. Gonggrijp had decided not only to donate his time and fly to Iceland to help, he also threw in €10000—approximately $15000. 'Julian can deal with incredibly little sleep and a hell of a lot of chaos, but even he has his limits and I could see that he was stretching himself,' he said. But even Gonggrip's cool manner couldn't calm the atmosphere.

To add even more pressure Assange had invited a journalist, Raffi Khatchadourian from the *New Yorker*, into what they now called 'the bunker'. To Jonsdottir's amazement, despite the paranoid concern about security she was unaware of even a basic check being carried out on Khatchadourian. He seemed like a well-intentioned person, but they were trying to deal with complex emotional and political issues and Khatchadourian was getting in the way. One day when Jonsdottir walked into the house, she caught Assange and Khatchadourian having a conversation 'about something that had nothing to do with the work we were doing,' she said. Jonsdottir told Assange to focus on the job at hand, something that did not please him, particularly in front of Khatchadourian.

The *New Yorker* article would do nothing to heal the growing rift between Jonsdottir and Assange, providing a distorted picture of Jonsdottir's role by portraying her as a woman with a walk-on part in the WikiLeaks production—wearing a short skirt, making the tea and cutting Assange's hair. If Assange was angry about the stereotypical way the traditional media reported the world, he made no complaints about the colourful *New Yorker* profile. In fact, he was pleased with the coverage, which painted him as proactive and decisive.

He was so happy he used the fact that he was in the *New Yorker* to garner favour with sources. Information corroborated elsewhere shows that Assange was in regular contact with anonymous informants and spent a lot of time and effort building up strong relationships—letting sources know in advance about the upcoming *New Yorker* story to make them believe they were privileged WikiLeaks insiders. 'They were being treated in a way which made them feel special.'

He developed a close relationship with a WikiLeaks activist who was also a source, a 17-year-old. According to Jonsdottir, Assange gave him direct access to WikiLeaks material, a secure computer, an encrypted phone and money, money she suspected 'he's never going to get back'. Jonsdottir described the teenager as like a 'young Julian', charming, disarming and dangerous. One day during a break in editing, she says she confronted Assange: 'Julian, there is something not right here—you cannot be trusting this guy so much, you cannot be investing so much time, effort, and money and trust into this person, because something, it's not right, trust me.'

She told him that the source could not deliver on his promises to hand over some transcripts of telephone conversations he said he had acquired. They were conversations that would have helped WikiLeaks greatly in one of the investigations. The trouble was, the transcripts didn't exist, according to Jonsdottir. 'I know for sure that there are no tapped phone conversations, and I just know it because I know this place [Iceland] very well. And he managed to tell Julian an incredible story,' Jonsdottir said. According to Jonsdottir, the boy told Julian that he used to get a very good salary and that he had been given three cars, 'really hot cars, you know, beautiful expensive cars. And Julian said "wow, fantastic" instead of, what's wrong with you? How can that be cool, you know that a 17-year-old kid has accumulated, through shady dealings with shady companies, three cars? How can you encourage that sort of behaviour?'

Yet the boy was useful and would play an important role in covering up the source of the Iceland US embassy cable. According to Jonsdottir, he concocted a story that Assange had been followed by two US Security agents because of the Icelandic cable when he flew out of Iceland, information he said he discovered by hacking into an airline reservation system. Jonsdottir thought it was not only untrue but also unhelpful given the pressure Assange was under. For Assange, it was a plausible story fitting perfectly his need to distance the Iceland US embassy cable from the 260000 pages of State Department documents which had yet to be released, and which he hoped the US government didn't know he had. According to Jonsdottir, Assange had been gullible to accept the information, from the teenager but had turned it to his own advantage.

Assange is fond of quoting Rahm Emanuel, President Obama's former Chief of Staff, who famously said that you should never waste a good crisis. Assange had certainly not wasted Iceland's, using it to enhance the chances of providing a safe haven for WikiLeaks, and now he would do it again, on a slightly modified scale. In apparent outrage at being followed by the US State Department staff and having his 17-year-old friend questioned by police for an unrelated incident, Assange went ballistic, according to Jonsdottir, sending tweets worldwide and a letter 'to the Icelandic press about the Icelandic authorities collaborating with the CIA'. Jonsdottir was blunt: Assange's allegation was 'a load of bollocks'. A later investigation by New York's Columbia School of Journalism, which made a detailed assessment of the allegations, came to a similar, if less colourful, conclusion. 'Icelandic journalists have been unable to substantiate his claims.' Assange was proving himself to be the master of deception, using smokescreens and false trails to mislead the intelligence organisations he was convinced were hunting him. The trouble was, some in the WikiLeaks team were also left wondering what was true and what was not.

Despite all the distractions, the video was still on track to be presented to the Washington Press Club just after Easter, during what was generally considered to be a slow news period. The tension between Assange and Jonsdottir was palpable. 'Julian was getting ready to go on stage in the United States in front of the firing squad,' Ragnar said. 'He was just trying to psyche himself up for that, but we were still trying to finish the video.' There were subtitles to do in many different languages; some of the translations were not matching up with the words spoken.

There were other problems too: disagreement over whether the voices of the helicopter pilots should be heard as the opening titles played out. Ragnar argued the case for keeping all the cockpit chatter out, saying viewers would form a bond with the pilots, not the point the video is trying to make. 'At the same time, we are displaying them as monsters,' one of the editors said. 'But emotions always rule,' Ragnar said. 'Well, what is your alternative?' Assange asked. 'Basically, bursts of sounds, interrupting the quiet,' Ragnar replied. The editor made the change, removing the voice of the soldiers and leaving just the sound of radio distortion and a few blips. Time was running out for any more changes. Assange gave the go-ahead. He well understood that while the facts may be sacred, emotional impact made sure they were remembered.

Late Saturday night, shortly before all the work had to be finished, Hrafnsson—who had gone to Baghdad—emailed Assange: they had found the two children in the van on the Iraqi video. They had also discovered the owner of the building that had been attacked by Hellfire missiles fired from the same gunship on the same day. In the video, the building is described as vacant, but it wasn't—seven residents had died.

WikiLeaks worked on its tactics, how best to handle this new information. The battle for the truth and human rights that had bought them together in the first place bound them once again in a common purpose. They discussed whether to hold back the discovery, or release it at the National Press Club. If the military justified the Hellfire attacks by claiming that there were no civilian casualties, WikiLeaks could respond by releasing the information in a kind of ambush. Jonsdottir turned to Gonggrijp, who was close to tears. 'Are you crying?' she asked. 'I am,' he said. 'It is just the kids.' By now Gonggrijp and Jonsdottir were both crying. They wouldn't be tipping the military off about anything; they would let them walk into an ambush.

The well-organised Jonsdottir knew the video had to be finished as soon as possible if they were to make the Washington deadline, but Ragnar also understood Assange's mental state: there was tension and 'Julian didn't want at that time to be practical, his mind was already in the States, he was already there preparing,' Ragnar said. 'He didn't know whether he would be arrested or whatever.' Assange was pretending that he was 'okay', but Ragnar had his doubts. Assange would be flying off to the United States within the next few days, carrying with him the finished videos, and Ragnar was concerned about their security. 'I actually didn't want him to take any computers along with him,' he said. Ragnar says he raised the issue about Assange taking his usual computer. 'It was like a PC, a portable machine like mine, with Windows and everything unencrypted on it, and I said, "He's not going to take this with him?"' Ragnar said he was told that the message would be passed on to Assange, but he heard nothing back. It might seem like bizarre behaviour, given Assange's obsession with security, but he believed he could enter and leave the US before the administration woke up to him being there. 'When you're dealing with a big bureaucratic state they just cannot respond that quickly.'

Concerned about what might happen not only to Assange but to the videos he'd been labouring over for the weeks leading up to Easter holiday, Ragnar took WikiLeaks' security into his own hands. 'I was convinced that Julian would be arrested on his arrival to the United States,' he said. Ragnar took a copy of the full, unedited version of the video and hid it in his house.

The cut down, 17-minute version would be for general distribution, and the 38-minute uncut edition would prove that the edited material had been faithfully reproduced. As they put the final touches to the shorter version, there was still considerable debate about what it should be called, with heated discussions between senior WikiLeaks supporters across the world about naming the video 'Collateral Murder'. It was felt by some that the name was clever, but would distract from the content or be seen as propaganda. It was contrary to the philosophy that WikiLeaks so publicly supported—of letting the facts tell the story. WikiLeaks could be rightfully accused of being the judge, jury and executioner without the evidence being tested. But Assange fought to keep it: 'The promise that we make to our sources is not only will we defend them through every means that we have available, technological and legally and politically but we will try and get the maximum possible political impact for the material that they give to us.' The title had been chosen for maximum political impact. So too had the location where the launch of the video would happen.

The National Press Club in Washington is housed in an imposing building, placed, some might say appropriately, halfway between the White House and the Potomac River, known locally as 'the river of death' because of the number of drownings. It was here on a brisk spring day that Assange and his team arrived. He admitted to being 'a little bit worried'—an understatement—as he flew in to the United States, but he had done his homework and his 'various sources in the US' assured him that officials weren't aware of what was about to happen. Assange had also set up a 'complex ruse' about the material they were carrying if they were stopped and interrogated.

Echoing the feeling at the time that it was a military-style operation, Assange said WikiLeaks would be able to move faster than any US legal counterattack. 'What I predicted would happen is precisely what happened,' he said. Assange and his group passed freely through border security. Nobody had recognised him and even if they had, he didn't appear to be on a wanted list. Certainly none of the officers took any interest in the array of laptop computers he carried in various bags. They may have been slightly more interested in the number of DVDs he and his colleagues had with them, particularly if they'd taken the time to play one of them.

Inside the National Press Club Assange took to the floor, telling the assembled media that what they were about to see was 'a very rich story'. The video screen shows signs of life and then the screen turns black. On it appears a quote from George Orwell: 'Political language is designed to make lies sound truthful and murder respectable and to give the appearance of solidity to pure wind.' The silence is broken by a burst of static. And then words fill the screen. 'On the morning of July 12, 2007, two Apache helicopters using 30 mm cannon fire killed about a dozen people in the Iraqi suburb of New Baghdad. Two children were also wounded.'

A slight pause, and then: 'Although some of the men appear to have been armed, the behaviour of nearly everyone was relaxed. The US military initially claimed that all the dead were "anti-Iraqi forces" or "insurgents".'

Another burst of static. 'The stories of most of those who were killed are unknown. But among the dead were two Reuters news employees, Saeed Chmagh and Namir Noor-Eldeen. In August 2007, Reuters used the Freedom of Information Act to request a copy of the video evidence taken from the primary helicopter involved in the attack. The video has not been released.

Until now.'

In the darkened room, an Apache helicopter with the call sign Crazy Horse is circling ... the audio crackles to life. On patrol in East Baghdad searching for insurgents, the helicopter comes across a group walking in the street. One or two may have been armed. But it is equally true the majority were clearly unarmed. A voice from the gunship says: 'He's got an RPG'—a rocket-propelled grenade launcher. The vision loses sight of the group as the helicopter swings around the back of some low-rise buildings. As the group appears again, a voice orders: 'Let's shoot. Light 'em all up.' Another voice, sounding agitated says: 'Come on, fire!'

The gunner starts firing. There is the loud clatter of heavy calibre munitions. For a split second the people down below continue walking, taking in the summer sun, unaware of their fate. Their bodies explode as the 30-millimetre cannon shells reach their target. The video records the jubilation of the gunship crew. 'Oh, yeah, look at those dead bastards.'

'Nice. Good shootin'.'

'Thank you.'

The gunship turns. By the roadside a survivor is still moving. Obviously severely wounded, he is trying to crawl away. One of the gunship crew says: 'Come on, buddy! Just pick up a weapon.' The US rules of engagement may allow the wounded man to be shot, if he were armed. But there is no weapon. The helicopter turns again. Now a dark-coloured van pulls into view. It stops to help the wounded man. As they carry him to the minivan, the helicopter opens fire again. 'Oh yeah, look at that. Right through the windshield! Ha ha!' The only survivors are two children sitting in the front seat with their father. The cannon shells rip into him. They live—protected by his body. Told of the injuries of one of the surviving children, one of the aircrew can be heard saying: 'Well it's their fault for bringing their kids into a battle.'

Just two hours after the Washington screening, the relatives of the victims watched the video on the other side of the world in Baghdad. It was given to them by Hrafnsson whose work on the ground, with Iraqi journalists, had managed to piece together so much of the story. In their tiny home in East Baghdad, the little girl who'd been so badly injured lifted her dress over her head revealing a long scar on her stomach. Her brother had also been badly injured. 'They are still traumatised and still suffer from the pain of their wounds,' their mother said. The friends of the family wept uncontrollably as they watched the carnage.

As the lights came up in the National Press Club, the US military were severely embarrassed. US Defense Secretary Robert Gates argued that the video was out of context and provided an incomplete picture of the battlefield, comparing it to war as seen 'through a soda straw'. 'There is no before and there is no after.' Assange admits that some soldiers have reported there was some action in the area before, but he makes the point: 'When you have unarmed people including a wounded prostrate man on the ground unable to even get away, to deliberately target and kill those people with 30 millimetre cannon fire—it's murder.' Lawyers who have reviewed this videoed evidence of the killing of an unarmed wounded man and the wounding of the children call it a war crime.

The fact the two journalists were working for the international news agency Reuters should have worked in favour of justice and a full public investigation of the killings. If you're going to get gunned down, it helps to be a journalist, if for no other reason than journalists would be more likely to go looking for your killers. Unfortunately for the journalists, Saeed Chmagh and his colleague, Namir Noor-Eldeen, who died that day, their deaths remained a mystery for the next two years. Though the US military did say the gunship had mistaken a camera for a RPG. Reuters tried repeatedly, under freedom of information, to get a copy of the video, but was refused by the US military. What is more disturbing is that at least one journalist did know what had happened, but no hard questions were ever asked of the US government.

On that spring morning in April 2010 in Washington, as the world digested the power of the extraordinary gunship video, frenetic activity permeated the corridors of the Pentagon, the five-sided squat building that houses the nerve centre of America's military. Senior officials were desperately trying to discover who'd leaked the vision. Across town on the other side of the Potomac River there should have been fevered activity too—but inside the nondescript edifice which is home to the newspaper that produced the world's greatest exposé in the history of journalism, Watergate, it was strangely business as usual.

The *Washington Post* might have been famous for the toppling of President Richard Nixon nearly forty years ago, but the WikiLeaks 'Collateral Murder' exposé posed many questions about what had happened to the once mighty media institution. David Finkel, a Pulitzer Prize–winning journalist with the newspaper, was embedded with the US troops in Baghdad that day, writing a book called *The Good Soldiers*. In the book, he gives a vivid description of the killings, and quotes much of the dialogue in the video. But when Finkel's book came out, the *Washington Post* carried a story about the killings that ended with a quote from the Pentagon: 'We think the safest way to cover these operations is to be embedded with US forces.' There was no follow-up investigation by the *Washington Post* on the killings of the journalists. Asked if he could say when he saw the video Finkel said, 'I can't,' and he added: 'I don't need advice from WikiLeaks how to do my journalism.'

Just what did the *Washington Post* know and when did they know it? This is difficult to ascertain. Assange has suggested that the *Washington Post* had a copy of the video but took no action. 'I assume they had the video, you know, close back to 2007 when these events happened. But I am sure that at least for the past year they have had it and it was not released,' he said.

The *Washington Post* has denied ever having a copy. Apart from a shocking frontline view of the war in which civilians were targeted as enemy combatants, 'Collateral Murder' also shone a bright light into the cosy relationships between journalists, journalism and the military in the United States. Compounding this perception, the *Washington Post* had also alerted the CIA that it was about to publish a story which revealed it had been involved in systematically kidnapping people in foreign countries as part of the so-called war on terror. Assange was at a loss to understand how the *Washington Post* could argue that it was necessary on the grounds of national security to tip off the CIA in advance the publication.

When WikiLeaks posted the video on its website, it ripped around the planet at viral speed. It looked like the world's media couldn't get enough of Assange. In the week following the release, 'WikiLeaks' was the search term with the most significant growth worldwide, as measured by Google. Yet for WikiLeaks, the overall coverage was disappointing. The international mainstream media treated it more like a video flick than a disturbing revelation about the war in Iraq. Most worrying for WikiLeaks was the coverage of the US cable news network, CNN. It was the one American network they expected to give the material a better run than most.

Hrafnsson, who had risked his life to bring the story home, was upset that 'CNN showed just a little clip of it,' he said. 'They didn't show the actual shooting of the people.' He said that when the CNN anchor asked his network's Pentagon correspondent why the killings weren't being shown, the correspondent said they were doing that 'out of respect for the relatives'. But as Hrafnsson pointed out, the relatives had already seen the full video the day before in Baghdad.

In Australia, the national broadcaster ABC TV's main evening news bulletin followed the Americans, with limited coverage of the attack. Like many other broadcasters around the world the ABC had not distinguished itself in its coverage of the Iraq war. Before the decision to attack Iraq was made, even the prestigious *Four Corners* program declined to investigate the role of oil in the invasion. But just when Assange was bemoaning the fact that the media was focusing on whether a camera could be mistaken for a rocket-propelled grenade launcher instead of the way the war was being conducted, another ABC program, *Lateline*, aired an extraordinary interview with one of the soldiers who'd been at the scene of the killings: former US Army specialist Ethan McCord. Without the WikiLeaks video, his story about the horrific reality of what happened that day would never have been known.

'I didn't know that there was actually a video, until the day that it was released and I dropped my children off at school, went home, grabbed a cup of coffee, sat on the couch and turned on the news, and saw myself running across the television screen carrying a child,' McCord said. 'My initial reaction was shock and anger. Anger that this scene that had been playing over in my head was now in front of my face.' McCord said he was one of the first six soldiers to arrive on the ground at the scene where the Apache's had opened fire.

'The first thing I saw was about four men, laying on the ground and, they were pretty much completely destroyed. I'd never seen anybody who had been shot by a 30-millimetre round before and, I don't want to see that again. It was, it almost didn't—it didn't seem real, in a sense that it looked more like I was looking at something that would be in a bad horror movie.'

He also noticed 'a couple of RPGs as well as AK47s when I got to the scene'. But his attention was drawn to the minivan. 'I could hear a small child crying, the crying was coming from the van that was shot up.' He ran over to the van and opened the passenger door with another soldier. 'The soldier that I was with turns around and started vomiting at the sight of the children, turned around and ran off not wanting to deal with that situation or, or even look at that.' When he got back to his base, McCord was overcome by emotion as he wiped the children's blood from his body armour. He spoke to his senior officer about getting some psychological counselling.

'He kind of chuckled and told me to get the sand out of my vagina and to suck it up and to be a soldier and told me that there would be repercussions if I was to go to mental health.' McCord said he was told he would be seen as a malingerer, which 'in the army is actually a crime'. He decided to bottle up his emotions. 'I started becoming very, very angry with the people around me.'

McCord believes the first attack on the group of men might have been justified but 'I don't feel that the attack on the van was warranted'.

The US military could see nothing wrong with any part of the action. The army continues to insist that there was no violation of the rules of engagement. For McCord, 'the WikiLeaks video only begins to depict the suffering we have created'. There was no difference between that day or any other day in Iraq other than that one was caught on video and the world got to see it, he said.

In a few months' time, WikiLeaks would produce the proof of McCord's assertion: Iraqi civilians were being killed in much larger numbers than was being reported. The US was covering up the numbers.

7

THE WHISTLEBLOWER

As the huge passenger plane began its final decent into Melbourne Airport, Julian Assange was worried about being arrested. It was May 2010, one month after he had released the secret footage of the US Apache helicopter gunning down unarmed civilians in a Baghdad street. The idea that the US might have put out a warrant was a possibility. But he'd also recently challenged the Australian Government, revealing a secret 'blacklist' of websites it hoped to use to control access to the Internet. He'd desperately tried to find out the likelihood of being stopped, but what worried Assange most as the plane hit the tarmac was the silence. He'd heard nothing from the government. As the aircraft taxied towards the air bridge, there was no way out.

No doubt many of the passengers were Aussies returning from holiday, sporting healthy tans and looking well, even after the long flight from Asia. Others looked more harried—business executives already on their mobile phones eagerly chatting as they made their way towards the customs barrier and Immigration. Assange, with his long, ghost-white hair, pallid complexion and piercing grey eyes, wasn't difficult to pick out from the crowd.

For the Australian Federal Police officers on border protection duty that day at Melbourne Airport, Julian Assange was an easy target. But this was a game of cat and mouse—and not what Assange was expecting at all. When he handed over his passport, the Immigration officer punched the data in to the keyboard. Assange's passport had the same look as its owner—frayed at the edges.

'Looks like we might have to get you a new one of these, mate,' the officer said, taking the passport and disappearing behind a glass screen which kept the activities that went on behind it hidden from public scrutiny. Assange was sanguine, a world traveller—this could be perfectly harmless. 'I mean I do travel a lot so my passport is a bit worn,' he had thought to himself at the time.

While Assange waited patiently, behind the screen the Immigration officer handed over the passport to a federal police officer. Slowly he peeled it open—Julian Paul Assange, born 3 July 1971, Townsville, Queensland, Australia. The passport was several years old but the face that stared back was unmistakably that of the man in the queue, though perhaps slightly more relaxed. Quickly he lifted the lid of the photocopy machine and placed the open passport face down on the glass. In a few minutes he was done. Back at the Immigration barrier, the officer handed Assange his passport and waved him through.

The officer had made some comments about the passport being cancelled, but then said they had merely been thinking about it.

Assange must have thought it was his lucky day. The passport problem had already cost him fifteen minutes and he had someone waiting outside to pick him up, so he hurried off to collect his bags.

But as he made his way to the luggage collection area, he caught the AFP rifling through his bags. They told Assange they had been 'instructed to investigate this matter a bit further', without revealing to him exactly what it was. It was possible to believe that it was payback; that the government had been far from happy with his exploits with their blacklist, and this was a kind of backhander. At least that's the way that Assange seemed to see it, brushing the whole episode off as 'a bit of a bureaucratic thing'.

As Assange finally caught up with his friend and headed into Melbourne along the eight-lane freeway that provides the sole access to the city from the airport, he may well have reflected on why his passport had been taken away for a quarter of an hour and the garbled explanation about whether it had been cancelled or not. Just what the AFP was up to in the baggage hall wasn't clear. The story didn't add up. And there was a very good reason.

Back at the airport the Immigration staff were busy filing a report on Assange. He'd been picked up by what is known as a Stop Alert. It involves a polished act of deception. The trick is to tell a person who is on this watch list that there is something wrong with their passport. It is important that the person is not unnecessarily alarmed and believes it is just normal procedure. When the passport is taken away it is photocopied—providing a list of every country visited that still stamps passports, and there are many of them. Linked with electronic records of travel, it gives a near complete record of a person's cross-border movements. This information might have been of little direct use to the Australian Government, but in the United States there were people who were far more interested in Julian Assange and his WikiLeaks team.

If Assange can call anywhere in the world home, it's Melbourne, the city where he developed much of his activist thinking and where his children live. It's as though he'd returned to catch his breath after the exhaustion of Iceland and the exhilaration of everything that 'Collateral Murder' exposed. The footage had put WikiLeaks on the map, but the consequences were profound both for the organisation and for him personally.

'Collateral Murder', like the Iceland US embassy cable, was only one element of the huge classified document drop WikiLeaks had received, supposedly from Bradley Manning, a US military intelligence officer stationed in Iraq. Already Assange and his team were working on the next big release. WikiLeaks had promised to publish any information it received as soon as possible. There's no doubt that what they had in the cables was perishable and the sooner it was released the greater its effect would be. Pushed for time, Assange also understood the importance of keeping the media onside. In one Internet conversation with WikiLeaks staff, he stressed the importance of dealing with journalists in a helpful way.

* * *

Tracking Assange down for an interview for ABC TV's *Foreign Correspondent* program proved to be an arduous business: conversations in lifts so that they couldn't be bugged, location changes at the last minute, and then, finally, in a wood-panelled, book-lined study in the heart of Melbourne Assange walked in and sat down. The camera rolled for the interview. His major concern was his treatment by the Australian government because of WikiLeaks' revelation of its secret list of banned Internet sites.

The list resembled a chamber of horrors: tens of thousands of the worst child porn sites in the world. The fact that a dentist's website and regular adult porn sites were also there only added to the media excitement. Australia was rushing to the barricades to erect an Internet barrier, not because of some extraordinary necessity to protect its citizens, but to help the government get the numbers it needed in the Senate to pass other legislation. The vote of one of Australia's more bizarre Christian members of Parliament, Steve Fielding, was needed to pass legislation through, and part of the price of his support appeared to be an Internet filter.

For Assange it was a perfect target to blow the whistle on: a list of sites the government wanted to censor, an example of what he saw as overbearing state control. What concerned Assange even more was the automated nature of the list and what it meant for the future of censorship. 'Should there be a centralised, automated, national censorship system between every newspaper and its reader, between every TV station and its viewer; between every political party and their membership; between us and our readers?' he asked. 'My answer is clearly no.' He argued that by embracing an automated system, Australia was heading down the Chinese path. He said that while the Australian government was not the Chinese government, it was possible to see 'slowly creeping authoritarian tendencies' in the Australian government. Because the filter was trying to catch people who were already acting illegally, Assange pointed out it was designed to control the law-abiding majority. It had opened up a system of what he called national mandatory, centralised, real time, instantaneous state censorship.

The government hit back by adding WikiLeaks to its banned list of sites. Communications Minister Senator Stephen Conroy had told the Senate he'd called in the Federal Police to investigate WikiLeaks. Assange wrote to the minister asking: 'What's the story? I am the publisher of this blacklist. I assume that these comments are referring to me. Is there a problem with me entering into Australian territory? Can my liberty be guaranteed or is there any information you have that may bear on this?' The minister's office, according to Assange, did not reply to his email or fax address. It was either a naïve or foolhardy action, asking the federal government if he would be arrested in Australia. It wouldn't be the last time that Assange, for all his political acumen, would so fundamentally misunderstand the way the world and its law enforcement agencies worked.

After our interview we arranged to meet up again the following day. My team would receive a message giving us precise details of the location later. Producer Mary Ann Jolley smiled and rolled her eyes. She'd been in too many unbugged lifts for her own good recently, and some of the fun was beginning to wear off.

When eventually the text came through, it said cryptically we should meet up at a pub across the road from Melbourne University. No particular time was mentioned. We arrived and stood in the bar, and after nearly forty minutes and with the thought that maybe the interview wouldn't take place that night, we ordered our first round of drinks just as Julian Assange walked in and saw us: 'Ah journalists,' he smiled. 'Can't do an interview without a drink!' Assange favours the element of surprise. He was having fun, but it wouldn't last.

Twenty-four hours later, in a private Internet chat room, events were unfolding that would have a profound affect on WikiLeaks and how it did business.

* * *

The Californian town of Carmichael, north-east of Sacramento, is a sleepy place where the local newspaper's front page is rarely more interesting than road traffic accidents or the fact that a local vet has been named businessperson of the year. It's hardly the kind of town where you'd expect to find Adrian Lamo. His exploits are legendary, not just in his home state, but everywhere the Internet reaches. He's described as a 'grey hat' in the Internet world where 'white hats' work for security companies, 'black hats' hack into everything with an open port, and 'grey hats' like the challenge of breaking in but say they do no damage. Lamo is an unusual character: a sometime journalist, he's been a habitual drug user, hospitalised with Asperger's syndrome—and convicted of breaking in to the *New York Times* and rifling through the personal data of its contributors. He also chewed up several thousands of dollars of free searches using its data research accounts. At times he's been broke, wandering America, living with friends where he has them, or just ending up in a new city with nowhere to stay but a park bench. However, among the hackeratti he's a celebrated star, a hero of the Internet. Lamo also has interesting relationships with members of US military intelligence.

In late May 2010 he received a message via an Internet chat room from Private First Class Bradley Manning, an intelligence officer with the 2nd Brigade, 10th Mountain Division, based at Forward Base Hammer in East Baghdad. Manning had access to two computers connected to SIPRNET: the Secret Internet Protocol Router Network and the Joint Worldwide Intelligence Communications Systems (JWICS)—systems of interconnected computer networks used by the US Defense Department and State Department to transmit information classified 'Secret'. Others, too, were plugged into the classified system, up to half a million people of both civilian and military staff, as the US government tried to share information more openly in the hope of heading off another 9/11 terrorist attack.

The dark towering walls do a good job of protecting the base from sandstorms that regularly sweep across the desiccated landscape outside—and other hostile forces. Inside, the military has tried to create some semblance of normality for the men and women stationed there, creating a 'town' with a supermarket, bars, a canteen and even a jazz band playing some nights. Even so, by many accounts Manning, aged twenty-two, had not been happy for some time. It seemed to be a repeat of his life at school where he had apparently been bullied and accused of being effeminate. According to ABC News America, he had been reprimanded for assaulting a fellow soldier and demoted from Specialist to Private First Class. He was also sent to a chaplain after officers noticed what was called 'odd behaviors'. His Facebook page gave an insight into his state of mind. 'Bradley Manning is not a piece of equipment,' he said, and quoted a joke about 'military intelligence' being an oxymoron.

At the beginning of May, he changed his Facebook status to: 'Bradley Manning is now left with the sinking feeling that he doesn't have anything left.'

Five days later he said he was 'livid' after being 'lectured by ex-boyfriend', then later the same day said he was 'beyond frustrated with people and society at large'. The Facebook page added: 'Take me for who I am, or face the consequences!' A few days later, on 21 May, he contacted Adrian Lamo.

> MANNING: Hi how are you, I'm an army intelligence analyst, deployed to eastern Baghdad, pending discharge for 'adjustment disorder'. I'm sure you're pretty busy. If you had unprecedented access to classified networks 14 hours a day 7 days a week for 8+ months, what would you do?

Lamo says when he logged into the chat room four hours later and discovered the message, he asked Manning for his MOS. Lamo said it was a sure way of discovering whether someone was a fake, because it is specific military jargon for Military Occupational Specialty. The reply came back: 'Intelligence analyst.'

According to the logs Lamo handed over to *Wired* magazine, Manning said: 'I can't believe what I'm confessing to you. I've been isolated for long. I just wanted to be nice and live a normal life but events kept forcing me to figure out ways to survive.' Manning added that he had been 'self-medicating' when he wasn't 'toiling in the supply office'—his new occupation since he was discharged—and was not officially 'intel anymore'. He said there were so many documents, 'it's impossible for any one human to read all quarter-million … and not feel overwhelmed … and possibly desensitised, the scope is so broad … and yet the depth so rich'.

LAMO: Give me some bona fides … yanno? Any specifics.

Manning then revealed that the classified cable from the US Embassy in Reykjavik on the Icesave bank had been 'a test'—presumably one of the first cables WikiLeaks had been sent.

LAMO: Anything unreleased?

According to Lamo's log, Manning said: 'I'd have to ask Assange.' 'Why do you answer to him?' Lamo asked.

MANNING: I don't … I just want the material out there … I don't want to be a part of it. I can't believe what I'm confessing to you.

Manning said that US security had also 'caught wind' that WikiLeaks had a video of an air strike in Afghanistan. 'It was an awful incident, but nothing like the Baghdad one.'

MANNING: I can't believe what I'm telling you.

The following day, Lamo is clearly interested. He instigates the first call at a little after 7.19 a.m.

LAMO: hey you

MANNING: whats up

LAMO: how're you feeling today?

MANNING: I'm feeling a little better …

Lamo is interested in the operational security at the base, but appears particularly interested in Assange. When Manning fails to respond he switches to personal questions about his religion and then tries again: 'Does Assange use AIM [an electronic instant messaging system] or other messaging services? I'd like to chat with him one of these days about opsec [operational security].'

MANNING: No he does not use AIM. He would come to you.

The following day, 25 May, the logs show Manning is particularly upbeat about how leaking the Iraq video to WikiLeaks connected him with Ethan McCord, the Army Specialist who apologised to the families of the victims.

MANNING: Amazing how the world works. Takes six degrees of separation to a whole new level. Event occurs in 2007, I watch video in 2009 with no context, do research, forward information to group of FOI activists, more research occurs, video is released in 2010, those involved come forward to discuss event, I witness those involved coming forward to discuss publicly, even add them as friends on FB … [Facebook] without them knowing who I am. They touch my life, I touch their life, they touch my life again … full circle.

Lamo asked Manning if he was concerned about counterintelligence 'looking into your Wiki stuff'. It might have seemed like an innocuous, or even supportive question, though it would later appear to have been nothing of the sort. Manning said there was no investigation, and though he believed the 'State Department will be uber-pissed', he didn't think they were capable of tracing everything. Anyone who went looking for evidence would find nothing because both of his computers had been 'zerofilled', meaning that both hard drives had been wiped clean. The evidence had been 'destroyed'. Asked if he was talking about embassy cables, Manning replies: 'Yes, 260 000 in all.'

Asked what he hoped to achieve by the leaks, Manning said he hoped for 'worldwide discussion, debates and reforms'. He says if that doesn't happen, 'we're doomed as a species. I will officially give up on the society we have if nothing happens.'

Manning confirmed that the Apache video had been seen by journalists well before it was released by WikiLeaks. The *Washington Post* 'sat on the video', David Finkel had 'acquired a copy' while embedded 'out here'. Echoing the manifesto of WikiLeaks, Manning said: 'I want people to see the truth, regardless of who they are, because without information you cannot make informed decisions as a public.'

The tipping point for Manning was a *New York Times* story reporting the killings, and the deaths of the two journalists in Baghdad. 'The American military said in a statement late Thursday that eleven people had been killed: nine insurgents and two civilians. According to the statement, American troops were conducting a raid when they were hit by small-arms fire and rocket-propelled grenades. The American troops called in reinforcements and attack helicopters. In the ensuing fight, the statement said, the two Reuters employees and nine insurgents were killed.'

The newspaper also quoted the US military: 'There is no question that coalition forces were clearly engaged in combat operations against a hostile force,' said Lieutenant Colonel Scott Bleichwehl, a spokesman for the multinational forces in Baghdad.

The misleading statement by the US military played on Manning's mind for weeks, 'probably a month and a half' before he took the next step with the video: 'I forwarded it to WikiLeaks through its whistleblower submission system at WikiLeaks.org.' Manning told Lamo that long-term sources, like him, got preference.

LAMO: How does that preference work?

MANNING: Veracity … the material is easy to verify because they know a little bit more about the source than a purely anonymous one and confirmation [sic] publicly from earlier material, would make them more likely to publish.

The earlier material he had sent to WikiLeaks gave him a great deal of credibility as a whistleblower with the organisation.

Inside Forward Base Hammer, Manning turned the culture of piracy and illegal copying of movies and videos to what he saw as a more worthwhile cause. The logs tell a story of a monotonous and difficult life at the base even in the intelligence section. 'You had people working fourteen hours a day, every single day, no weekends, no recreation,' according to Manning. 'Everyone just sat at their workstation, watching music videos/car chases, buildings exploding, and writing more stuff to CD/DVD—the culture fed opportunities.' To check out how strong the security was Manning asked the local National Security Agency (NSA) officer 'if he could find any suspicious activity coming out of local networks'. According to Manning: '… he shrugged and said… "it's not a priority"' and went back to watching *Eagle's Eye*, a movie warning about how governments shouldn't be trusted with personal data. For Manning, the coast was clear. He apparently downloaded the material onto a music disc he'd first wiped clean. As he told Lamo, he 'listened and lip-synced to Lady Gaga's "Telephone" while exfiltratrating [sic] possibly the largest data spillage in American history'.

As the logs record, Manning reflected: 'Weak servers, weak logging, weak physical security, weak counterintelligence, inattentive signal analysis, a perfect storm.' Manning cited the video of an air strike in Afghanistan. 'Iraq war event log, the "Gitmo Papers", and State Department cable database,' as the highlights of the material he gave to WikiLeaks. 'Not too shabby,' said Lamo, which might have sounded like a statement of admiration but it was far from it.

Within hours Lamo had called his friends in military intelligence and met up with the FBI, in midtown Sacramento not far from Carmichael. Lamo said the reason he turned Manning in wasn't about the cables specifically; it was about the fact he was grabbing what he could and 'firing bullets into the air without thought to the consequences of where they might land or who they might hit'. As he sat in a diner, Lamo portrayed himself as an honest American defending the interests of US troops.

But Lamo's motives—and the truth about his relationship with Manning—remain oblique. Since meeting the FBI and talking to military investigators, Lamo has changed his story several times, from saying the first contact from Manning came 'out of the blue' to that Manning contacted him via Twitter. He has also asserted that

Assange 'groomed' Manning and that Manning had said he had been given access to a series of 'special servers' reserved only for those who submitted the most sensitive documents. But none of that is in the published logs and not in the unpublished ones either, from what can be made of statements by *Wired*, which apparently has a full copy. Ellsberg said there was a real possibility that Lamo was 'just making this stuff up'. As Lamo spoke with the investigators, he knew that Manning was having a tough time in Forward Base Hammer. What he didn't know is that it's probable Manning, far from being treated like a privileged source as erroneously asserted by Lamo, had been pushed to one side by Assange and felt increasingly isolated. This was why he was looking for friendship on the Internet.

It was a crucial moment for WikiLeaks: if Manning had not felt so alone he may not have started his Internet 'confession' to Lamo. It appears that Manning wanted to get his story out—and was looking for someone to tell it to. He had every reason to believe that Lamo, who had a reputation as a WikiLeaks financial supporter, would be sympathetic: 'I have encouraged people to donate and I still do,' Lamo said.

Manning also may have believed that in Lamo he had a trusted journalist who could offer him protection. Later on, respected Salon.com journalist Glen Greenwald asked Lamo: 'So early on in the conversation you had discussions with him about the fact that because you were a journalist you could offer him protection, confidentiality protection, as a source?'

LAMO: Under the California reporter shield law, not federally but yeah–

GREENWALD: I know, but you talked about that with him?

LAMO: That is correct …

This is one explanation for why Manning may have been so extra-ordinarily open in his online discussions. Apart from believing that Lamo was sympathetic to WikiLeaks—even a trusted journalist—what Manning clearly didn't expect was that Lamo would hand everything over to the FBI. The following day, 26 May, Bradley Manning was arrested by military police at Forward Base Hammer.

Blithely unaware of the unfolding drama, Assange carried on business as usual in Melbourne, preparing for a huge drop of US documents, a total of 91 000 reports on the war in Afghanistan. As he hurried across Melbourne's busy streets carrying his backpack or riding on trams to get to the homes of friends where he stayed, he was increasingly preoccupied with the problems of his rapidly expanding organisation. Though the world thought that WikiLeaks was staffed by hundreds of people, the fact is that WikiLeaks had no more than ten people who were engaged full-time—and many of those also had permanent jobs. Assange was to all intents and purposes WikiLeaks. When he said as much, it wasn't hubris as many saw it—it was the truth. It was the last time, though, that WikiLeaks would operate as a near one-man band—in the future he would include media partners from around the world.

* * *

Just as we were beginning to edit our *Foreign Corresponent* report ready for broadcasting Assange put in an unexpected call to the story producer. He was in a bind; something had happened. Assange had been going to go to the United States and now he couldn't. Manning was languishing in a Kuwait military prison, waiting to be sent to the US. 'None of us knew that Bradley Manning was under arrest.' Jonsdottir said. 'Assange knew but told no one,' she said. When Jonsdottir found out she was livid. As someone whose name was on the 'Collateral Murder' video she pointed out to Assange that she had a right to know such facts.

Exactly when Assange knew isn't clear, but by 2 June—four days before the news broke publicly—he was concerned enough to abandon any thought of travelling to the United States to meet Daniel Ellsberg for the first time. He had arranged instead to video Skype in to a conference in Manhattan where Ellsberg would be on stage at what was called a 'Personal Democracy Forum'.

What Assange—who had managed to hack into the Los Alamos nuclear weapons facility in his youth and now ran the biggest Internet whistleblower site in the world—wanted was our help. With Skype, of all things, the free Internet video conferencing system. He didn't have broadband big enough to carry the signal. Seeing this as an opportunity to get much needed extra vision of Assange, *Foreign Correspondent* agreed to assist. We had pictures of him walking down the street, in a manner not dissimilar to a John Cleese impersonation of the Ministry of Silly Walks, but that was all. He had refused to let us film him playing the piano because we might use the pictures to suggest the keys were a computer keyboard and he was still hacking. Assange appeared obsessed with how pictures might be represented.

People might draw the wrong conclusions based on what they saw and what they knew, he told us. The pressure of WikiLeaks was clearly having a big effect on its founder.

Assange, looking slightly rougher than usual, seemed mildly on edge. But as the conference got underway he hit his stride, telling the New York audience that 'leaking is inherently an anti-authoritarian act, it is inherently an anarchist act'. He was clearly delighted to pay homage to the man he called his hero, Ellsberg, making the point that, while he was busy leaking the Pentagon Papers, Assange was just being born.

Over in midtown Manhattan, Assange appeared on a huge screen like a ghostly image hovering over the stage. Ellsberg and the audience of journalists, activists and technical enthusiasts had trouble at times hearing him, something Ellsberg jokingly put down to 'the Australian accent'. But there was nothing humorous about the warning Ellsberg gave his young admirer. He was sure it was a 'high priority' for the US Government to 'neutralise him one way or another and I wouldn't exclude physical danger'. Ellsberg added that 'trying to find ways that discredit him or to keep him from communicating with possible sources, is a very high priority' for the US government.

While Ellsberg strongly supported Assange and the work he was doing at this time, Ellsberg feels that it is Manning, rather than Assange, who is more like him, if indeed he is the leaker.

'The analogy is not with Assange so much, but with Manning. And he's the first person in forty years to really do what I did, in the sense of a large amount of material, with the large risk and expectation of a very long prison sentence, and when I read that he's said, "I am ready to go to prison for life" or even be executed. You know when I read the "executed" I thought, that's a little melodramatic or extreme. It turns out not to be of course, they're calling for his execution.'

As we drove through the darkened streets of Melbourne the night of the New York conference, Julian Assange sat quietly in the car. He'd eaten our cold leftovers of risotto and drunk a can of Coke. If WikiLeaks was a money scam as some have suggested, Assange should get an Oscar for his performances. A block from his hotel he asked us to pull over. We had strict instructions to drop him off on a nondescript stretch of road. Julian Assange disappeared down the street; he was going into hiding with a bag full of secrets—including, 92 000 documents on the Afghanistan war.

He began moving from house to house, never staying in the same place for more than a few nights. It wasn't just the Afghan documents the Pentagon believed Assange was carrying. It was convinced he had the entire State Department dump as well—and there were no other copies. 'The Pentagon was of the belief that I was carrying two-hundred-and-sixty thousand classified US cables in my pocket and a whole bunch of other things.' The Pentagon was right, but Assange had made plans.

The material had been disseminated to a number of different people and places, but for Assange they were not diverse enough to guarantee its complete safety. 'The difficulty at that stage is that the material had not been spread very wide,' Assange said. If the US managed to track down one source, it could well lead to the others. Assange began working on disseminating the material to so many places that, even if one location was discovered, the US would never find them all. 'We started hearing the reports that they were hunting for me,' he said.

* * *

Nick Davies, a leading investigative reporter for the *Guardian*, had read about Manning's arrest and combed through the logs of his chats with Lamo. What attracted his attention was the blunt statement that he had given WikiLeaks secret US diplomatic cables, including 260 000 yet-to-be revealed State Department documents. Davies, like dozens of journalists before him, began trying to contact Assange, but unlike most Davies didn't want an interview—he wanted access to the cables themselves.

After emails to Assange got no reply, Davies began trying to contact people close to him. The fact that he repeatedly drew a blank was hardly surprising. Assange wasn't taking any calls—even an encrypted conversation can be traced if an organisation like the Pentagon really puts its mind to it. Davies discovered that Assange would be going to Europe in a few days' time. Assange was keen to get the Afghan War Logs out as soon as possible. 'He was genuinely concerned about being killed by the Americans,' said one of his friends. It would be possible to do the work from Melbourne, but difficult, and much easier to work out of Europe where much of WikiLeaks' infrastructure and supporting personnel live. He decided to take a chance.

Assange had established a cover story: in case he got stopped at the border on his way out of Australia he had managed to secure an invitation to speak at a conference sponsored by the European Union about freedom of speech and censorship. Assange gambled it would prevent the Australian government 'detaining me at the border on behalf of the United States'. It would cause an 'uproar', he said.

In Europe, Davies persuaded the *Guardian*'s Brussels reporter to get word to Assange and tell him he was on his way. As Davies clambered aboard the Eurostar train he would have had little doubt that persuading Assange to hand over the documents could produce the story of the decade, and would almost certainly be the pinnacle of any journalistic career. 'While I was on the train going under the Channel, I had tried to work out what I would say to him,' remembers Davies. 'It wasn't going to work if I said "I'm a greedy reporter, I'd like to take all your information and put it in my newspaper."' Instead, Davies planned to lay out a plan he thought would be appealing. The *Guardian* would set up a special team of reporters to comb through the WikiLeaks material—singling out those unreleased documents that would benefit from the kind of forensic analysis and examination the *Guardian* is famous for the world over.

During a six-hour meeting in a Brussels café on 22 June, Davies says he and Assange agreed that the *Guardian* and the *New York Times* be given an early look at some information WikiLeaks had on the Afghanistan war, with each newspaper publishing their own takes on the documents.

Assange didn't feel he had much time before he was hunted down. With the *Guardian* on board, he had found a way to move ahead with the Afghan documents, and since he would be working closely with established news outlets it took some of the heat off him. The Pentagon would think twice about attacking him while he was working with the *Guardian* and the *New York Times*. It was a masterstroke, and thanks largely to Nick Davies. But within a few days the *Guardian* received a call from *Der Spiegel* saying they were part of the deal too. 'We agreed to let them in,' said Davies, but their presence had never been part of the deal. For Davies, it was a warning. 'He taught us we couldn't trust him.'

Standing in Brussels with the possibility that he had just secured access to a world-beating story, Davies was tempted to call his boss, the quietly spoken yet adventurous editor of the *Guardian*, Alan Rusbridger. But hours of talking to Assange would make even the most cavalier person cautious about telephone intercepts, and Davies was a naturally careful journalist, especially when it came to protecting sources. He left the mobile in his pocket. Early the next morning he went to the railway station and caught the Eurostar home, and headed straight to the *Guardian*'s offices, which are walking distance from the London terminus at St Pancras.

Davies told Alan Rusbridger what was on offer. Rusbridger picked up the phone to Bill Keller, the executive editor of the *New York Times*. It was the beginning of something very new.

WikiLeaks had had an ongoing relationship with the *Guardian* for years. They seemed to share a common, simple journalistic goal: exposing information that powerful vested interests wanted kept secret. What made this relationship more complex, and potentially more difficult to handle, was the inclusion of two other media outlets, the German *Der Spiegel*, and the *New York Times*. The three media organisations had never worked together before on such a huge scale—and they had certainly never worked with WikiLeaks as a group. There was hope that if it worked it could be a blueprint for other collaborative efforts. It would be an interesting experiment.

8

GOOD TIMES, BAD TIMES

For nearly a century, the neo-Gothic *New York Times* building on 43rd Street in the centre of Manhattan was viewed as the heart of American journalism. It was here that the Pentagon Papers were published in 1971, and the newspaper's coverage of Watergate further bolstered its reputation for gutsy journalism. The *New York Times* has won more than a hundred Pulitzer Prizes, the most prestigious award in US journalism. But despite the building's grand history, few were sorry to leave behind the narrow corridors and the dingy office space when the newspaper moved in 2007.

The *New York Times'* new home, a 52-storey steel and glass tower just a few blocks away on 8th Avenue, was more suitable for a newspaper of the modern age. Yet by and large, the journalists who crowded inside this open and airy building were motivated by the same beliefs and aspirations as those who had occupied the old offices for the last ninety-seven years—they, too, were chasing the big story that would make a difference to the world. Exclusives were hard won and took dedication, time and sometimes courage to deliver. And that meant money, and taking risks.

In recent times, the *New York Times* had been bedevilled by a mixture of misfortune and controversial editorial judgement as it tried to balance its journalistic principles with a changing mood in the United States after the 9/11 terrorist attacks. From its often unquestioning coverage of the White House in the lead-up to the Iraq war, to reporters found guilty of plagiarism and fabrication, the newspaper has gone through a difficult period. It led to the resignation of two senior editors in 2003. The present executive editor, Bill Keller, not known for reticence, had also come under fire for holding back a story about how the NSA had been spying on the US public, accepting the argument from President George Bush that publication might compromise national security.

The phone call from Alan Rusbridger, editor of the *Guardian*, offered what the paper needed: a strong revelatory story with the promise of more to come. In Washington, Eric Schmitt had just returned from a reporting stint in Pakistan. He'd barely had time to settle back into his office when the *New York Times* bureau chief, Dean Baquet, told him he'd have to be on a plane quickly for a special project in London. Schmitt had covered the military for many years and Keller saw him as a journalist with 'excellent judgment and an unflappable demeanor'.

Schmitt arrived in London late on Saturday 26 June. The next day he met with the *Guardian*'s investigations editor David Leigh and they began discussing how to tackle what was emerging as one of the biggest ever stories about the Afghan war.

It would be an interesting collaboration between arguably the best of British and US journalism, with all the inherent cultural differences of the two newspaper institutions thrown into the mix. What made this venture unique was the addition of WikiLeaks, a child of the anarchic blogosphere, and Assange, its editor-in-chief.

Before they got down to the details of the cables, Schmitt was shown a large office positioned a discreet distance from the *Guardian* newsroom and the prying interest of other journalists. The room was tucked away on a floor used by the *Guardian*'s advertising staff on the well-founded belief that no self-respecting journalist would be seen anywhere near the advertising department. The room would become the centrepiece of the operation: just half a dozen desks and smart, large-screen computers, with a huge window that stretched from the floor to the ceiling overlooking the internal lobby of the building. But there wouldn't be much time for gazing out of it as the journalists plunged into the twilight world of military cables and seemingly impenetrable jargon.

With Assange still in Stockholm it fell to the *Guardian* reporter Nick Davies, who had originally talked him into taking part in the joint venture, to maintain contact with him. The level of anxiety and even paranoia reached way outside what was inevitably known as 'The Bunker'—the same name given to the Cold War nuclear shelter that housed some of WikiLeaks' servers in Sweden. Security-conscious Davies was worried about his phone calls being intercepted by the NSA and the British equivalent, GCHQ, the General Communications Headquarters. Davies thought that if the NSA and GCHQ were doing their jobs they would be trying to figure out what WikiLeaks would leak next.

John Goetz, a *Der Spiegel* reporter, arrived at the *Guardian* offices on the following Wednesday, making up the troika of print media interest. That afternoon, Assange arrived too. He was a day late, not unusual for someone who has been known to turn up at an airport without an airline ticket, or arrive with a ticket on the wrong day, but also not a good start for the beginning of such an important set of relationships. It may well have coloured the view of *New York Times* journalist Eric Schmitt, a snappy dresser with an eye for detail, when he wrote an email to his boss Bill Keller describing his first encounter with Assange.

'He's tall—probably 6-foot-2 or 6-3—and lanky, with pale skin, grey eyes and a shock of white hair that seizes your attention.' Schmitt added disparagingly that although Assange was alert he was also 'dishevelled, like a bag lady walking in off the street, wearing a dingy, light-coloured sport coat and cargo pants, dirty white shirt, beat-up sneakers and filthy white socks that collapsed around his ankles. He smelled as if he hadn't bathed in days.' Schmitt's immediate dislike for Assange did not augur well for the relationship.

Assange dropped his huge and heavy backpack to the floor and began removing a treasure trove of electronic gadgetry, from laptops to mobile phones and memory sticks. Some of the juiciest secrets of the diplomatic and military world were being unloaded like so much dirty washing all over the floor of the *Guardian* offices.

In their new home, the reporters began preliminary work on the Afghan reports, mainly dispatches from US soldiers in the field, using a large Excel spreadsheet to organise the material, then creating search terms and combing through the documents for newsworthy content. But the reporters ran into a puzzling incongruity. Although

Assange had said the data included reports from the beginning of 2004 until the end of 2009, the material ended eight months short, in April. Many of the documents appeared to be missing. Assange was unfazed by what was clearly causing consternation among the technically challenged journalists, some of whom had written their first stories on manual typewriters. 'Open a second spreadsheet,' he said. As they followed his instructions the spreadsheet electronically unfolded—revealing all 92 000 reports, which gave an extraordinary insight into the Afghan war and its consequences.

Schmitt emailed his boss back in New York. There was no question that the Afghanistan dispatches were genuine. They provided a fascinating insight into a troubled war from the ground up, but just as importantly there was the promise of more to come—half a million classified State Department cables from US embassies around the world. Keller believed WikiLeaks was holding back extra material presumably to see how the relationship with the establishment media worked out.

Assange seemed to be enjoying the game, teasing the journalists with his classified treasure trove. According to Daniel Domscheit-Berg, WikiLeaks' second in charge, he was 'running around like he had like a shop … selling cigarettes', 'opening up his stuff', being a 'cool guy' and giving away all sorts of material which was 'against all the agreements we had internally'. Domscheit-Berg said that Assange had shown the *New York Times* some of the other cables he had. It wasn't part of the agreement, and angered others in the WikiLeaks' team.

Though she had been representing WikiLeaks to the international media while Assange was hiding in Australia, Birgitta Jonsdottir was unaware of the deals that Assange was doing. He was acting alone.

He had not had 'any prior discussion' with his WikiLeaks colleagues before making many of his decisions. Assange's one-man band approach was causing serious rifts inside the organisation.

* * *

Though Assange had worked with mainstream media before, this was the first time he had really ventured into the big time. The audience reach and impact provided by collaborating simultaneously with three of the most influential publications on the planet was huge for WikiLeaks, but then so too were the stakes. Assange would have to relinquish some control over the WikiLeaks information—their demand for exclusivity would be a catalyst for conflict later on. He would soon be involved in a struggle between the old and the new media, played out on the home ground of the old players.

Drawing together any journalists for a collegiate effort is difficult at the best of times; they are traditionally competitive and are not known for showing much largesse towards one another. Expecting them to work together is normally wishful thinking. But because of the detail that needed to be understood, self-interest forced them to collaborate and share resources, research and analysis.

Though each paper had its own focus, many of the stories extracted from the Afghan War Logs were based on similar information. Everyone was totally absorbed in the material on their computer screens, said Goetz, shouting to each other whenever they found an interesting piece of information.

After working their way through the documents, the reporters sat down to check their findings, bouncing ideas and views off each other—and fact checking all the time. For Davies it was an unusual experience to see a group of journalists working so closely together.

Davies, more than anyone else, understood what Assange wanted. Assange had been staying at his home near London part of the time and the two had struck up a close friendship. He was convinced that Assange wasn't just putting documents on the Internet for the sake of causing trouble. He wanted the world to understand whatever was the subject of that information, and linking up with the *Guardian* helped him achieve that goal.

While they had a common purpose in the early stages of the project, Davies would later have a bitter falling out with Assange. Davies thought he had got exclusive rights for all the material Assange had agreed to hand over in Belgium. Assange disagreed and had started talking to television stations, eventually bringing in Britain's Channel 4.

But that crisis lay ahead and the big issue remained when to publish. While the *Guardian* and the *New York Times* were daily newspapers, *Der Spiegel* was a weekly magazine. In the end they all agreed to go online on Sunday 25 July at 10 p.m., London time, and hit the streets the next day—Monday, the day that *Der Speigel* normally publishes its weekly magazine. Assange was in a bind. He wanted to delay publication at one time because he was concerned about Bradley Manning's safety. 'He didn't want to make his [Manning's] position worse,' said Davies. Yet at the same time, with Manning in detention and being questioned, WikiLeaks might be put out of business. Assange was still 'spooked' by reports from the US the previous month that the Pentagon had launched a manhunt for him. If that had happened, some of the reporters had the impression that Assange was ready to publish the documents on the WikiLeaks site immediately, whether the print outlets were ready or not.

According to Assange, the *New York Times* was quite happy for WikiLeaks 'to scoop them, and for the other two papers to publish first', so they could claim, 'We weren't involved, we are just reporting what someone else did'. There was little doubt that of all the publications, the *New York Times* would probably face the strongest criticism from its readership about the secrets of the Afghan war and would be more cautious in its reporting.

Assange's 'publish and be damned' attitude added more strain to an already tense atmosphere. It amplified the problem of 'redacting' or removing the names of the huge number of people who had been secretly working for the US-backed regime in Kabul. David Leigh had a very firm view: 'We were starting from: "Here's a document. How much of it shall we print?" Whereas Julian's ideology was, "I shall dump everything out and then you have to try and persuade me to cross a few things out." We were coming at it from opposite poles.'

It wasn't just the *Guardian* that was having problems with redactions. During one clandestine meeting at a café, Daniel Domscheit-Berg says reporters from *Der Spiegel* told him they were still waiting for WikiLeaks to redact the names from all the material it was going to post online. 'Five days before publication the *Spiegel* guys asked me how far we are with the redaction and I am saying "What redaction?" and they're saying, "Julian in London promised all of the three media companies that all the material would be redacted."'

Schmitt told *Der Spiegel*: 'I just don't know anything about it.' He promised to check and called his WikiLeaks colleagues. 'I asked the people that were processing the material making it ready for publication, and they said, "We don't know anything about this"'.

Daniel Domscheit-Berg was concerned that with just four days now to publication, time was running out to remove the names from the Afghan documents that WikiLeaks was going to publish online.

On Thursday, Domscheit-Berg says he contacted Assange again to ask him about the redactions. According to Schmitt, Assange said: 'Oh yeah I wanted to tell you tonight.' Domscheit-Berg says he told Assange: 'Man we're talking about ninety thousand documents here. It's Thursday, we need to go live on Monday. The production of the website takes twenty-four to forty-eight hours just to render the stuff.' The following night, the White House spokesman, Robert Gibbs, asked the *New York Times* reporter Eric Schmitt to relay a request to Assange that WikiLeaks not publish information that could lead to people being physically harmed.

The next day, Saturday, Assange replied in an email that Wikileaks was withholding close to 15000 of the Afghan documents, which had the heaviest concentration of names, for review.

Eric Schmitt said Assange wrote that WikiLeaks would consider recommendations made by the UN-backed security mission in Afghanistan, known as the International Security Assistance Force, 'on the identification of innocents for this material if it is willing to provide reviewers'. In other words, WikiLeaks was prepared to talk to the White House about a redaction process that would remove contentious names from the war logs on its website.

Eric Schmitt said he forwarded the email to White House officials and *New York Times* editors, but curiously, and with no explanation, he added: 'I certainly didn't consider this a serious and realistic offer to the White House to vet any of the documents before they were to be posted.' The White House did not take up the offer to talk.

As the countdown to publication started, Assange and the WikiLeaks team had set up a temporary headquarters at the Frontline Club, spreading themselves across the handy trestle-style tables and plugging into the high-speed wi-fi. Assange, like his parents who were travelling entertainers, had inherited a touch of the showman. He pulled out a mobile phone and explained to his audience how to use it to confuse any government agency that might be on the prowl.

'If you think you have a hot phone, you charge the battery up fully, and then you post it overseas,' he said, sending it not by airmail but by surface delivery. As the phone headed cross-country by train, boat or truck, anyone in pursuit would be led on a false trail—following a phone in a parcel. It was a trick that both amused and impressed those in the room.

For Assange it was an echo of his nomadic and theatrical roots. He was 'pretty much doing something that his family did when they were involved in theatre and the movie business,' he said, 'heading off to a certain location, bring all your people, get ready for a production launch, bang, go'.

It was almost showtime again and the WikiLeaks team, including new recruit Sarah Harrison, eagerly prepared to monitor the rush of interest. At 10.03 p.m.—three minutes after the deadline—the *Guardian* story appeared on the web, focusing on what it called 'a huge cache of secret US military files' providing a 'devastating portrait' of a 'failing war' in Afghanistan. It revealed that coalition forces had 'killed hundreds of civilians' in unreported incidents, and also that NATO commanders feared that neighbouring Pakistan and Iran were fuelling the insurgency. The *New York Times* went live with the story but, steering away from civilian casualties, said the war logs revealed the US military had long harboured 'strong suspicions' that Pakistan's military spy service had guided the Afghan insurgency—even though Pakistan received more than a billion dollars a year from Washington for its help in combatting militants.

The stories covered a huge arena of the war, from the existence of a covert US assassination squad, Task Force 373, which had been roaming Afghanistan targeting Taliban leaders, to the story of Shum Khan, who lived in a remote village in the mountains near the Pakistan border. When a CIA paramilitary squad charged into a village and ordered him to stop, he kept running and was shot dead. What the CIA didn't know was that Shum Khan was deaf and had not heard their commands.

As the international media digested the material, Assange received a call from *The Larry King Show*. If he wasn't already a household name in the United States he was about to be. 'Afghanistan bombshell: leaked documents rip the lid off the war. The man whose website WikiLeaks published the classified documents for the world to see is here. It's next on *Larry King Live*,' screamed the announcer.

Both men gave smooth performances. King quoted Assange as saying: 'These leaked documents contain evidence of war crimes by United States forces.' King asked: 'What kind of evidence?' Assange, in a clear and measured baritone, replied: 'In the end it will take a court to really look at the full range of evidence and decide if a crime has occurred.'

As interest in the Afghan War Logs surged, all was not well with the WikiLeaks site. In footage aired on SBS's *Dateline* program, Sarah Harrison told Assange people were complaining that the site was overloaded and they couldn't get on. Seemingly unaware she was being filmed, she said people were getting 'really agro'. She asked Assange: 'Are you happy to ignore them?' He nodded. 'OK good,' she said, and threw a Post-It note in the waste bin. Every decision was being managed by Assange.

The following day the Afghan War Logs dominated coverage by all the main British newspapers. In the *Dateline* footage, Assange looked pleased, as Harrison laid out the newspapers on the floor. 'I'm untouchable now in this country,' he said, before correcting himself … 'for the next couple of days'.

Neither the *Guardian*, the *New York Times*, nor *Der Spiegel* carried any Afghan names considered suspect, and in the end WikiLeaks held back close to 15 000 of the 92 000 Afghan files on the grounds that the names could not be redacted in time. But WikiLeaks had made mistakes and some names, even the names of villages where people lived, still remained in some of the 77 000 documents posted on the WikiLeaks website. When they became apparent, Assange was under fire for endangering the lives of others.

Even as the international media moved off from outside the Frontline Club where they had been camped with their satellite dishes and telephoto lenses, questions about how WikiLeaks had dealt with the redaction of names returned to haunt Assange and seriously undermine the credibility of WikiLeaks. He had already made the point to a packed press conference that WikiLeaks had 'tried hard to make sure that this material does not put innocents at harm ... All the material is more than seven months old'.

Yet some of the credit he claims for 'harm minimisation' isn't really credible. It came too late for WikiLeaks technicians to do an effective job redacting the names.

The issue would not go away. In the first hint of dissent among WikiLeaks' traditional supporters, Amnesty International sent an email to Assange asking him to 'censor' the names of the Afghanis mentioned in the reports. A few days later, Reporters without Borders published a personally addressed letter to Julian Assange praising WikiLeaks' past usefulness in exposing 'serious violations of human rights and civil liberties' but criticising WikiLeaks over a perceived absence of editorial control, saying 'indiscriminately publishing' the classified reports reflected 'a real problem of methodology and, therefore, of credibility'. Reporters Without Borders subsequently clarified its statement as a criticism of WikiLeaks' release procedure and not the organisation itself, stating 'we reaffirm our support for WikiLeaks, its work and its founding principles'.

But the damage was done and the dialogue with Amnesty International ended in acrimony when Assange dismissed the group as 'people who prefer to do nothing but cover their asses'. That's not what he felt about Amnesty the previous year, when it showered him with praise and gave him an award for journalism. It pointed to a fragile ego—evidence that Assange had problems dealing with criticism.

But there was one person Assange took notice of, and that was Daniel Ellsberg. When Ellsberg told Assange he would have questioned 'putting stuff out that you haven't read', Assange wrote

Ellsberg a message saying: 'You're right'. Assange said WikiLeaks had taken his advice and done a 'much bigger job of redaction' on the next tranche of documents they were about to release.

Despite its threats, from what had been known by early 2011 the Taliban hadn't killed anyone on the list and the excited reporting of one dead was already revealed, on closer reading, to be about a person who died several years earlier. In the United States the Pentagon was forced to admit that no one had died as a result of being named in the leaks. While Assange read this as a vindication of sorts, his credibility was still tainted over his handling of the leaks. He had also gained a reputation, as Bill Keller pointed out, as someone who was 'smart and well-educated, extremely adept technologically but arrogant, thin-skinned, conspiratorial and oddly credulous'.

Assange, somewhat simplistically, has hit back at journalism's modus operandi, criticising the selection of stories based on what is going to 'make the most money for the newspaper', or have 'the most professional advancement' for the journalist or make them the 'biggest celebrity on TV'. It wasn't only bad journalism; it was 'bad for people's characters'. He knew people who had been involved in this area and he didn't like what it turned them into. 'That's why I do what I do and the way that I do it,' he said.

If Assange was underlining the divide between the 'old' media and his organisation, it was also a division between the journalists, who dealt with what was, and a man who dreamed of what might be. Yet despite his criticisms, he spoke of working on the Afghan War Logs 'in a collaborative basement' and identified the three outlets—the *Guardian*, the *New York Times* and *Der Spiegel*—as Wikileaks' 'media partners'.

Eric Schmitt, in particular, was furious by that description of the relationship. If Keller had sent him to London because he was unflappable, he'd certainly shaken off that moniker.

'I've seen Julian Assange in the last couple of days kind of flouncing around talking about this collaboration like the four of us were working all this together,' says Schmitt. 'But we were not in any kind of partnership or collaboration with him. This was a source relationship. He's making it sound like this was some sort of journalistic enterprise between WikiLeaks, the *New York Times*, the *Guardian*, and *Der Spiegel*, and that's not what it was.'

Schmitt portrayed the relationship with Assange as verging on hostile. Assange would arrive and 'you'd ask him questions about certain types of data, and certain questions—some of them he answered and some of them he didn't'. Schmitt appeared to be almost goading him. 'Where did you get this material? He wouldn't answer that.'

Schmitt admits that he even pressed Assange to divulge the name of the source of the material. 'Did it come from Bradley Manning?' he asked. It was a mischievous question that revealed how the relationship between the *New York Times* and Assange had broken down. Not surprisingly, Assange, who believed he was bound by the journalistic code of ethics to protect sources, didn't answer.

On the other side of the Atlantic at the Pentagon, the issue of whether or not Assange was a journalist became more than a matter of pride or professional jealousy. It had implications that went all the way to the top of the *New York Times*. It's generally accepted by the US courts that journalists are covered by a freedom of speech provision enshrined in the Constitution. Not so the sources that provide that information, particularly if the source has put at risk the security of the US.

When US Defense Secretary Robert Gates said WikiLeaks had endangered lives, it set off alarm bells at the *New York Times*. WikiLeaks might well be able to argue it was protected by the First Amendment for the material it published online, but even that argument could be swept away if it could be proved that WikiLeaks had deliberately conspired to publish information damaging to the security of the United States.

'The battlefield consequences of the release of these documents are potentially severe and dangerous for our troops, our allies and Afghan partners, and may well damage our relationships and reputation in that key part of the world,' he said. 'Intelligence sources and methods, as well as military tactics, techniques and procedures, will become known to our adversaries.'

The Chairman of the Joint Chiefs of Staff Admiral Mike Mullen portrayed WikiLeaks as recklessly endangering people in order to satisfy its 'need to make a point'. 'Mr. Assange can say whatever he likes about the greater good he thinks he and his source are doing, but the truth is they might already have on their hands the blood of some young soldier or that of an Afghan family,' Admiral Mullen said.

Ominously, for Assange, Gates said he had called in the FBI to assist army investigators. This was no longer a military matter: by calling in the FBI Gates had broadened the investigation to the wider instruments of the US government.

The *New York Times* reported unnamed sources in the Justice Department saying that lawyers 'are exploring whether Mr Assange and WikiLeaks could be charged with inducing or conspiring in violation of the Espionage Act, a 1917 law that prohibits the unauthorised disclosure of national security information'. The author of that report, Eric Schmitt, and his editor Bill Keller, were anything but impartial observers.

By arguing that Assange was only a source, the *New York Times* could distance itself from Assange, stressing that it just took the information and had nothing else to do with him. If he was a journalist, the relationship was much closer and the *New York Times* ran the risk of being implicated in any connection Assange had with Bradley Manning.

The *New York Times* had cut Assange adrift. And to make life even more difficult, Keller implied Assange had a political agenda— potentially stripping him of any free speech arguments he may be able to run as a journalist. Keller reported that Assange was 'openly contemptuous of the American government' and self-servingly added, 'I would hesitate to describe what WikiLeaks does as journalism'.

After hanging Assange and WikiLeaks out to dry, it was disingenuous in the extreme for Keller to then argue that it was 'chilling to contemplate the possible government prosecution of WikiLeaks for making secrets public'. Keller had gone out of his way to strip Assange of even his journalistic protection. Keller might not have liked Assange, and Schmitt almost certainly took a dislike to him. But as an act of bastardry it took some beating.

The most damaging allegation for Assange is that he 'groomed' Manning; that, rather than being in receipt of illegally leaked material, he actively conspired with Manning to obtain it. When I asked Assange specifically if he had ever directly contacted Bradley Manning, Assange replied, 'No'. Asked if he ever spoke to Manning 'indirectly', Assange did not answer the question, and when pressed said: 'I would never, never, never comment'. Despite lengthy investigations, at the time of this book going to press the US was still working on the case against him.

In an interview with him in December 2010, Assange was talking carefully and deliberately. 'So if they're trying to say I conspired with Bradley Manning, anyone who conspires with me, is, if you like, a chain in the conspiracy, so that's all about fear and management.' Assange added: '… but if you're going to do that I understand you've been forced into certain positions by real politic process'. It might be necessary 'for legal reasons [to call WikiLeaks] a source, fine, but don't fuck'n denigrate us'. He understood that the *New York Times* may 'need to be not truthful because of threats'. In a final word on the issue, he points out that if he is a source and only a source, shouldn't the journalists that used him as a source protect him?

That was certainly the view of Max Frankel who had 'overseen the defence of the *New York Times* in the Pentagon papers case forty years earlier'. Frankel wrote to the *Guardian* editor Alan Rusbridger after the first Cablegate material, attaching a copy of a memo he had written at the time when his newspaper was under pressure to reveal the identity of its source, Daniel Ellsberg. 'We reject collaboration or revelation of our sources for the larger reason that ALL [his capitals] sources deserve to know that they are protected by us, he wrote.' These seem to be words from another era, because it's not how Julian Assange was treated if he was *just* a source.

Whatever he was to the *New York Times* others consider him a journalist. After interviewing Assange for six hours, the US *60 Minutes* reporter Steve Kroft said, 'I definitely consider him to be a publisher which is the important thing. I mean if he is not a publisher then people at *60 Minutes* online, or the *New York Times* online, aren't publishers either. I mean he operates an Internet site and he publishes material.'

The federal secretary of Australia's Media and Arts Alliance, Christopher Warren, underlines this view, 'What Assange and his colleagues are doing is journalism. There's no doubt about that,' he said. 'One of the most important tasks of journalism is to uncover and inform people of things that other people would rather keep hidden. They've certainly done that.'

The US would do all it could to get their hands on Assange. Almost to the day that the Afghan War Logs were launched, the US ramped up its investigation into WikiLeaks.

* * *

As the aircraft made its final approach to Newark Airport, New York, Jacob Appelbaum, a WikiLeaks volunteer and acknowledged authority on computer security, could be forgiven for feeling deeply apprehensive. He was re-entering the United States for the first time since he'd spoken at a New York computer conference in place of Assange who had been hiding out in London. Appelbaum used the event to ask for funding and volunteers for WikiLeaks, but fearing the FBI were in the audience, instead of returning to the stage after playing the 'Collateral Murder' video he left by a side entrance, using a decoy with a similar hooded top to throw the police off his trail. What happened next would be an indication of whether the level of paranoia was reasonable, or not.

As he approached customs, he was taken to one side. Though Appelbaum has refused to discuss what happened, the reputable online news site CNET says he was pulled aside by customs and border protection agents, who told him that he was randomly selected for a security search.

Appelbaum was taken into a room and frisked, and his bag was searched. Receipts were photocopied, and his laptop was inspected. Officials from Immigration and Customs Enforcement, and from the US Army, then told him that he was not under arrest but was being detained.

The officials asked questions about WikiLeaks, asked for his opinions about the wars in Iraq and Afghanistan, and asked where WikiLeaks founder, Julian Assange, could be found. Appelbaum declined to comment without a lawyer present but he was not permitted to make a phone call, the sources cited by CNET said.

After being held for three hours, Appelbaum was given his laptop back, but the agents kept his three mobile phones. As he made his way through the airport on to the next leg of his journey the irony of the situation would not have been lost on Applebaum. He was on his way to give a workshop on how to deal with censorship in China, planning to pass on the tricks of the trade. He would help US businesses, and even tourists who planned to travel there, cope with what's known as 'The Great Firewall of China', a system designed to prevent free speech and control any criticism of the government. The fact that the workshop was being held in the gaming capital of the world, Las Vegas, only added to the absurdity.

The Riviera Hotel and Casino is a glittering star-spangled altar to the American dream: everyone can be rich, you just have to be lucky.

It boasts eleven kinds of draught beer and a business centre, but it's unlikely anyone would have been brave or foolhardy enough to send even a fax from there during the first few days of August 2010. It was at the Riviera that what's known as the DefCon conference was held, a jamboree of computer nerds, hackers, conspiracy theorists and freedom of speech champions who moved out of their darkened rooms and into the soft lights of the chandeliers to compare notes and share their thoughts with the world. For anyone considering travelling to China, Appelbaum's presentation gave them valuable information, including details of software and tools used to bypass Internet and content censorship.

What he didn't know at the time was not everyone in the room was particularly interested in his talk, entitled 'The Power of Chinese Security'. When he let slip the fact that his phone had been seized, two casually dressed men who introduced themselves as FBI agents approached him and asked to talk.

'We'd like to chat for a few minutes,' one of the men said, adding, 'We thought you might not want to'.

Appelbaum asked them if they were aware of what had happened to him.

One replied, 'Yes, that's why we're here'.

'I don't have anything to say,' Appelbaum told them.

One of the agents said they were interested in hearing about 'rights being trampled' and said, 'sometimes it's nice to have a conversation to flesh things out'.

A lawyer with the Electronic Frontier Foundation asked if the agents were at the event in an official capacity or for personal reasons. 'A little of both,' one of them said.

Appelbaum, clearly concerned about the mobile phones that had been seized, asked when they would be returned. 'We aren't involved in that,' one of the FBI agents said. 'We have no idea.' When Appelbaum refused to talk any further they walked away.

With the FBI actively gathering information and the net closing in on WikiLeaks, Julian Assange decided on a high-risk move. Within hours of the FBI talking to Appelbaum, he posted what he called an Insurance Policy on the Afghan War Logs site. The 'policy', in the form of a giant encrypted file, was available for anyone to open once WikiLeaks released the key. It is widely accepted that the file contained the unreleased copies of the 260 000 US State Department Cables.

Assange says he only posted the file so he could have confidence in WikiLeaks' ability to withstand what he called 'even a massive multi-continental roundup'. In other words, the information would survive if, somewhat melodramatically, the WikiLeaks team didn't.

Assange need not have been concerned with the survival of the information. A short time later he would give a copy of all the documents he possessed to the *Guardian* newspaper for safekeeping, under the agreement that they wouldn't publish until he said so and they would store the secret documents safely away from the Internet. What he didn't know then was that the *Guardian* would also give the *New York Times* a copy of the documents though they would say it was a different version—an act that would lead to full-scale acrimony between Assange and the newspaper.

The insurance policy that Assange had posted on the web was a blackmail threat to the US Government not to go after him. It revealed an extraordinary level of hubris—that Assange believed he would be able to intimidate the most powerful country on earth. It might have given the State Department a few sleepless nights but it did nothing to stop the FBI investigation. In fact it arguably forced their hand, because a couple of days later the US called in its allies for help. The Obama administration asked Britain, Germany and Australia to consider bringing charges against Assange concerning the Afghanistan leaks and 'limiting his travels across international borders'.

The Australian Defence Association, representing the country's retired and active military personnel, said WikiLeaks could have 'committed a serious criminal offence in helping an enemy of the Australian Defence Force'. The insurance policy was looking more like a failed Mafia style intimidation—a brick through the window from a passing car that had been picked up and lobbed back at the driver.

9

SEX MONEY POWER

In mid-August 2010, Julian Assange arrived at Stockholm Airport. He was on his way to a conference he'd been invited to, run by 'The Brotherhood', a leftist Christian faction of Sweden's Social Democrat Party. As Assange made his way out of the spacious airport he might have had pause to stop and check the credentials of the person he'd be dealing with at the conference. Assange has a brilliant mind, but he does get a touch of the Bazza McKenzies about him at times, and though he exudes an air of worldliness, he also has an extraordinary naiveté, trusting people he'd be best to steer away from.

If he had googled Anna Ardin he'd have come up with a blog entry written by her entitled: 'Seven Steps to Legal Revenge on a Cheating Lover'. It was potentially far more damaging for Assange than his fears about a CIA hit squad.

Not that Ardin wasn't suspect in that area too. Though she'd been called a leftist, she'd been connected with 'US-financed anti-Castro and anti-communist groups in Cuba'. By the time that information emerged, Sweden had issued a warrant for Assange's arrest on allegations of rape and sexual molestation.

As Assange travelled in to Stockholm he had plenty to occupy his mind. The possibility that Iceland might not be the safe haven he originally hoped for WikiLeaks had begun to concern him. There were questions about how close the Icelandic government was to the United States and, on a personal level, his relationship with Icelandic MP Birgitta Jonsdottir had cooled considerably, and was even hostile at times. Sweden was in many ways a Scandinavian mirror image of Iceland. It had good infrastructure, excellent communications systems and, at the time, better laws to protect journalists.

These laws offered an unusual protection to sources. Based on Sweden's Freedom of the Press Act, whose origins trace back to 1766, journalists are legally forbidden to reveal a confidential source unless it involves a direct threat to national security or treason. While the laws covered newspapers and magazines, they didn't automatically give protection to the electronic media and that included organisations like WikiLeaks. Assange would need to register WikiLeaks as a media organisation in Sweden, and to do that he needed to be a resident of the country.

In the meantime, WikiLeaks would have to make do with the kind offering from the Swedish Pirate Party—a legitimate political organisation in Sweden with a member in the European Parliament. It offered to donate servers and bandwidth to WikiLeaks free of charge, until the WikiLeaks registration was approved. It would also provide technicians to make sure that the servers were maintained and kept in working order. What was almost as attractive to Assange was that the Pirate Party planned to set up an Internet Service Provider (ISP) to offer anonymous Internet connections. The organisation would offer anonymity by not storing a copy of its users' Internet Protocol (IP) addresses, a unique identification number used to locate every computer, mobile phone or other device on the Internet at any given time. IP addresses are used by law enforcement and intelligence agencies to track everything from illegal downloads to terrorism suspects.

The robust laws protecting freedom of expression in Sweden are matched by equally tough laws that protect the right of the individual. They grew out of the feminist movement of the 1960s and extended themselves to the whole gamut of sexual activity.

These laws protect the rights of both partners during sex, but it is accepted that the laws are designed to allow women to decide what kind of sex they want and under what circumstances. Sweden might have strong laws enshrining what might at first look like libertarian values, with the age of consent at fifteen, but they are balanced by strict rules relating to sexual conduct. In his search to find the perfect environment for his WikiLeaks endeavour, Assange seemed to have missed a few things that might have been useful for him to understand.

One thing Assange has never had to concern himself with is where he will spend the night, and Stockholm was no exception. Ardin was so pleased he had agreed to speak at a conference where she was the publicist, she offered him a bed at her apartment. What happened next is rather routine for Julian: he bedded the hostess. It's difficult to know what might have been had he left it at that. On Saturday at the conference Assange addressed, he met a younger woman, a 26-year-old photographer named Sofia Wilen. They flirted and then went off to the movies together. Nothing much unusual about that. But by this time Ardin seemed so taken by her lover she sent out a tweet that she was looking for a couple of places at a crayfish party—a more formal version of an Australian BBQ, with lobsters instead of meat, but with just as much grog. Discovering there were no free places round town she threw her own—just for Julian.

On the following Monday, Assange and Wilen went to Wilen's home in Enkoping, an industrial town that is the birthplace of the adjustable spanner and the base for the Swedish Army's electronics warfare centre. Assange stayed the night and they had sex. The trouble seemed to start for Julian, as is often the case with relationships, when the two women started talking—or in this case Wilen sent a text to Ardin and they met. It might have been a coincidence but it seems unlikely that subsequently Ardin asked Assange to move out of the apartment. The following Friday the two women went to a Stockholm police station. There they told their stories and the prosecutor—a stand-in during the Swedish summer break—concluded there may be grounds for Wilen to pursue charges of rape and *ofredande*, a misdemeanour which can be translated as 'annoyance', and for Ardin, a charge of *ofredande* alone against Assange.

In a country so heavily regulated by the right to privacy it came as a surprise to Assange that within hours of the two women going to the police station, the local Stockholm tabloid, *Espressen*, splashed the rape allegations across the front page. Contacted by the paper, the duty prosecutor had confirmed the allegations, an act that is illegal under Swedish law. The duty prosecutor was later quoted as not being aware that they had broken the law.

Within the next few days the story took on a life of its own. On holiday, Eva Finne, the chief prosecutor for the Stockholm region, heard the Assange case on the news—and called for the file to be couriered to her. She could find no evidence of rape in Wilen's case—and struck it from the charge sheet leaving just the lesser offense of molestation.

It was about this time that the allegations against Assange moved into the surreal, where the Swedish law protecting the rights of the individual gave no protection at all. Assange, who planned to use the Internet as a force for openness in the world, now became its victim. A Swedish feminist blog called Revell, run in part by Ardin, posted an article warning: 'Even WikiLeaks heroes can do crappy things'. It gave a one-sided story of events, alleging Assange had continued having sex after a condom broke—against Ardin's wishes. The freedom of the net also produced a trap for her. Seemingly spurned by a fiancé some time ago, Ardin had posted a strange list of how to get even.

It bore a striking resemblance to what would happen to Assange. Headlined 'Seven Steps to Legal Revenge' by Anna Ardin, it starts off in a conciliatory way.

> Step 1—Consider very carefully if you really must take revenge.
>
> It is almost always better to forgive than to avenge …
>
> Step 2—Think about why you want revenge.
>
> You need to be clear about who to take revenge on, as well as why. Revenge is never directed against only one person, but also the actions of the person.

Step 3—The principle of proportionality.

Remember that revenge will not only match the deed in size but also in nature.

A good revenge is linked to what has been done against you. For example, if you want revenge on someone who cheated or who dumped you, you should use a punishment with dating/sex/fidelity involved.

Step 4—Do a brainstorm of appropriate measures for the category of revenge you're after. To continue the example above, you can sabotage your victim's current relationship, such as getting his new partner to be unfaithful or ensure that he gets a madman after him.

Use your imagination!

Step 5—Figure out how you can systematically take revenge.

Send your victim a series of letters and photographs that make your victim's new partner believe that you are still together which is better than to tell just one big lie on one single occasion.

Step 6—Rank your systematic revenge schemes from low to high in terms of likely success, required input from you, and degree of satisfaction when you succeed.

The ideal, of course, is a revenge as strong as possible but this requires a lot of hard work and effort for it to turn out exactly as you want it to.

Step 7—Get to work.

And remember what your goals are while you are operating: ensure that your victim will suffer the same way as he made you suffer.

A similar list had been published on a US website as a joke, but Ardin made it clear she was serious. When chided about it in a comment online she said she had been broken-hearted by a fiancé and wanted to pay him back.

By the end of August this cyber theatre of the absurd became even weirder. Ardin and Wilen had now linked up with a lawyer, Claes Borgstrom, Sweden's former equality ombudsman, famous for proposing that Sweden boycott the 2006 Soccer World Cup in Germany because of an expected surge in prostitution during the month-long tournament. The idea was immediately rejected by the Swedish soccer federation.

Borgstrom took the case of Wilen and Ardin to the head of a special unit that focuses on sex crime laws, two hundred kilometres away in Gothenburg. In Sweden it is not unusual to shop around for an opinion. The Swedish law allows complainants to take their cases to other representatives in the ombudsman system, and that's what they had done. The head of the unit, Marianne Ny, began working on the case—including re-examining the rape allegations which had already been thrown out.

To complicate matters even more, Assange was now interviewed by the original prosecutor's office on the lesser charges. He must have been feeling confident because on the same day, he applied for a work and residency permit which would allow him to base

WikiLeaks in Sweden with its protection of journalism shield laws. Ironically, the laws he wanted to use to expose what he saw as large international crimes were the same ones protecting journalists who were writing about his personal life and gathering information about him from administration insiders who were themselves possibly breaking the law.

The tweet that Ardin had posted the night after she'd had sex with Assange, expressing the thrill of meeting 'cool' people, as well as her 'Seven Steps to Legal Revenge', mysteriously disappeared from the Internet. But Ardin had kept one thing: the condom that she said had broken while she was having sex with Assange. Whether she retained it as a souvenir, a trophy, or as evidence for what might come up in the future, it's not known.

Iceland had suddenly become a whole lot more appealing again as a base for WikiLeaks.

* * *

In Reykjavik, the weather for August was unusually dry and warm. The last time Daniel Domscheit-Berg was there it had been as chilly as his relationship with Assange. Now he had returned from Germany and he had reason to be happy—he had brought his new wife with him. But Assange's rape allegations forced his attention back to WikiLeaks.

Domscheit-Berg met up with Jonsdottir and Hrafnsson to discuss how to handle the situation. There are various accounts of what happened at the meetings, but whatever the truth, it was clear that the way Assange was dealing with his problems in Sweden created even more divisions in the WikiLeaks camp. Factions were becoming apparent, split down the lines of sex, money and power.

Assange said that when the Swedish sexual allegations were first made public Domscheit-Berg was overjoyed. According to Assange, the feeling must have been: 'Control problem solved. I am not going to be marginalised anymore.' Assange said that as WikiLeaks had grown, Domscheit-Berg's 'stature' and power became more and more 'unstable'.

When Jonsdottir made a public call for Assange to be replaced as the spokesperson for WikiLeaks while the investigation was underway in Sweden, Assange took it badly, interpreting it as an act of disloyalty. But for Jonsdottir, who says she had 'known him quite intimately for a chunk of time', his response didn't come as a surprise.

Assange's mother Christine believed her son interacted well with women because he had been brought up by a single mother, and that women liked men raised by single women 'because they were comfortable about women'. Jonsdottir had a different view. She noticed that Assange had what she described as 'a bit of an Aussie attitude towards women'. Jonsdottir had been married to an Australian. She said she was not saying that all Australian men were like that, but she believed there was a cultural attitude that jarred with Swedish women. Assange had come up against what she called the 'Scandinavian female'. And while not all women in Scandinavia were like that either, they were 'extremely firm about their rights'. 'If a guy acts in a certain way to a Scandinavian female, he is going to encounter big trouble, particularly when it comes to sexuality, and the boundaries.'

She believed that Assange had run into a cultural challenge. People were much 'wilder in Australia', she said. The 'wild streak' was 'very, very strong in Julian'. Jonsdottir described Assange as a 'wild child', adding that it was as if 'he's just come out of the jungle, or something, in a good way'. She said he was 'uninhibited', which is very different from Scandinavians who want to 'organise their freedom'.

But her praise fell well short of adulation. Jonsdottir said that Assange did not know how to relate to women unless it was to 'flirt' with them, which was a game and 'a perfect way to get into trouble'.

Did he flirt with you? 'Of course.'

A lot? 'I don't want to get into that, it's too personal.'

Assange does not deny he's a flirt and reveals it's part of the tactic he uses. 'What it means with some women in positions of power is that you can encourage them to talk to you for longer,' he said. He described 'flirtatious conversations' as being 'enjoyable'. He added that it hadn't 'backfired too many times', but when it did—'Oh boy!'

What is perhaps not so attractive is that Assange was also given to boasting about his various relationships. According to Domscheit-Berg, after a conference in 2008 he went out to dinner and bragged to the table that 'he had children on all continents and doesn't pay for them'. Domscheit-Berg said he was left wondering 'what is the point of boasting about that stuff; that's lame'. For Domscheit-Berg the desire to impress people in that way was 'really weird'.

When I asked Assange how many children he had he wouldn't comment. He said 'the children are under threat' because of his

WikiLeaks work and explained that was why he could not talk about them.

Domscheit-Berg claims that Assange had also given him some advice when he met his wife that he should 'get as much dirt' on her as he could. Schmitt asked: 'What the hell. Why?' To which Assange explained that he had to 'have some leverage in case I run into a problem with her'.

Sitting talking to Assange, it is easy to understand his attraction. He's witty, charming, intelligent and passionate. He's also intellectually seductive and not just to women. Jonsdottir says she has 'seen guys that were critical of him' meet Assange and be turned around in a few minutes. 'It's very hypnotic,' she said. It was the same sort of admiration when a person was 'blindly in love'. But when the charm wore off there was a very different Assange, as Domscheit-Berg would discover when their close relationship soured irreparably.

Three months earlier Domscheit-Berg had had an extraordinary conversation with Assange. He was working with sensitive WikiLeaks documents when Assange confronted him with an astonishing threat.

'If you fuck up I will hunt you down and kill you.'

Assange's recollection isn't that much different. He said he had told Domscheit-Berg: 'If your actions result in the terminating, incarceration or execution of my sources I will kill you.'

The attack greatly disturbed Domscheit-Berg and he asked Assange what he had done to give him any reason to make such a statement. Assange said he had 'warned him on numerous occasions previously [about not] taking care of some security procedures or sources,' something that Domscheit-Berg argues he was scrupulous about. Did Assange mean that he would kill Domscheit-Berg?

'I meant for him to hear it.'

'No, but did you mean it?'

'At the time, I meant it, yes. At the time, that was the feeling.'

But do you think you would have killed him if he had revealed sources who were subsequently executed?

'The jury is out.'

Assange added that people's lives were at stake, and the threat was the only way to get through to Domscheit-Berg that he needed to 'stop fucking around with something that was so serious'. Then he smiled an impish grin: 'It might be a good precedent to set for all our staff.'

Domscheit-Berg saw it differently. The two had been arguing since Assange accused him of claiming to be a co-founder of WikiLeaks— something Domscheit-Berg denies. He says that Assange didn't like him because he challenged him on issues involving the running of WikiLeaks, describing Assange as a 'control freak' who believed he could handle people by 'containing' them. He said that Assange thought of him as 'like a dog' that needed to be 'contained'.

In his book published in February 2011, Domscheit-Berg spends much of his time describing his alienation from Assange and eventually WikiLeaks, likening it to a religious cult. He describes WikiLeaks as 'a system that admits little internal criticism. Anything that went wrong had to be the fault of something on the outside. The guru was beyond question.' Domscheit-Berg wrote that anyone who offered too much criticism was punished by having his rights suspended or by being threatened with possible consequences.

Domscheit-Berg was certainly angry that Assange's promises he would one day be paid for his work were not being fulfilled. He had sunk his life savings into WikiLeaks, €30 000, buying servers and 'helping WikiLeaks get onto a sustainable level'. He believed that when WikiLeaks became established it would start paying its staff. He wouldn't be able to work for nothing for the rest of his life.

WikiLeaks had been on a huge fundraising exercise over the new year and was now flush with cash. Domscheit-Berg had raised the question of being paid again, but the discussion hadn't gone anywhere. The Internet was rife with rumours. Where had the money come from, and more importantly, where was it going? Domscheit-Berg was among those asking the questions.

Much of it was passing through the German Commerzebank in the tenth-century township of Kassel, north-east of Frankfurt. The account belonged to the Wau Holland Foundation, a charitable organisation that in October 2009 had become the de facto financial manager of WikiLeaks, handling donations and paying the bills. The Foundation was established in memory of the co-founder of Germany's Chaos Computer Club, an organised group of hackers and freedom of speech activists. Wau Holland had campaigned strongly against censorship in the early days of the Internet and developed 'refined concepts' like 'hacker ethics'—teaching young people how to balance natural curiosity with respect for others.

As a tax-deductible foundation, it handles and transfers donations to WikiLeaks according to strict German law. 'We have certain responsibilities for this money, and we are taking this seriously,' Hendrick Fulda, the foundation's vice-president said. Run on a part-time basis, however, the Wau Holland Foundation was ill-prepared for the requests for disclosure about WikiLeaks' financial state of affairs when the organisation burst into public prominence in the early part of 2010.

The demands for financial scrutiny came not only from those who opposed WikiLeaks' activities in principle, but also people who accused Assange of 'gross mismanagement' of the organisation's funds. Much of this public brawling took place on John Young's Cryptome site. A shadowy group calling themselves WikiLeaks Insiders said that 'only a full audited financial disclosure' of WikiLeaks' global donations and expenditures would finally reveal just 'how loose' Assange had been with WikiLeaks' donor funding. They clearly didn't believe that Assange was only remunerated for travel expenses and that he travelled 'coach class'.

The Wau Holland Foundation eventually produced a partial snapshot of WikiLeaks' funding. Not surprisingly, it revealed that in times of crisis the money poured in from donations. Shutting the organisation down completely when it was short of cash was a masterstroke by Assange. In the months before WikiLeaks had closed down over the new year in 2010, pleading poverty, the foundation said it received about US$6000. But in January, with the site shut and its supporters realising WikiLeaks was in trouble, donations began pouring in: a total of US$800000 swelled the WikiLeaks coffers from PayPal or bank money transfers alone. Yet it wasn't pulling the plug on the WikiLeaks site that gave the organisation its biggest boost. After WikiLeaks published 'Collateral Murder', donations soared—lifting the total income for the year until August to more than US$1 million.

Even so, as the money was coming in, the overheads were going up. There were also more disputes, mainly arguments about staff being paid. WikiLeaks tried to bring a professional discipline to its business practices and eventually, after months of argument,

Assange decided to pay some of the WikiLeaks staff, including himself. The Wau Holland Foundation would reveal it had paid more than '€100 000 in salaries for 2010, including about €66 000 to Mr Assange', and Fulda said it's estimated other senior staff could be paid in the region of $5500 a month.

But the decision to pay staff would be too late to save Domscheit-Berg's WikiLeaks career. He would be suspended by Assange and later quit to set up his own WikiLeaks-style website, OpenLeaks, a system bearing a striking resemblance to an idea that Assange had in early 2010, allowing whistleblowers to make direct submissions to media outlets.

Wau Holland's statements had dealt with the main issue of WikiLeaks' funding, but it hadn't silenced all of the critics, especially not Domscheit-Berg. He said there were 'all sorts of other money trails' that Assange 'refuses to share'. 'No one else knows about all sorts of other money,' Domscheit-Berg said. Assange apparently had registered '"Wikileaks ICT" [Information Communication Technology] in Australia', which Domscheit-Berg understood was an Australian non-profit organisation. Domscheit-Berg said that 'everyone knows how much money is in the German fund', but whenever someone asked about Australia, 'How much is the total?' Assange said: '"That's none of your business" and no one knows where the money has gone, what it's being spent on.'

Though there appears to be no non-profit organisation or charity registered as ICT in Australia, there is an 'ICT Building' on the University of Melbourne campus, not far from the post office where a WikiLeaks PO Box was registered. Its address is ICT, PO Box 4080. In what might be called highly suspicious circumstances, Australia Post decided to shut down not just the post office boxes but also the post office itself, just before Christmas 2010, citing declining patronage as the reason for the closure. Assange gave a hint about what may be behind the WikiLeaks PO Box activities during our interview in May 2010 when he spoke of 'high security money' which needed to be 'anonymised' to allow WikiLeaks to buy 'encrypted telephones' and 'certain bits of internet infrastructure', and 'postal addresses' that were involved in 'running an organisation like this'.

He said that 'nearly all the money goes through the [Wau Holland] Foundation that are [sic] audited' and 'some of the money goes through unaudited accounts', but he pointed out that was not money from the 'general public' but from 'particular individuals who have faith in us personally'. It is quite extraordinary that an organisation that is so paranoid about its security should publicly advertise its PO Box number on a university campus—a PO Box apparently registered in the name of Julian Assange.

By checking the contents of the mailbox it would be easy for any government agency to discover the names of donors sending in money. It was another symptom of just how sloppy the organisation could become. A good friend of Assange's in Australia handed him some sound advice about getting a proper organisational structure in place. Even the AFP officer who had arrested Assange twenty years ago was prepared to help. Ken Day came with not just a federal police officer's knowledge of the difficulties of running an intelligence-gathering organisation like WikiLeaks, he also understood business. He had worked as a senior security consultant for large corporations. After the 'Collateral Murder' video, Day publicly supported Assange, believing that one of the 'strengths of democracy' was having a strong media, what he called an 'independent voice', to challenge what government and corporate worlds were doing. He offered to help WikiLeaks, but perhaps unsurprisingly Assange wasn't interested.

He said WikiLeaks needed a 'charter', a 'strategy' and an end game. He said Assange needed to identify the problem, find a solution and in the next five years develop an executive strategy. He said he thought there was a gap, 'a vacuum' in WikiLeaks' thinking.

One of the other proposals involved an extensive corporate plan specifically tailored to WikiLeaks' unique situation: a management structure with accountability and responsibility. It was something the organisation desperately needed and at least one of Assange's friends worked hard to convince him it would be invaluable for WikiLeaks. But it all came to nothing.

Inside the WikiLeaks camp the arguments were becoming more strident. The most pressing involved whether or not to help Bradley Manning who needed thousands of dollars in financial support to mount his defence. There were some in WikiLeaks who believed that there was a moral case for supporting Manning as a charged whistleblower who was held in solitary confinement in a US jail. But there was always the difficulty that if WikiLeaks gave money it might incriminate Manning. In the end WikiLeaks made the decision in principle to help, but it was up to Wau Holland to decide whether they were able to hand over any money. They would have to seek legal advice.

It was estimated Manning's case, if he decided to take a civilian lawyer, could cost up to US$200 000 dollars. WikiLeaks would eventually make a paltry payment of US$15 100 towards his defence. Manning had been charged with transferring classified data onto his personal computer and adding 'unauthorised software' to a 'classified computer system' in connection with the leaking of a video of a 'helicopter attack in Iraq in 2007'. He was also charged with 'communicating, transmitting and delivering national defense information' to an 'unauthorised source'. But it was the last charge under the 1917 Espionage Act which, if he was found guilty, carried by far the biggest sentence: 'Disclosing classified information concerning "national defense"' with reason to believe that the information could cause 'injury to the United States'. In all, the charges carried a maximum possible sentence of fifty-two years in prison.

As Manning was moved from Kuwait, where he'd been held after his arrest, to Quantico, a particularly desolate military prison near Washington, it may have cheered him to know that the marine base where he was now imprisoned was also the FBI headquarters where one of the most celebrated whistleblowers in US history, W Mark Felt, the FBI's associate director—better known as the *Washington Post's* Deep Throat during the newspaper's investigation of the Watergate break-in—was stationed. In his early years with the FBI he'd taken part in illegal activities himself, but had received a presidential pardon. Nothing could have been less probable for Manning.

Not far from the prison, the Pentagon had set up a team of nearly 150 intelligence experts and a number of FBI agents in what it called the 'WikiLeaks War Room'. One of their tasks was to assess whether the leaking of names in the Afghan War Logs had put the lives of US troops or informants in danger. They were painstakingly going through the 77 000 logs that had already been released, trying to second-guess what might be in the 15 000 documents Assange was still holding, and trying to discover what else Assange was preparing to leak. As they pored over the documents and the online chat logs in their suburban Virginia hideaway, the team was also trying to figure out whether Assange had manipulated Bradley Manning to hand over the huge cache of files he had openly boasted about leaking. If they could prove the relationship with Manning, they had a chance of charging Assange under the US Espionage Act as a co-conspirator. In a sign of the anxiety WikiLeaks had created within the Obama administration, the number of staff in the team, known formally as the Information Review Task Force, had jumped by nearly 50 per cent in the previous month. The US administration had put one of their top military intelligence experts in charge of the WikiLeaks program. As deputy head of operations at the giant US Defense Intelligence Agency, which worked closely with both the NSA and the CIA, Brigadier General Robert A. Carr had a formidable reputation for achieving results. WikiLeaks, and its connection with Manning, was now under full-scale surveillance facing all the might of the US administration's intelligence-gathering and counterintelligence operations. Assange had to move carefully and swiftly.

It was tricky territory. Some in WikiLeaks wanted him to hold off any more releases until Bradley Manning's investigation was over. But Assange argued another course: maintain the targeted approach with a limited number of documents, but include other media outlets to broaden their reach and impact. A month earlier, Assange had spoken at a conference organised by the highly regarded Gavin MacFadyen, who'd made a name for himself in the 1970s with the investigative TV program *World In Action*. MacFadyen, director of the Centre for Investigative Journalism at London's City University, was also on the board of the Bureau of Investigative Journalism at the same university. He immediately called its director Iain Overton after meeting Assange.

'I got a flurry of urgent phone calls and texts saying, "You've got to meet him, he wants to meet you,"' Overton said. Over the next few days Overton and Assange began meeting up at irregular hours of the day and night. 'I kind of kept on disappearing out and not really telling my wife where I was going,' said Overton. 'I think she was wondering whether I was having an affair or something.'

Eventually Overton negotiated 'the broadcast' element of WikiLeaks' next big drop, giving the bureau the exclusive rights for two documentaries based on nearly 400 000 field reports relating to the Iraq war that WikiLeaks was holding. Though Overton says Assange had no editorial input into the documentaries, he was often a presence reminding all concerned of the importance of security.

Guardian journalist David Leigh says his newspaper agreed to delay the Iraq War Logs report to allow the bureau to collaborate in the making of the television documentaries—one with the commercial broadcaster Channel 4's *Dispatches* program, and the other for the English version of Al Jazeera. There could be several reasons why the newspaper agreed to wait, but the most obvious was it wanted to keep the relationship going and get its hands on the treasure trove of documents WikiLeaks had: the US State Department Cables—secret messages that gave an unvarnished view of what US diplomats thought of nations around the world. And in the end that's exactly the concession that Leigh rung from Assange. WikiLeaks could do its TV deal but the *Guardian* would get a copy of the classified State Department Cables. There were strings attached but Leigh was still happy.

Next to the State Department Cables, the Iraq War Logs seem a pale second best. But they were still extraordinarily revelatory about American foreign policy, which had been 'transformed' after 9/11. Speaking on ABC's *Four Corners*, managing editor at the *New York Times* Dean Baquet said: 'As journalists who've had to rely on third hand, fourth hand, you know, late night interviews with people who knew pieces of this [the Iraq War], we had the whole story. So we were elated, of course we were.'

All involved—the *Guardian*, the *New York Times* and *Der Spiegel*—agreed secrecy was paramount to gain maximum impact for the story. But holding it back for as long as six weeks, and with so many different outlets involved, would make it difficult to stop others finding out.

When the leak came it was as a result of dogged, if somewhat questionable, journalism.

Newsweek broke the story, quoting Overton that the Iraq War Logs would be WikiLeaks' next big hit. Overton said he felt he had been tricked into confirming the story but he was merely trying to make sure the report was accurate, more than worrying about 'upsetting the sensitivities of relationships'—pointing to Leigh at the *Guardian*.

If one small leak caused feathers to be ruffled, what happened next caused feathers to fly. All media outlets were scheduled to go with their reports at the same time, 10 p.m. in London. But Overton said Al Jazeera had broadcast its report at 9.20 p.m.—breaking the deadline by a full forty minutes.

The story was sensational—thousands more civilian deaths than the US had admitted; the same helicopter gunship which killed the Reuters journalists in Iraq killing civilians again, and the US turning a blind eye to torture.

'The *Guardian* was furious,' said Overton. It caused the newspaper to publish early on its website and gave some of the other newspapers enough time to 'do a cut and paste job' and run prominent stories about what the *Guardian* had found. Overton said he was sure Leigh was 'pissed off' about it, but at the same time accused him of 'making a mountain out of a molehill'.

As Assange witnessed the squabbling over leaks and security, he condemned the whole business, saving a particular level of vitriol for the *Guardian* and the *New York Times*. He said the editors of both newspapers often spoke on open, unencrypted phones and communicated by Gmail. With its main servers in California, Gmail was instantly accessible by the United States government. He pointed out what he saw as the sickness in journalism: 'The *Guardian* doesn't care that the government knows, the *New York Times* doesn't care if the government knows. The *New York Times* just doesn't want the *Washington Post* to know and the *Guardian* just doesn't want the *Telegraph* to know, or *The Times*. *The Times*, they don't care, because they're not trying to get a maximum reform impact.'

He said stories were all about increasing the 'journalistic prestige' of individual journalists, to get 'awards and so on'. There was also 'institutional prestige' based on sales, and that was the industry culture that has been bubbling along for 150 years. It was, he said, 'quite disgusting'.

Despite his criticism of the mainstream media, WikiLeaks had now clocked up two major hits with its media partners. The third and biggest was yet to come.

With the pace quickening, the Swedish sex allegations were beginning to overwhelm WikiLeaks. While the US had not been able to charge Assange with any crimes to date, the US had been keeping him under close surveillance. The challenge for Assange now was to get the third shot left in the WikiLeaks armoury out— before he ended up in jail, or worse still for him, in the United States of America.

10

CABLEGATE

Harold Hongju Koh, a lawyer for the US State Department in Washington, is responsible for giving legal advice on everything from trade disputes to inter-government relations. The work is arcane and often tedious. But as Koh made his way to his office on 26 November 2010, a message arrived that promised to shake things up. WikiLeaks' lawyer Jennifer Robinson had written to the US ambassador in London with a request for the US government. She said that WikiLeaks was about to publish a number of the 260 000 classified communiqués between the US State Department and its embassies around the world dating from 1966 to early 2010—and they needed his help to remove the names of people who might be harmed if they were published.

Ambassador Louis Susman's reaction to this is not recorded, but as a long-time Democratic Party financial backer and former banker he hadn't landed the plum London posting because of his diplomatic skills. Ambassador Susman had passed on the request to the State Department. He didn't know it then, but it would turn out that Susman had a vested interest in the outcome. One of the cables was written by him, reporting on a conversation he had with Australian High Commissioner John Dauth, in which Dauth said he thought the international community should pack up and leave Afghanistan. Another cable from his embassy said the British government had promised to protect the United States from probing questions during its investigation into the Iraq war.

It was Koh's job to fire off a blunt response. 'Dear Ms Robinson and Mr Assange,' he wrote. 'If any of the materials you intend to publish were provided by any government officials, or any intermediary without proper authorisation, they were provided in violation of US law ...'

Publication would put at risk the lives of 'countless innocent individuals', threaten ongoing military operations and just for good measure, 'place at risk ongoing cooperation between countries—partners, allies and common stakeholders—to confront common challenges, from terrorism to pandemic diseases to nuclear proliferation, that threaten global stability'. The United States wanted the material back, or at least destroyed and removed from the WikiLeaks website.

Just a few weeks earlier the *New York Times* had published an exceedingly unflattering report about Julian Assange and his WikiLeaks organisation. Though it was written by Pulitzer Prize–winning reporter John F Burns, it had the look and feel of a tabloid-style hit. Burns told the *New York Times* readers it wasn't just governments that were denouncing Assange. His former supporters were also abandoning him for what they saw as 'erratic and imperious behaviour and a nearly delusional grandeur'. They were also becoming more aware that 'the digital secrets he reveals can have a price in flesh and blood'.

The *New York Times* article was attacking someone who had just provided the newspaper with its best and biggest stories in years. Assange described it as a 'smear' against him.

It was certainly true that many in the organisation were angry at what they saw as Assange's high-handed and autocratic behaviour. Rebuffing a critic who questioned WikiLeaks' failure to redact names from the Afghan War Logs, Assange wrote: 'I am the heart and soul of this organisation, its founder, philosopher, spokesperson, original coder, organiser, financier and all the rest. If you have a problem with me, piss off.'

Assange called Daniel Ellsberg and told him he was going to cut out the *New York Times* from all future document releases. 'I said I thought he was absolutely right in being mad at John Burns and John Burns was inexcusable, but that I wouldn't make an enemy of the *New York Times*. He should try to work with them,' recalls Ellsberg. 'He just said: "Fuck them". He was mad at them and I know how he feels.'

The truth is the *New York Times* simply didn't need Assange any more. And as it prepared to negotiate the difficult political terrain that came with publishing a major exposé of US foreign policy, it sought to distance itself from him. An article like Burns' would certainly help the newspaper deal with the avalanche of criticism that was bound to pour in after publication of the leaks.

It was now clear that the *New York Times* and the *Guardian* were in cahoots. They had set a publication date, 5 November, for the first tranche of Cablegate material. The two newspapers were going to ambush WikiLeaks, only telling them of the plans to publish two days before they went to press. At *Der Spiegel*, there was a growing sense of discomfort amid the possibility they might be dumped. The planned publication date was a Friday—and *Der Spiegel* is published on a Monday.

When Assange got wind of the plans to publish early he threatened to put all the Cablegate material online. He was particularly angry that the *New York Times* was being included. If the *New York Times* was in, the whole world would get access to the Cablegate material. There would be no exclusive. For Assange it wasn't just the profile by Burns that turned him against the *Times*. He had been angry that while *Der Spiegel* ran a front-page story on Task Force 373—the US assassination squad in Afghanistan—it received far less prominent treatment in the US newspaper, prompting the question of who was protecting who.

Over at the well-appointed *Der Spiegel* offices near the Brandenberg Gate in central Berlin, the Germans looked on in horror. They demanded a meeting to sort out the differences. The magazine's editors were worried that the entire cooperative venture would fall apart and, as they put it, partners would turn into competitors. They scheduled a meeting at the *Guardian*'s offices for 6 p.m. on 1 November. Assange, wearing the attire he saves for special occasions, a blue suit and white shirt, was his customary half an hour late. But it was the team he brought with him that caused the most interest—his lawyers Mark Stephens and Jennifer Robinson. *Guardian* editor Alan Rusbridger quickly called for the newspaper's legal representative. *Der Spiegel* didn't bring any lawyers but did have a full complement: Holger Stark, Marcel Rosenbach and the magazine's editor-in-chief, George Mascolo. It would have been a complete team of old and new media but for one group that was missing. Perhaps unsurprisingly, *Der Spiegel* reported, the *New York Times* did not attend.

Assange walked in, sat down and got straight to the point. Does the *New York Times* have a copy of the Cablegate material? He repeated the question and, according to the *Der Spiegel* team, 'it sliced through the room', which by now was very still. 'And if so, where did it get a copy?' he asked. According to Assange, his next question to the group was: 'Did you give it to them in violation of our agreement?' Assange says that Rusbridger scanned the room and refused to answer the question. Assange said: 'What's the point in making an agreement if people will dishonour it?'

The story seemed to be that the *Guardian* had acquired another copy of the WikiLeaks cables and shared some of the information on it with the *New York Times*. If it was another copy, it wasn't governed by the same agreement as the one Assange had given to the newspaper. The *Guardian* says that it got the copy of the cables from freelance journalist Heather Brooke, who was apparently given it by one of the Icelandic WikiLeaks supporters, Smari McCarthy in early October. But according to WikiLeaks, McCarthy said he wiped that copy from Brooke's computer. So when did the *Guardian* get its own copy? Possibly it came much later, according to one source familiar with the case as late as November 1st, just four days before the planned publication date. The clear suggestion is that the *Guardian* produced the Cablegate stories using the WikiLeaks files they were supposedly holding in trust. While Assange called it theft, someone in the room pointed out: it's all stolen material. Rusbridger was more urbane. He simply made the point that the leaker had been leaked.

Der Spiegel was not sure what was going on. Understandably nervous that it might be shut out of Cablegate again, it asked the *Guardian* for a copy, but at the time of publishing this book they had not received one.

What the *Guardian* did by bringing Brooke onto the Cablegate team was smart. Rusbridger, who had written a foreword for one of her books, bound her exclusively to the newspaper for the duration of Cablegate, preventing her from selling her copy to one of the newspaper's competitors. WikiLeaks was playing in the cutthroat world of journalism and it was losing control.

More than three hours later, as everyone decamped downstairs for some food at the Rotunda Restaurant, Assange was by all accounts still fuming about the *New York Times*. What Assange wanted was no more negative stories about him and even a front-page correction. His lawyer Mark Stephens, who was playing the role of mediator, came up with what seemed like the best solution to end the stand off: the *New York Times* should publish an opinion piece by WikiLeaks.

Rusbridger got up from the table and called Bill Keller, the *New York Times'* executive editor in New York. When he came back the news wasn't encouraging. Assange would be treated like any other complainant—he could write a letter to the newspaper. The only guarantee Keller could give was that the *New York Times* wasn't planning any sleazy hit pieces. Assange was not happy. He even gave an indication that he was going to pull out of the deal with both newspapers.

Rusbridger summed up: Assange could cut out the *New York Times* and go with the *Washington Post* instead, but since he had lost control of the material that would result in chaos. The best decision was to go with the existing arrangements. Persuasively he argued in what must have been one of the most syrupy diplomatic pitches on record: 'We're good at working together, we like each other. We've communicated well with your lot. It's gone well. Why on earth throw it away?'

As they parted that night, Assange shook David Leigh's hand. Though Assange felt he'd been duped by Leigh, he had a grudging respect for him. 'He is genuinely interested in the journalism that he does, that is a big tick from me, that he actually does care about his story. But that's all he fucking cares about. So it doesn't matter who he fucks to do it—it's immoral, duplicitous behaviour to get as much exclusivity, as possible.' Yet from the outset Assange had been trying to control who had the right to use the material and how it was released. He had given five big media organisations access to the exclusion of every other media outlet in the world, forcing them to play catch up on the cables. It was hypocritical for Assange to argue about exclusivity.

The next day Rusbridger sent an offer for a settlement. The *Guardian*, the *New York Times* and *Der Spiegel* were still involved, and now Assange also wanted to formally include France's *Le Monde*, which had negotiated a side deal for access to the Iraq material, and also Spain's *El Pais* newspaper. Assange was keen for WikiLeaks to extend its reach far into the French- and Spanish-speaking areas of the world, which until then had been largely neglected. The decision to include *Le Monde* was designed to cause problems for the dictatorships in former French colonies in Northern Africa. The extraordinary events that would eventually unfold there would surprise Assange as much as the rest of the world.

As Assange mulled over the offer he examined the alternatives: 'We still had some levers in this meeting, we could have gone—right, we can give the whole lot to Al Jazeera, we can give it all to AP [the wire service Associated Press] and NewsCorp, fuck 'em.' But Assange said with 'too many cables coming out too quickly' this would 'saturate the market', reducing the number of investigative stories which in turn would limit the level of what he called 'political reform'.

Importantly, Assange secured a caveat that if there was a critical attack on WikiLeaks he would be free to release everything immediately. In the coming weeks that particular part of the agreement would be heavily tested.

There was something else Assange had to consider as he ruminated over whether to accept or reject the offer. 'We would have the *Guardian* and the *New York Times* campaigning against us and those are two big cannons ... at the very moment the Pentagon and the White House was campaigning against us.' Assange finally accepted the offer—he didn't need any more enemies than he already had. He was increasingly worried about being picked up off the street in London by US intelligence and whisked away to the United States. He had been lying low with people from the Frontline Club in Paddington, West London, run by its amiable founder, Vaughan Smith.

They made an odd couple: Smith, a former Grenadier Guards officer, had made a name for himself as a daring journalist covering the first Iraq war. Here was a right-wing libertarian supporting a hybrid lefty-libertarian, but their views meshed on one big issue: the problems of state power and individual privacy. Smith had another great quality: Ellingham Hall, a ten-bedroom Georgian manor in Norfolk—the perfect bolt-hole if the going got too tough in London. And early in November, with the deal settled with the *Guardian*, it became less necessary for Assange to remain there. He had already agreed that WikiLeaks' role this time would be to post the documents online as the newspaper wrote the stories.

He must have been growing tired of his treatment by the *Guardian* a newspaper he admired and believed was socially progressive. One witness to a discussion between Assange and senior Guardian staff including its editor and deputy editor said they were conceited and dismissive. This witness was surprised by their treatment of Assange; describing it as "shitting on the goose that had laid the golden egg" for their newspaper. [source: author informant]

One night, wearing a ridiculous-looking wig, he was driven the three and a half hours over some of the flattest countryside in Britain to the surprisingly quaint village of Bungay, and then through the winding streets to Ellingham Hall. As the car carrying Assange and his group made its way up the driveway and through part of the 600-acre wooded land that surrounds the property, Assange had every reason to be anxious about the security of WikiLeaks. The organisation was in deep trouble.

When Domscheit-Berg left WikiLeaks in September after a protracted falling-out with Assange, Assange suspected he'd taken with him more than his personal laptop. Domscheit-Berg had access to the codes and servers that not only stored WikiLeaks' data in Germany—they were the key to the system that protected the identities of whistleblowers and allowed them to download secrets in complete safety. Remarkably, for all his computer wizardry Assange did not have access to the codes. Without them the system couldn't work, so for the past two months at least WikiLeaks had been off-air—unable to take submissions. WikiLeaks posted an explanation that the site was down due to maintenance and engineering issues, but it wasn't true.

On several occasions he asked for Domscheit-Berg to return the codes and arranged for him to have meetings with WikiLeaks representatives. But this only caused more frustrations. On one occasion Domscheit-Berg agreed to return them, but when he did hand over the data the 'hard drives were empty [and] there was nothing there,' according to Assange.

Just a few weeks before the Cablegate exposé, an Australian woman working with WikiLeaks travelled to Germany to ask Domscheit-Berg for the codes. She is a calm and intelligent person and did her best to explain that WikiLeaks was about to go through its most severe test yet—and it needed maximum security. After the niceties had been dispensed with she asked Domscheit-Berg the question: Where are the access codes?

'What access codes?' he said.

'For all these servers,' she said.

'He has these already. It's all been handed over.'

Assange has been accused by many people of being difficult to work with, and one of the biggest complaints is that he says one thing to one person and something else to another. In late November I travelled to a town in the far east of Germany near the Polish border to talk with Domscheit-Berg. When we discussed the fact that Assange claimed Domscheit-Berg still had the codes he refuted that saying he had returned them: 'This is all sort of weird misinformation that he's spreading to people. And it's again—you see one-to-one conversations of him telling everyone a customised version of the truth.'

But it was Domscheit-Berg who was having difficulty with the truth has since admitted publicly that he and another activist known as 'the architect'—who built the submission system and the original WikiLeaks infrastructure—had taken the codes. Their actions shut down the whistleblower submissions system just before they both left the organisation. By early 2011 WikiLeaks was still unable to handle whistleblower material. Effectively, Assange had been locked out of his own organisation.

Domscheit-Berg now says he and 'the architect' will give them back when they decide that the system is secure. One of the reasons they took them, he says, is because security was lax at WikiLeaks, something Assange denies.

As Julian Assange settled down for his first night at Ellingham Hall it wasn't just the internal problems in WikiLeaks that were giving him concern. The US investigation was gathering pace.

* * *

Across the Atlantic, David House was returning home after a holiday with his girlfriend in Mexico. It had been a well-deserved break. As a founder of the Bradley Manning Support Network, he had worked hard to set up the website to raise money for Manning's defence when the world's attention was fixed on Assange. But at Chicago's O'Hare Airport, House was pulled aside. He said officials who told him they were from Homeland Security seized his laptop, mobile phone, flash drive and other electronic equipment, and asked him for names of others in the support network.

House knew Manning, but not that well. They had met when Manning turned up at a workshop on hacking in Boston. When Manning was arrested House decided he would help, and visited him three times in his Quantico Marine Corps Base prison cell. It was about this time that military intelligence began focusing in on Manning's friends in the Boston area where House also lives, apparently trying to recruit members of the hacking community to spy on WikiLeaks. With House they went one step further, following him in the street and staking out his home. On one occasion, he said, four people came to his door: two identified themselves as military investigators, the others said they were from the State Department. When he invited them in they spent more than an hour talking about WikiLeaks and Bradley Manning, and pumping him for information.

The investigators were getting anxious, and little wonder. WikiLeaks had just announced it was going to release the drop of cables that were seven times bigger than the Iraq War Logs. Journalists with their pocket calculators came up with an extraordinary figure: nearly three million documents. What Assange deliberately omitted was that he meant it was seven times the number of words—not documents. 'It appears that the State Department thought we had a lot more than we did,' Assange told me later with a mischievous smile.

The Thanksgiving holiday is usually a period when even politicians get some time to relax with their families; many of them make it a long weekend. But on the last Friday of November, the gloomy day perfectly reflected the atmosphere at the State Department where

Hillary Clinton, the secretary of state, was preparing for a press conference. She looked stressed and exhausted: Clinton had been informed of what was coming. The biggest leak in history—an exposure of the inner workings of the US Government and its foreign policy. But she couldn't say she wasn't warned.

Nine days before publication, the *New York Times* told her administration to get ready for the firestorm of information that was heading its way. Two days later, the newspaper's Washington bureau chief, Dean Baquet, and two of his colleagues made their way down to the State Department. Apart from the *New York Times*, they were also representing the interests of the *Guardian, Der Spiegel, Le Monde* and *El Pais*. After they passed through security, they were shown into a 'windowless room' where they encountered an 'unsmiling crowd'. It was an impressive turnout. Gathered around a conference table were representatives from the White House, the State Department, the Office of the Director of National Intelligence, the CIA, the Defense Intelligence Agency, the FBI and the Pentagon. Others, who did not identify themselves, added to the packed room.

It was 'fair to say the mood was tense' according to the *Times*', Bill Keller. Another said there were signs of suppressed outrage and frustration. Here the old tests were about to be applied with vigour: the fine balance between the government's right to hold secrets and the public's right to know. This would be the Internet age's biggest test of that balance.

WikiLeaks, though not directly represented, was a powerful presence in the room. Though the *New York Times* would be the last to admit it, WikiLeaks' ability to disclose everything on the Internet without challenge tilted the balance very much in favour of the newspaper's representatives, as the group worked their way through the amount of disclosure the government would accept.

Baquet understood the most important issue was to protect individuals who had spoken candidly to American diplomats in countries that had oppressive regimes. The second category of importance included sensitive US programs, usually related to intelligence. The *New York Times* agreed to withhold some of this information.

It was the third category the newspaper had the most disagreement about. The State Department feared that publication of cables that disclosed candid comments by and about foreign officials—including heads of state—would strain relations with those countries. The *New York Times* was mostly unconvinced by this argument.

In what must have come as a great comfort to the newspaper, the US government's fury was directed at the presumed source of the leaked material, Bradley Manning, and in particular WikiLeaks. According to *Der Spiegel*, the US government was not interested in quarrelling with the media organisations involved. Two days after the meeting, the US Ambassador to Germany, Philip Murphy, reinforced the message: 'I'm incredibly angry. I don't begrudge *Der Spiegel* and the press, who are just doing their jobs. I am criticising those who stole this material.' It was a convenient argument for the United States—it retained its relationships with the powerful old media while demonising the newcomer.

Assange had a very straightforward view of how to correct the power imbalance. You get the impression that if he really had his way the US would receive virtually no warning at all. He was unhappy that the 'perpetrator' was aware before the 'victims', and that the State Department would be able to have enough time to spin the stories its way. Yet as the deadline approached and Hillary

Clinton embarked on a global tour to quell the anxiety of many of the world's leaders, others had developed a different tactic to blunt the WikiLeaks attack. Just before the launch, a massive distributed denial-of-service (DDoS) attack hit the WikiLeaks site. Thousands of computers linked through one controller began simultaneously trying to contact WikiLeaks. As the attack continued it grew stronger and stronger. In the end the 'requests' were asking WikiLeaks to deliver the equivalent of 114 full-length movies every second. As the site was collapsing it must have crossed Assange's mind to fire off all 260 000 cables at once, as per his agreement with the *Guardian*, if the situation got too hostile. Instead Assange kept his cool and WikiLeaks shut down the US server that had come under such ferocious attack, and switched all requests to Sweden. It's never been revealed who was behind the cyber assault but all it did was draw even more attention to the impending stories—and they rolled onto the Internet as planned, unimpeded by the crisis.

The front-page headline in the *Guardian* said: 'US Embassy Cables Leak Sparks Global Diplomacy Crisis.' The report said that the United States had been catapulted into a worldwide diplomatic crisis with the leaking to the *Guardian* and other international media of 'more than 250 000 classified cables from its embassies'. It focused on calls by the Saudi king for the United States to attack Iran to put an end to its nuclear weapons program, as well as the fact that Hillary Clinton had ordered US State Department officers to spy on the UN's leadership, gathering everything from frequent flyer numbers, health records and samples of DNA.

Der Spiegel's headline followed the *Guardian*'s global perspective: 'A Superpower's View of the World' it said, pointing out that 'never before in history has a superpower lost control of such vast amounts of such sensitive information'.

Le Monde headlined: 'WikiLeaks: A Behind the Scenes Look at US Diplomacy'. The serious French afternoon paper even managed a little humour, pointing out that despite all the hype the documents did not cast new light on who shot President Kennedy.

The *New York Times'* coverage was more muted. 'Leaked Cables Offer Raw Look at US Diplomacy,' the headline murmured. Although it did report that the cables contained 'brutally candid views of foreign leaders and frank assessments of nuclear and terrorist threats'. In what is known in journalism as 'burying the lead', the newspaper failed to mention Hillary Clinton's directive to spy on the United Nations Secretary General, Ban Ki Moon, or that Arab countries were urging an attack on Iran. High up in the story Clinton was given a free kick to say what a terrible thing it was to have her government's dirty washing aired in public, with no hint that she had directed what at first glance looked like a case of criminal activity against the United Nations.

But it wasn't all high-end politics. There was plenty of gossip from the cocktail circuit. Libya's Muammar Gaddafi starred with the revelation that he wouldn't go anywhere without his voluptuous, blonde Ukrainian nurse, and hates flying so much he will only travel short distances by air, something he may have to re-evaluate as demonstrators took to the streets demanding his ousting in early 2011.

Vladimir Putin, the Russian prime minister, was referred to as an 'alpha dog' and the only mildly disparaging comment about Italian prime minister Silvio Berlusconi appeared to be that his late-night partying left him insufficient energy for his day job.

While the *New York Times* was trying to balance its relationship with the Obama administration, its more conservative readership and those who don't believe in any form of censorship, it certainly wasn't honouring the motto it has carried on the masthead for decades: 'All The News That's Fit To Print'.

The slow release of stories, taken from just a handful of the leaked documents, was partly a tactic by Assange to create maximum impact over many months and partly to keep the Americans guessing about what was in the vast bulk of the remaining Cablegate documents. The day by day leaking of individual documents gave journalists the upper hand in their dealings with the State Department. But on 3 December, five days after the first Cablegate release, the plan came horribly undone. The *Guardian* posted the identifying information of every single one of the 251 286 cables on its website. Assange, who was still hiding out in the country manor house and having nothing to do with the *Guardian*'s publication process, was appalled. It tipped off the US administration to the contents of every cable. 'They released all the metadata ... the date of every cable, the subject of every cable, which embassy it was from, where it was to, subject, date, time,' he said.

It was 'one thing' to say it was 'inevitable' that WikiLeaks would release a certain number of cables, Assange said, but 'which of the 251 000?' That was the important question and the *Guardian* had just shown the US government exactly which ones. It would allow the United States to 'prepare their own spin' now that it knew the identity of the cables, and thus the material they contained.

The *Guardian* material potentially provided ammunition for the Americans to attack Assange and Manning. There were reports that a grand jury had been empanelled in Virginia to investigate possible charges against them. If the US military computer logs line up with 'every goddamn record of what we release, that's very strong evidence,' he said. It seemed that Assange himself had been caught in the new online world of openness and full publication.

Yet for all its intelligence gathering, the US government still did not understand what WikiLeaks was doing. The White House said it anticipated WikiLeaks would make public 'several hundred thousand' cables on Sunday night, according to the *New York Times*. This was incorrect—Assange would release only a handful of cables at that time. As Ellsberg points out: 'About half a dozen people in the country are giving Julian credit for having withheld 99 per cent of the 260 000 cables. He has put out 1900 cables—less than 1 per cent. No one seems to know that'. It has been called the 'zombie lie' that Assange had 'indiscriminately dumped everything out'. By February 2011 only 4000 cables had been released, leaving approximately 247 000 other documents still to come.

What had been redacted by WikiLeaks and released was sensational enough. Yet still serious errors were made, not by WikiLeaks, but by the newspapers that reported on the released files. A story on Iran reportedly obtaining missiles from North Korea that were capable of attacking Russia and Western Europe was merely speculation, but it was reported as near fact by the *New York Times*. The newspaper was on safer ground with revelations that the US had been trying to remove highly enriched uranium from a Pakistan nuclear research facility in the fear that it could end up in a terrorist device, and that China would not necessarily support North Korea indefinitely, weakening the rogue nation in the eyes of the world. And in Yemen the US had been secretly bombing terrorist targets, with the Yemini president saying: 'We'll continue to say the bombs are ours, not yours.' Soon after the Yemini people read this story, they took to the streets in an attempt to topple the government.

The fact that WikiLeaks was on occasions more careful than the mainstream media made no difference to the attacks against the organisation that followed the Cablegate releases.

'Let's be clear. This disclosure is not just an attack on America— it's an attack on the international community,' Hillary Clinton said. Such leaks 'tear at the fabric' of responsible government. 'There is nothing laudable about endangering innocent people, and there is nothing brave about sabotaging the peaceful relations between nations,' she added.

Clinton emphasised that she wanted to 'make it clear to the American people and to our friends and partners that we are taking aggressive steps' to hold those who leaked the documents to account.

Within hours an official from the office of Senator Joe Lieberman, who chairs the Homeland Security Committee, was on the phone to Amazon who had been hosting WikiLeaks during the Cablegate release. Twenty-four hours later, the company announced it was disconnecting the WikiLeaks service, forcing it to switch to another server based in the Cold War bunker in Sweden.

Lieberman said that Amazon's 'decision to cut off WikiLeaks now' was the right decision and should set the standard for other companies that WikiLeaks was using to distribute its 'illegally seized material'. He called on 'any other company or organisation that is hosting WikiLeaks to immediately terminate its relationship with them'. In a message sent via Twitter, WikiLeaks fired back that if Amazon was 'so uncomfortable with the First Amendment, they should get out of the business of selling books'.

As the flood of attacks continued Vice President Joe Biden weighed in, describing Assange as a dangerous 'hi-tech terrorist', while right-wing politicians set the temperature to boiling point by inciting violent action against Assange and Manning.

The former governor of Arkansas and a Republican presidential hopeful Mike Huckabee said: 'They've put American lives at risk. They put relationships that will take decades to rebuild at risk. Whoever in our government leaked that information is guilty of treason, and I think anything less than execution is too kind a penalty.'

Sarah Palin, a likely presidential candidate in 2012, posted on her Facebook page: 'He is an anti-American operative with blood on his hands. His past posting of classified documents revealed the identity of more than 100 Afghan sources to the Taliban. Why was he not pursued with the same urgency we pursue al-Qaida and Taliban leaders?'

University of Calgary Professor Tom Flanagan who helped organise the campaign of the Canadian prime minister, said: 'Well I think Assange should be assassinated actually. I think Obama should put out a contract and maybe use a drone or something.'

As the clamour increased, PayPal cut off the account used by WikiLeaks to collect donations. PostFinance announced it had frozen Assange's accounts and MasterCard and Visa announced they had stopped payments to WikiLeaks, seriously imperilling its financing and future of the organisation.

* * *

Even in the bucolic surrounds of Ellingham Hall, the world was closing in on Assange. At Sweden's request Interpol had issued a red alert for his arrest to face questioning in Sweden over the sex allegations, and his lawyers were negotiating with the British police extradition squad about where he might hand himself in. A bail hearing would decide whether he remained free or was held in prison while he waited for the extradition case to start after Christmas. When he finally arrived at Horseferry Road Magistrates Court for the hearing he appeared in dark suit and sunglasses, looking less the hacker from Melbourne and more like the star he had become.

Jemima Khan, former wife of Pakistani cricketer and politician Imran Khan, was there to back Assange, with bail money if necessary, as was director Ken Loach, famed for his insightful films on social justice, and Australian filmmaker, author and journalist, John Pilger.

In arguing against Assange getting bail, Gemma Lindfield, the lawyer from the British Crown Prosecution Service appointed to represent the Swedish case, made a big play of Assange's peripatetic nature—the fact that he moved from town to town and country to country with little more than a backpack and a couple of computers to keep him company. Looking around the court, the same description might have been applied to half the journalists covering the case.

Inexplicably, despite the fact that the WikiLeaks website is always pleading poverty and appealing for money, Lindfield asserted that 'it was clear' that Assange had access to money. What she appeared to have missed was that the biggest credit card companies in the world had all frozen WikiLeaks' funds.

When Assange's lawyer Mark Stephens got to his feet, his argument for Assange to be released on bail included the simple fact that he 'had nowhere to go', 'was instantly recognisable' and, besides, he had already handed in his passport.

The feeling in the Assange camp was positive and though their confidence was shaken when Judge Riddle muddled up WikiLeaks with the free online encyclopedia Wikipedia, they still thought the prosecution had failed to make its case. Assange was bound to be released on bail. Sitting in his glass cage in the courtroom, his signature grey hair shorter than usual, Assange was paying particularly close attention. After what seemed like an eternity, but was only a few minutes, Judge Riddle concluded of Assange that despite it all, 'There are substantial grounds to believe he could abscond if granted bail'.

There was a collective, audible gasp. Jennifer Robinson indicated she was shocked by the decision. Assange was led out of his cage and back to the cells below. Outside, Mark Stephens said: 'Many people believe Mr Assange to be innocent, myself included. Many people believe that this prosecution is politically motivated.'

The closest the cameras got to Assange as he was driven through the crowds in a white prison van was a shot through the window. He made the front pages the next day with a defiant stare and a victory salute.

One week later, Assange returned to court for a second attempt at bail. If the star-studded cast had failed to impress the judge last time, Assange simply doubled the number of the cast—and increased the star quality.

He might be someone who at times had trouble keeping long-term friendships, but he certainly knew how to make them fast. Geoffrey Robertson QC, the celebrated Australian human rights barrister, had cut short his holiday to represent Assange. The documentary filmmaker Michael Moore also put up US$20 000 bail for someone he didn't know. Bianca Jagger wandered in offering a further touch of the exotic, and the author and investigative journalist Phillip Knightley added credibility.

Conspicuously absent were many of the journalists Assange had worked closely with on Cablegate. At this hearing, Judge Riddle granted bail because Assange had put up better surety, and provided a good address—Vaughan Smith's country home, Ellingham Hall.

Assange and his team believed he would walk free, but two hours later the prosecution announced it was appealing the bail decision to the High Court. Until the appeal, Assange would be returned to Wandsworth prison and solitary confinement, where he would spend another three days.

With all the time he had for reflection, he found 'I rather liked myself'. He also discovered he still had a voice from inside prison. 'We now know that Visa, MasterCard and PayPal are instruments of US foreign policy. It's not something we knew before.' The message delivered via his mother, Christine Assange, also called on 'the world to protect my work and my people from these illegal and immoral acts'.

Assange was talking like a political prisoner, and though he denied it, his supporters took it as a call to arms. Within hours MasterCard had been knocked off the air in a similar attack to the one that had crippled WikiLeaks itself. A group calling themselves Anonymous took responsibility for the attack, which they called 'Operation Payback'.

As Assange sat in his Wandsworth prison cell he placed a call to Daniel Ellsberg, who had come to his support during the attacks on him in the US. Assange left a spirited message on Ellsberg's phone, saying he was 'calling from a Norman Basement Slammer and just called to see how it's all going'.

It's a good job Assange didn't call the *New Yorker* veteran Seymour Hersh, another of his heroes, most famous for exposing the cover-up of killings by US troops at My Lai during the Vietnam War, and more recently, the torture of prisoners at Abu Ghraib. He'd met Hersh earlier on, before 'Collateral Murder'. Hersh said he saw Assange at a conference where 'he took me aside'. Asked if he had given Assange any advice, Hersh said: 'He's not interested in advice.' Hersh said that Assange was now discovering that he 'has the same problems that newspapers do'. He said he felt that Assange 'just made it worse for himself', but didn't elaborate.

Ellsberg too was having difficulty with some of the decisions being made by WikiLeaks. It had posted a secret document—marked NoFor, meaning not to be seen by any foreigners, which identified key infrastructure the US considered critical to its national security. The sites ranged from the Nadym gas pipeline junction in Siberia, which it described as 'the most critical gas facility in the world', to a factory that makes parts for nuclear submarines in Scotland, to the Sydney landings for two giant undersea communication cables, as well as many other sites. Ellsberg had grave misgivings about the direction WikiLeaks was taking. He contacted them.

'I said, "Well I would not have put that out", and they came back with an answer from somebody saying: "Well, it's really all on the public record, it's not all a secret". I said, "You know, a terrorist could find this stuff easily enough anyway, why give them a lift, I wouldn't give them a lift. It doesn't look responsible to me."' He added: 'I don't know why they put that up. That wrecked it ...'

WikiLeaks disagreed with any assessment that the release was dangerous, arguing that the sites were not directly identified. But losing Ellsberg's support on such a key issue should have caused some consternation. It was a reminder of the Afghan War Logs fiasco where informers were named, helping the White House continue its attacks on WikiLeaks. Yet the degree to which US national security is compromised by the cables is debatable. Reuters news agency reported that 'a congressional official … said the administration felt compelled to say publicly that the revelations had seriously damaged American interests in order to bolster legal efforts to shut down the WikiLeaks website and bring charges against the leakers'. In truth, internal US government reviews of Cablegate had determined that the leaks had caused only 'limited damage to US interests abroad'.

In lock step with the Obama administration, Australian Prime Minister Julia Gillard echoed the White House's public statements. She declared that Assange had broken the law, although she couldn't name exactly which law he had violated. She also announced that the Australian Federal Police had been briefing her on security implications of Assange's actions.

The Attorney-General Senator Robert McClelland said that the Australian authorities would do all they could to help the US investigation. He even went so far as to say he would look at the possibility of revoking Assange's Australian passport. Why the government should have taken such an extreme view about one of its citizens may well have had less to do with national interest and more to do with cosying up to the US, or that is how it was perceived.

Cablegate revealed just how close that relationship is. One cabinet member had been snitching to the US Embassy in Canberra on the Labor party's power struggle before Gillard was elected. Right-wing Labor powerbroker Mark Arbib was one of the major players in the removal of Kevin Rudd as prime minister. The documents identify Arbib, now a minister, as a valuable source of information on the attempts by Rudd to prevent a move against him by Gillard, his then deputy. Arbib's comments were contained in documents that said his identity should be guarded as a 'protected' source.

It's possible Gillard thought being pro-American and taking a tough line on Assange would play well with the Australian public. It didn't. Assange has his biggest support base in Australia where opinion polls have said that two thirds of the people agree with the work he has done. What is more surprising is the degree of support he has received from news outlets in the country. In an unprecedented move, representatives from all the major media outlets in Australia with the exception of *The Australian* newspaper, signed a letter criticising the Prime Minister for her actions: 'To aggressively attempt to shut WikiLeaks down, to threaten to prosecute those who publish official leaks, and to pressure companies to cease doing commercial business with WikiLeaks, is a serious threat to democracy, which relies on a free and fearless press,' it said. When the activist organisation Getup.org launched a major campaign, thousands filled the streets at protests in Sydney and Melbourne. Public opinion rallied behind Assange, casting Gillard into the political wilderness on the issue. Assange told the crowd by video: 'It is interesting how some politicians single out my staff and myself for attack while saying nothing about the slaughter of thousands by the US military or other dictatorships. It is cowardly to bully a small media organisation, but that is what is happening here.'

With Gillard looking vulnerable on the issue, her foreign minister Kevin Rudd dissented from the government line. In Cairo, where WikiLeaks would play a role in what was to unfold in the following months, he took a swipe at the Americans, saying that it was up to them to look after their own secrets. He may well have been irked by their description of him in one cable as a 'control freak'. But he was also playing to the audience back home, countering McClelland's threat to revoke Assange's passport. He said that was his responsibility, not McClelland's, and even offered to arrange for a computer to be sent to Assange in jail so he could prepare his defence.

The Australian Federal Police would eventually discover that there was nothing they could charge Assange with in Australia. But that didn't stop the ongoing US inquiry, and the assistance offered by the Australian Attorney-General, who has direct charge of ASIO, Australia's internal intelligence service.

I have been reliably told that ASIO played an active part in the investigation into Assange, trawling through his life and activities in Australia. But what must be just as worrying for him, and has also never been revealed before, is the fact that the inquiry also included officers from ASIS, Australia's overseas intelligence agency, which has strong links with the US.

* * *

Over in Britain, Assange successfully fought the appeal to the High Court over his bail, and was eventually freed from Wandsworth prison. He had to meet stringent conditions, which included remaining under curfew on Vaughn Smith's estate, reporting daily to the local police and wearing what's known as a Glasgow Rolex, an electronic bracelet to track his every movement.

As he emerged victorious from the High Court hearing snow fell, promising an unusually white Christmas. Flanked by his legal team, Robertson, Robinson and Stephens, Assange waved amid a barrage of TV lights and flashing cameras. He might have been tired but he hadn't lost his sense of irony in prison. 'It's great to smell the fresh air of London again,' he said.

In front of the world's media he was on message: 'During my time in solitary confinement in the bottom of a Victorian prison, I had time to reflect on the conditions of those people around the world also in solitary confinement, also on remand, in conditions that are more difficult than those faced by me.'

The next the crowd saw of him, he was being driven off in Vaughan Smith's white four-wheel drive through the heavy London traffic, up The Strand and towards Fleet Street, the former heart of British journalism. Assange would have plenty of time over Christmas to prepare for the extradition hearing, when Swedish prosecutors would finally reveal full details of the allegations against him.

With a hostile prime minister in his country, the most powerful nation on earth chasing him and the Swedish legal system demanding he be extradited, Assange was embarking on the fight of his life.

11

CAUGHT IN THE NET

When the fax machine at Twitter's headquarters in San Francisco spat out its latest complaint just before Christmas 2010 it might have been just another dissatisfied customer writing in about a phishing scam or someone else up to no good on the Internet.

But it was in fact the latest development in the WikiLeaks investigation. Addressed to Twitter's Trust and Safety Department, the four-page fax carried the United States Justice Department letterhead. It wasn't seeking assistance: it was demanding information about some of Twitter's highest profile clients on behalf of an unnamed authority, probably the FBI. Twitter was told it should tell no one about the fax, which named Julian Assange, Bradley Manning, Birgitta Jonsdottir, Jacob Appelbaum and Rop Gonggrijp. It was known in the WikiLeaks camp that an inquiry was underway, but it had been difficult to assess exactly which course it was taking. The investigation may have been trying to discover who leaked the

'Collateral Murder' video, but the inclusion of Appelbaum's name suggested the hunt was much wider. Appelbaum operates a Tor, the special Internet system that allows people to communicate without revealing their identities. It was probable that the FBI were trying to link Manning to Assange through this 'cut-out' operated by Appelbaum.

Whoever wrote the court document spelt Rop Gonggrijp's surname incorrectly (there are two 'g's), a likely indication the document had been pulled together quickly. Twitter was told it had just three days to comply with the demand to hand over the information.

The court order requested everything that Twitter knew about those named in the fax: where Assange and the others lived, how they paid their accounts, who they sent their tweets to, who they received them from, the telephone numbers they used and their bank account details. The order demanded every shred of information Twitter held on them dating back to November 2009, when it's believed WikiLeaks first began receiving the initial trickle of classified documents from its well-connected source. Such was the secrecy, the Justice Department's court order instructed Twitter not to even reveal receipt of the fax, or anything else that related to what it called an 'ongoing criminal investigation'. The orders had been 'sealed' by the Federal Court.

Unlike other US corporations who had rolled over and abandoned WikiLeaks, Twitter decided to confront the government and not release the information without a fight. It had nothing to lose. By standing up to the US administration Twitter made Washington look like Beijing, using heavy-handed tactics to silence free speech. Had Twitter given in it would be seen as weak, and possibly receive the treatment meted out to other companies, like PayPal and MasterCard, who had handed over information without a fight. They'd been knocked offline by activists, their businesses and their reputations badly damaged. Whether or not Twitter took that into account is not known. But as an Internet company that prides itself on supporting freedom of communication, what it eventually did made sound business practice. It stuck by its stated policy that it would only hand over personal information about its users if compelled to by law.

Though Twitter took the fight to court, because of the secrecy order it couldn't tell anyone in WikiLeaks what it was doing. The Justice Department made it clear that Twitter had to keep the request for information secret. Only when the judge lifted the secrecy order and the court documents were unsealed, was it possible for the names to be revealed, along with exactly what was going on.

Considering the demand was for detailed information about key WikiLeaks personnel, it was clear the grand jury investigation was more than a rumour: it was almost certainly a fact, and more importantly, it was possibly the first step in prosecuting Bradley Manning and Julian Assange under the 1917 Espionage Act. As the Justice Department dug into the WikiLeaks case it called witnesses before the grand jury, examining information and sifting the evidence to see whether the basis for criminal charges could be established.

After the Cablegate revelations it wouldn't have come as a surprise that the United States government was prepared to brush aside diplomatic niceties to prosecute Manning and WikiLeaks members. The fact that Birgitta Jonsdottir was an elected member of parliament in Iceland, a friendly democracy, did not matter.

Freed from the non-disclosure provision of the sealed court order, Twitter called Birgitta Jonsdottir to break the news. Jonsdottir was furious, and demanded a meeting with the US ambassador. She said the Justice Department had gone completely over the top. 'I have not done anything that can be considered criminal. It's not against the law to leak information, it's not against the law to be a source,' she said. She is right: it is not illegal to leak material in the United States, which is why there was an attempt to prosecute Ellsberg under the Espionage Act all those years ago when he leaked the Pentagon Papers.

Assange described the Twitter revelations as 'an outrageous attack by the Obama administration on the privacy and free speech rights of Twitter's customers—many of them American citizens'.

The tables, however, were about to be turned on the Justice Department. Three of the WikiLeaks group—Birgitta Jonsdottir, Jacob Appelbaum and Rop Gonggrijp—asked the court to 'unseal' other information that was being kept from view—details of the investigation itself. They were represented by the Electronic Frontier Foundation [EFF] and the American Civil Liberties Union [ACLU]. It's a standing joke that from the ACLU's Manhattan office it is only possible to catch a glimpse of the Statue of Liberty, and justice can be similarly elusive. Nevertheless, it had already successfully argued that the attorney general had been in breach of the First Amendment's right of free association and the Fourth Amendment's protection against unreasonable search. Now the EFF wanted to test the constitutional right to question government to the limit. It argued that unsealing the court documents and revealing the details of the investigation would contribute greatly to the public's ability to 'participate meaningfully in this ongoing debate' about freedom of the press. The case presented a rare and valuable opportunity for the public to learn more about the nature and scope of the government's use of electronic surveillance orders, the EFF said.

As Judge Theresa Buchanan mulled over the arguments in the Eastern District Division Court, not far from where a special Pentagon team had been working on the case, Julian Assange's legal representatives were noticeable by their absence. WikiLeaks described the hearing as 'the first round in the US Government's legal battle against Julian Assange' but said neither it nor Assange would be present for the hearing because they believed that in this case the United States lacked jurisdiction over 'activities beyond its borders'.

While the case was being heard in America, Twitter was making an impact on events in a former French colony perched on the northern coast of Africa. From the regional towns to the backstreet bazaars and the wide boulevards of the Tunisian capital Tunis, everyone knew that President Zine el-Abidine Ben Ali was corrupt. The people had watched government ministers become millionaires, while the regime siphoned off the nation's wealth.

Like many revolutions it wasn't one event that started the protests. First came the death of a street trader who set himself alight, protesting he'd been humiliated by a local official. This was closely followed by the release of the Cablegate documents. Thousands of Tunisians tweeted a link to a WikiLeaks story that said Ben Ali had presided over an orgy of corruption: the boats, the homes, the businesses, had been bought with money that rightfully belonged to the people. Significantly, the cables also revealed that Ben Ali did not have the guaranteed backing of his ally, the United States, indicating that the dictatorship only had the army's support. The people of Tunisia took to the streets—convinced for the first time that the US would not intervene to support Ben Ali.

Le Monde journalist Florence Beaugé, who had been expelled from Tunisia in 2009 for writing critical articles about Ben Ali, knew first hand the importance of the cable to the Tunisians. 'It was as if for the first time someone told the Tunisians: "You are not insane. You are right to hate him. You deserve better,"' Beaugé said. 'Tunisians could read what an official said from the outside: Ben Ali and his family were crooks and robbers and he was a dictator. It gave them tremendous encouragement to bring down the president.' Even Bill Keller from the *New York Times* was fulsome in his praise: WikiLeaks cables in which American diplomats recounted the 'extravagant corruption of Tunisia's rulers' helped fuel a popular uprising that overthrew the government.

As Ben Ali and his family fled into exile in Saudi Arabia, Assange was wary about claiming credit for the downfall. Assange's plan had been to link up with the 'old media', *Le Monde*, to widen WikiLeaks' reach into the French-speaking world. But in Tunisia the newspaper had no impact: *Le Monde* had been banned since Beaugé was ejected. In the end it was the new media—WikiLeaks links being spread by Twitter, Facebook and Al Jazeera—that cut through.

WikiLeaks was a brilliant example of what had been known for some time: the power of information from a legitimate source, disseminated via social networking systems, to threaten the power of the state and its institutions. And it made no difference whether a country was democratic like the United States, or autocratic, like

Tunisia and Egypt, where president Hosnai Mubarak had ruled with US backing for nearly thirty years.

In Cairo on 29 January 2011, when demonstrators moved into Tahir Square for one of their biggest rallies in opposition to Mubarak's rule, they too were spurred on by evidence from WikiLeaks. Just a few hours earlier WikiLeaks had released cables from US Ambassador to Egypt Margaret Scobey, reporting police brutality was 'routine and pervasive' and that there had been 'standing orders' from the Interior Ministry for police to 'shoot, beat and humiliate judges in order to undermine judicial independence'. The demonstrators who, like their Tunisian counterparts, used Twitter and Facebook to organise, had other messages flashing across their mobile phones: a US embassy cable also said that the Americans suspected the Egyptian government of torturing a Facebook activist who had organised a strike, to scare others into 'abandoning their political activities'. While the world looked on with fascination and a large degree of dread about the escalating bloodshed, Mubarak was ousted from power after just eighteen days of protest, replaced by the military until promised democratic elections.

Ironically, at the same time in the US, WikiLeaks was facing the possibility of being prosecuted for leaking the documents that were playing a significant role in achieving what the White House wanted: free speech in other parts of the world. In an address on censorship in January 2010 at Washington's Newseum, a museum of news, Secretary of State Hillary Clinton made special mention of Tunisia and Egypt, naming them as countries where the 'free flow of information' was threatened. She added that any nation which restricted free access to information risked 'walling themselves off from the progress of the next century'.

Assange was buoyed by her comments, hoping they marked a change of direction in US policy by demonstrating Washington's support of a more open form of government—in the United States as well. He saw it as a possible shift away from the hard line against whistleblowers that had been pursued by the Obama administration.

Assange believed that the United States had used the principle of free speech as a 'stick' with which to beat the former Soviet Union. This was something that united the hawks (hard line anti-communists), and the liberals during the Cold War—the hawks because it attacked communism, and the liberals because it allowed them to argue that if free press was good for the Soviet Union it must also be good for the United States. The problem, as Assange saw it, was that with the end of the Cold War, the free speech argument was no longer important so the hawks were reasserting themselves. 'They're annoyed by people publishing, they're annoyed by a free press, they're annoyed by leaks, so they want to get rid of the free press,' he said. It may sound far-fetched, but there's some evidence to support his view. Despite Clinton's championing of an unrestricted Internet, which she described as 'the public space of the 21st century—the world's town square, classroom, marketplace,' the Obama administration has been cracking down on freedom of speech at home. In the past two years it's outdone all previous administrations in pursuing those who leaked classified information. According to US author Jonathan Alter, Obama was 'fearsome' on the subject and went on an 'anti-leak jihad' over some of the disclosures.

'They're going after this at every opportunity and with unmatched vigour,' said Steven Aftergood of the Federation of American Scientists.

Bradley Manning and Julian Assange are just two in a long line who are under investigation. An FBI linguist has already been jailed for twenty months for leaking information to a blogger, and an employee of the National Security Agency (NSA) has been charged for allegedly handing over classified information to the *Baltimore Sun* about an intelligence project which even the NSA admitted in the end had wasted a billion dollars of taxpayers' money on a failed contract.

* * *

On 7 February 2011, Assange was back in court in London fighting the extradition request from Sweden. The nearby Belmarsh Prison, known as Britain's Guantánamo Bay because of the number of terrorism suspects who had been held there without trial, was a constant reminder to Assange of what his lawyer Mark Stephens repeatedly said might be his fate if the Swedes got their hands on him. His legal team argued that there was a strong possibility that US prosecutors would seek Assange's extradition from Sweden to the United States. Geoffrey Robertson QC said there was a suggestion that the Swedish prime minister had meddled in the case with his remarks in parliament. Assange's defence relied heavily on attacking the Swedish legal system, arguing that he wouldn't get a fair trial there.

They brought in Britta Sundy-Weitman a retired Swedish judge, who suggested Swedish prosecutors illegally leaked information of the sex crime accusations and that the media in Sweden had 'turned very hostile' towards Assange. She saved her most damning assessment for the Swedish prosecutor, Marianne Ny, claiming Ny was 'anti-men' and prejudicial towards Assange.

Forty-eight hours earlier, the entire contents of the case against Assange—sent to his lawyers by the Swedes—had been published online. Just who it benefitted wasn't clear but it did reveal that one of the women who accused Assange of rape had let him carry on having sex with her when she woke up even though he wasn't wearing a condom.

Inside court, the focus was on the allegations themselves, which, for the first time, were being examined in public. The Swedes wanted Assange for questioning and possible prosecution for the 'unlawful coercion' of one of his accusers, which involved 'a firm hold of the injured party's arms and a forceful spreading of her legs'; 'sexual molestation'; knowing that although it was 'a prerequisite of sexual intercourse that a condom be used, consummated sexual intercourse without her knowledge'; a second allegation of 'sexual molestation' in that 'Assange deliberately molested the injured party by acting in a manner designed to violate her sexual integrity—that is, lying next to her and pressing his naked, erect penis to her body'; and finally, rape: in an 'aggravating circumstance' knowing it was a 'prerequisite of sexual intercourse that a condom be used, still consummated unprotected sexual intercourse with her'.

Much of the argument in court revolved around whether or not rape meant the same thing in English as Swedish.

Assange, dressed in a dark suit, sat behind a glass screen while Robertson argued that the sex was consensual, citing evidence given by one of the women that sexual relations occurred four times over the night after [which] both parties fell asleep. 'It is hyperbolic and irrational to suggest there was wickedness involved.' Robertson also made much of the fact that Assange had made himself available for interview with the Swedish prosecutor, Marianne Ny, on several occasions, even offering to talk by Skype while he was in England.

It seemed like an open and shut case of prejudice: a man-hating prosecutor who bent the rules and sought extradition unreasonably. The problem was, it wasn't true: Ny had in fact sought an interview with Assange, damaging the defence's argument. Assange's case collapsed and Judge Riddle ordered the extradition to go ahead.

Assange had barely left the court when his legal team announced they were heading back to the High Court to appeal the extradition decision. It was set to be a protracted legal fight. Next time the stakes would be much higher and if they lost there would be only two more appeals they could make—the British Supreme Court and finally, if all else failed, the European Court of Human Rights in Strasbourg. The stop after that would be Stockholm.

The reason Assange was resisting extradition to Sweden so vehemently is intriguing. When I spoke to him in December 2010, Assange said he was worried he wouldn't get a fair trial in Sweden. He has a point, part of the hearings would be heard in private, something which Judge Riddle pointed out is 'alien as far as our system is concerned'. He was also concerned about what he said was the close relationship between Swedish intelligence and the United States. If that really concerned him, he's certainly worse off in Britain. There are no two countries closer in intelligence sharing than Britain and the US, with the possible exception of the US and

Israel. It's generally accepted that Britain's extradition laws heavily favour the United States, much more so than in Sweden. In the end, Assange may have been better off just facing the music in Sweden, unless of course his real concern was the strength of the case against him.

Throughout the court hearings it seems that Daniel Ellsberg, though not uncritical of Assange, had been playing the long-distance role of father confessor to him. The two had been in regular contact since Assange came under attack after the 'Collateral Murder' video. Ellsberg had spoken to Assange about the Swedish sexual assault charges and believed that Assange had been telling the truth when he said he was innocent, but he thought he hadn't handled the issue well. It was no use just saying that he didn't do it: he had to explain himself, Ellsberg told Assange. WikiLeaks' 'media handling' had been bad. 'He denies the allegations which is fairly ambiguous because it could mean that he denies that this stuff was illegal, he denies the interpretation of it.' Was Julian Assange denying that the events occurred at all? It was too unspecific and wasn't convincing, he said.

There is often a conflation between the trouble Assange gets into with his work as editor-in-chief of WikiLeaks, and his personal life. Assange himself often points out the need to draw the difference between public issues and personal privacy. And yet, as he stood outside Belmarsh Magistrates Court he blurred the boundaries himself asking why he, as the head of a non-profit organisation, should be subjected to what he believed was unjust treatment. Assange was saying: if you support WikiLeaks you should support me.

* * *

WikiLeaks prides itself in demanding answers to tough questions—but what assessment is to be made of Julian Assange and WikiLeaks itself?

Assange has travelled a long way from Townsville, his nomadic childhood days with his mother and a wandering life in adulthood before arriving on to the world stage. He has turned himself and WikiLeaks into a significant political player, but precisely identifying his politics is difficult.

His world view was shaped by the Australia of the 1970s and 80s, especially its hacker community. He's been described by the US State Department as an anarchist, but that's not how Assange sees himself. Back in May 2010 when we first met, Assange did not answer the question of whether he was an activist or a journalist, pointing out that his objective was what he called an 'end state'—the creation of a 'more just world'. He was goal-driven and it was extremely satisfying to him, he said, 'to push all of my abilities to the very edge in pursuing that goal'. It wasn't exactly a 'whatever it takes' philosophy, but it wasn't far from it, and it indicated a certain kind of hubris.

His beliefs sprawl across the political spectrum, with unlikely support from right-wing libertarians. He is certainly no classic lefty, and appears to be primarily motivated by anti-authoritarianism, not anti-Americanism. His support of the First Amendment is testament to that. It may well be that Julian Assange simply has an Emperor complex, as some former WikiLeaks friends have said. Whatever Assange is politically, he has built an empire of ideas that are intellectually and socially challenging.

Nick Davies, the investigative reporter who landed the cables and war logs deal for the *Guardian* says of Assange: 'He has grown up being the cleverest person in the room.' Lisa, the mother of his daughter, put it this way: Julian 'always wins because he is smarter, and he's right'. He rationalised everything and became upset when someone 'didn't think of his feelings'.

The contradictions in Assange abound. Davies said of him: 'He was brave and I liked him' but as time went by he found he couldn't trust him. Assange didn't seem to understand the 'normal human feelings' that were involved in the betrayal of trust. Davies said Assange had told him when they were in Stockholm together: 'I am somewhere on the autistic side,' and added, apparently jokingly: 'Aren't all men autistic?' Whether or not it was a joke, there are some in the WikiLeaks camp who believe his humorous self-diagnosis could have had a strong element of truth in it and may explain some of his difficulty with both professional and personal relationships. It takes someone with an extraordinary cast of mind and character to make the enemies he has made.

Despite it all, Davies is still intrigued by what Assange has achieved. 'It is like he is in a fantasy world,' he said. He fantasised in Melbourne about creating a system that could take on governments. And that, is what he has done.

Just five years ago, WikiLeaks was a name carefully written on a whiteboard in a Melbourne terrace. The International Subversives made some contribution to the idea that eventually became WikiLeaks, but it was Julian Assange who brought it all together. WikiLeaks harnessed twin powers: Assange's intellect and commitment to social justice, and the emergence of the greatest revolution in communication since the printing press, the Internet. It might be too early to make an assessment of WikiLeaks' impact, but there are many who believe that it has changed the world already. Oddly enough, one of its greatest supporters, Daniel Ellsberg, has his doubts.

Ellsberg is not optimistic that WikiLeaks will win the battle against secrecy and force organisations to be more open. Nor does he believe the secrecy of closed organisations will eventually destroy them, which is the view Assange takes. Ellsberg, who has been championing more open and accountable government for the past forty years has an interesting perspective on why Assange holds the beliefs he does.

'I think it's because he's thirty-nine years old, not seventy-nine years old. I think it's the kind of political naïvety which for me doesn't damn him, it doesn't mean he's worse than a lot of other people, but I really don't agree with it.' Ellsberg believes instead that governments will get more secretive to preserve themselves. He cites the Stalinist regime of the old Soviet Union, which lasted 'only seventy years or so' but it was long enough: 'to kill scores of millions of people'. While he applauds much of the work done by WikiLeaks, what Ellsberg fears is a backlash in the US and the introduction of an Official Secrets Act, which would curtail parts of the First Amendment. If that happened it would be a huge defeat for Assange, whose stated goal is to bring the benefits of free speech enshrined in the First Amendment of the US Constitution to the entire world. The unintended consequences could be that WikiLeaks achieves just the reverse of what it hopes—a lessening of free speech in the United States.

What's significant about WikiLeaks is not that it has leaked material—leaks have occurred for years—but that it has shifted such a huge volume of data into the public domain and it has been able to do this without sources being discovered. (If Bradley Manning is the leaker of the biggest document dump in history, he was only caught because he confessed.) It is the welding of a desire for change and the capability to affect that change that has created such a powerful force. Ellsberg's argument that large organisations and even countries will become more secretive under the threat of WikiLeaks may be right in the long term, but recent examples suggest that in the short term at least there have been great benefits to democratic movements in Tunisia, Egypt, Yemen and Bahrain.

If WikiLeaks had existed before the Second Gulf War it's not unimaginable that the invasion of Iraq may have been averted. There was enough concern inside intelligence agencies, including the CIA, for those working there to plausibly have sent incriminating documents to WikiLeaks. Plenty spoke up after the invasion, but only one, Australia's Andrew Wilkie, an intelligence officer at the federal government's Office of National Assessments, had the courage to quit and reveal the truth publicly *before* the invasion. WikiLeaks has lifted the bar even higher on what the public can expect. Governments cannot be trusted on their say so. Journalists, too, will have to be more demanding of governments if they are to be believed or trusted.

* * *

The cast of characters scattered throughout this book is a who's who of old and new journalism. They were all caught up with the pursuit of truth of a kind, but how they went about it is as interesting as the final outcome. Maybe it was the cutthroat world of journalism, mixed with the new speed of instant communications and huge data drops, that led to some unprincipled behaviour on the part of a number of parties.

It is hard to imagine a greater degree of fear and loathing from people supposedly on the same side of an issue: the disclosure of information the public has the right to know about. Most have been damaged in some way by their experiences in the murky world of cyberspace, where ethics are often whatever you think and theft is covered by a pervasive belief system that information is a free commodity. Many of the actors in this drama, including the *New York Times* and the *Guardian*, have published their own version of their experiences, which is probably as much about getting their version of history out first as it is about settling old scores and comforting themselves that they didn't behave too badly.

The real victim in all this is Bradley Manning, whether he is guilty or not. He had already been accused of illegally downloading classified material, but in early March 2011 further charges were added of 'aiding the enemy', an offence for which he could be sentenced to death. He's been held in solitary confinement for twenty-three hours a day since May 2010 without trial, something his supporters say amounts to psychological torture, an allegation being investigated by the United Nations. For many, Manning is a truth-telling hero, as Ellsberg—a steadying voice of reason throughout—portrays him. For others he's a treasonous villain. The man who dobbed him in, Adrian Lamo, has the dubious distinction of making many of the others involved look honourable. His role as an online celebrity posing as a journalist-turned-informer is probably the least appealing of them all. Lastly, there's Julian Assange, who emerges as a fearless and charismatic character, but also someone who is complex and mercurial. He's either a man of little credence who has fanned the cult of personality around him, or a journalistic saviour, depending on your point of view.

WikiLeaks is now in danger of unravelling. The safe haven for journalists in Iceland, with shielded offshore bank accounts providing protection from vexatious legal action, are still to be achieved and WikiLeaks' financial security is not looking good. In early 2011 the organisation still can't take whistleblower submissions because Assange still doesn't have the keys to the system. Yet whether WikiLeaks survives or not it has spawned a huge number of copies around the world, including websites like Domscheit-Berg's OpenLeaks, making it difficult for authorities to prevent further leaking.

Whatever the future brings for Assange and his organisation, WikiLeaks has provided a new way to achieve better journalism by challenging powerful institutions, be they governments or corporations. There will be difficult issues, as always, over what to publish and what to keep secret. But the old journalistic maxim 'publish and be damned'—a phrase first used by the Duke of Wellington to dismiss a blackmail attempt nearly 200 years ago—seems to capture the feeling of the moment. WikiLeaks and Julian Assange have delivered to journalism an old-fashioned idea reborn: real journalism is simply the disclosure of whatever powerful vested interests want kept secret.

ACKNOWLEDGEMENTS

Sincere thanks to the following people for the various contributions they made during the making of this book. First to Louise Adler, who had the original idea; Publisher, Elisa Berg, who not only kept me on the straight and narrow but seemed to relish telling this story as much as I did; Kate Torney, the ABC Director of News who enthusiastically endorsed the project; Steve Taylor, *Foreign Correspondent* program's Executive Producer, who was equally supportive; Jane Burridge, who helped me negotiate the new world of publishing; *Le Monde*'s Florence Beaugé for her insight into the WikiLeaks affect in North Africa and the Middle East.; Daniel Ellsberg, for his objective analysis; Suelette Dreyfus, for her historical perspective of the Melbourne hacker scene; Mary Ann Jolley, Guy Rundle, Heather Forbes, Lorelei Vashti, Gillian Hutchison, Mark Davis, Paul Williams, Peter Cronau, Phil Dorling, Wayne Harley and Pete Curtis for their assistance and encouragement; also to Julian Assange for challenging the orthodox. And my wife, Pamela and our daughters, Elouise and Sophie, who kept me sane and provided invaluable feedback.

NOTES

Some interviews were conducted in confidence, and the names of the interviewees are withheld by mutual agreement.

INTRODUCTION

p. xi 'These charges against him in Sweden are absurd and were judged absurd by a senior Swedish prosecutor' John Pilger, in author's notes, December 2010.

p. xii 'He'd just come out of nowhere and flop for a few days … then he'd be gone' Interview with anonymous author source, August 2010.

p. xiii He was 'not safe physically wherever he is' ABC TV, *Foreign Correspondent*, May 2010.

p. xiii one of his friends confided, 'He enjoys taking risks' Interview with anonymous author source, August 2010.

NOTES

p. xiii 'The citizenry have a right to scrutinise the state' Julian Assange, televised speech, Federation Square, Melbourne, 4 February 2011.

p. xv Assange … had been asked whether he thought his life would ever return to normal. 'I hope not,' he replied Julian Assange, in author's notes, December 2010.

CHAPTER 1

p. 2 She'd had a tempestuous relationship with her father, and has been described as 'very strong-willed' *Northern Star*, July 2010.

p. 2 He is remembered by one person who worked with him as a 'staunch traditionalist' *Northern Star*, 'WikiLeaks Founder's Lismore Roots', 29 July 2010.

p. 3 She wrote that she lived 'in a bikini' and was 'going native with my baby and other mums on the island' Magnetic Island Visitors Centre guestbook.

p. 3 Together they travelled around Australia with Christine's puppetry company, spending much of their time 'in Lismore and the Adelaide Hills' Christine Assange, author interview, February 2011.

p. 3 they had to 'slash [their] way to the front door with a machete' Magnetic Island Visitors Centre guestbook.

p. 4 'He was a geeky, smart kid' *Northern Star*, op. cit.

p. 4 'He always stood up for the underdog' Brett Assange interview, Channel Seven news, December 2010.

p. 4 'We were travelling and touring around many different places, so this was quite a rich environment' Julian Assange, author interview, May 2010.

p. 4 'We try to develop free thinkers and people of independent thought here and Julian would be the ultimate example of that' *Northern Star*, op. cit.

p. 6 It was said Dr Johnson's goal was to 'understand the meaning of life' Parnaby, Owen, biography of Johnson, Raynor Carey (1901–1987) in *The Australian Dictionary of Biography*, Volume 17, Melbourne University Press, Carlton, 2007, pp 590–591.

p. 7 'Bleached blonde hair singing like the Von Trapp family ...' Channel Nine, *Sixty Minutes*, October 2009.

p. 8 'We watched them trying to stifle their sobs, trying to be brave' Hamilton-Byrne, Sarah, *Unseen, Unheard, Unknown*, Penguin, Australia, 1995.

p. 9 Assange said neither he, nor his mother or half-brother, had ever been involved in the cult Julian Assange, author interview, May 2010.

p. 9 For Christine that was more than enough evidence Christine Assange, author interview, January 2011.

p. 10 Assange said he was told Hamilton used several different identities Julian Assange, author interview, May 2010.

p. 10 'children with IQs up to 150 get along in the ordinary course of school life quite well, achieving excellent marks without serious effort' IQ.org, http://web.archive.org/web/20071020051936/http:/iq.org/#WilliamJamesSidis

p. 11 Assange had an IQ 'in excess of 170' *Sydney Morning Herald*, 'The Geek Who Shook the World', 12 December 2010.

p. 11 He said he liked learning 'and telling people what I learnt' Julian Assange, author interview, May 2010.

NOTES

p. 11 'We were bright sensitive kids who didn't fit into the dominant subculture and fiercely castigated those who did as irredeemable boneheads' Khatchadourian, Raffi, 'No Secrets', *New Yorker*, 7 June 2010.

p. 13 'Back then there was no Internet' Julian Assange, author interview, May 2010.

p. 15 'We were watching them watching us' Ken Day, author interview, May 2010.

p. 15 like a shipwrecked man washed ashore on a Tahitian island Dreyfus, Suelette, *Underground*, Reed, Australia, 1997.

p. 17 'They were into the core systems, the heart of our comms' Ken Day, author interview, May 2010.

p. 18 it was an 'extremely educational experience' Julian Assange, author interview, May 2010.

p. 18 Assange vividly recalls the siren from the local fire brigade sounding like 'the start of World War Three' ibid.

p. 19 He claimed that they were bound by 'ethical codes and ethical standards' ibid.

p. 19 'We had total control' ibid.

CHAPTER 2

p. 24 an individual's right to 'privacy is necessary for an open society in the electronic age' Hughes, Eric, *Cypherpunk Manifesto*, 9 March 1993, published at http://www.activism.net/cypherpunk/manifesto.html

p. 25 'What you have then is a Church based on brainwashing yuppies and other people with more money than sense' Cryptome, http://cryptome.org/

p. 26 He wrote that 'censorship, concealment and revelation (for a fee) is the Church's raison d'etre' ibid.

p. 27 The Church had already won several court cases by what Assange called 'its manipulation of the legal system' ibid.

p. 29 the FBI, the NSA and the Department of Justice were demanding tough laws Zimmerman, Philip, 'PGP for Personal Privacy', published at http://www.philzimmermann.com/

p. 30 he 'wanted cryptography to be made available to the American public before it became illegal to use it' US Senate testimony, http://www.philzimmermann.com/EN/testimony/index.html

p. 30 'The government has a track record that does not inspire confidence that they will never abuse our civil liberties' ibid.

p. 31 'I want to read you a quote from some email I got in October 1993' ibid.

p. 32 'put it in a frame and put it on your wall to remind you to be a good boy for the next three years' Melbourne County Court judgement.

p. 32 'It's an unusual experience when the judge says "the prisoner will rise" and no one else stands up' Julian Assange, author interview, May 2010.

p. 35 'We like to put up original documents so people can make up their own minds' Wired magazine, October 1999.

p. 36 'It's the greatest thing since love' Wired magazine, January 1999.

p. 36 Readers Digest described the website as 'an invitation to terrorists' Cryptome, op. cit.

p. 38 Assange signed off his Cypherpunks message quoting the French aviator and author, Antoine de Saint-Exupery ibid.

p. 38 [Assange] insists that though he worked for large corporations he only did consultancy work Julian Assange, author interview, December 2010.

p. 39 'Normally NGOs beg, but I'm no good at that sort of thing' Cryptome, op. cit.

p. 40 He formed a particularly close relationship with one woman student, Lisa. Lisa is not her real name.

p. 40 'He was special to know' 'Lisa', author interview, September 2010.

p. 42 In other words, Julian Assange was asking the founder of Cryptome ... to be the silent partner in his venture Cryptome, op. cit.

p. 43 'As soon as you have opened your mind to a malcontent you have given him the material with which to content himself' ibid.

CHAPTER 3

p. 45 Riseup ... promises to provide 'secure communication' for people involved in 'struggles for liberation' Riseup, https://riseup.net/

p. 45 Part of its recruitment drive assured supporters in emails that Riseup had an established lawyer and 'plenty of backbone' Internal WikiLeaks emails published by Cryptome, http://cryptome.org/

p. 45 WikiLeaks would also cater for those in the West 'who wish to reveal illegal or immoral behaviour in their own governments and corporations' ibid.

p. 45 WikiLeaks aimed for 'maximum political impact' ibid.

p. 46 It was also, they declared 'within our means to achieve' ibid.

p. 46 WikiLeaks wanted Riseup to be one of the 'stable and trustworthy' ibid.

p. 46 a 'deniable drop off' ibid.

p. 46 A 'regular drop' ibid.

p. 47 CJ Hinke ... confirmed he had regularly been consulted by WikiLeaks 'on such issues as credibility and importance of leaked materials' *Wired* magazine, September 2009.

p. 47 But that he has since developed 'great regard and trust for their mission' ibid.

p. 49 Ellsberg's recent statements on leaking had been followed with 'interest and delight' Internal WikiLeaks email published by Cryptome, op. cit.

p. 49 Assange informed Ellsberg that WikiLeaks had crossed over from 'prospective' to 'projective' ibid.

p. 50 Ellsberg had said to himself: 'Who's this coming out of the blue?' Daniel Ellsberg, author interview, January 2011.

p. 50 'I didn't get anything back and then I just put it out of my mind; I just didn't think it would come to much' ibid.

p. 50 Ellsberg would have provided a much-needed guiding hand as the WikiLeaks activists struggled to define the organisation and its 'new kind of journalism' Internal WikiLeaks emails published by Cryptome, op. cit.

p. 51 There was no easy way for the reader to check 'whether they are being lied to by the journalists' Julian Assange, author interview, May 2010.

p. 51 Assange said that many organisations involved in the reconstruction only had 'three or four days' ibid.

p. 53 'There he is, flame on his chin, holy book in his hand and anti-aircraft cannon between his legs' Internal WikiLeaks emails published by Cryptome, op. cit.

p. 54 [Assange] was concerned about the readership, which, though large, 'tends to pal up on one pew and sometimes even sings and claps' ibid.

p. 55 'until all is dancing confetti and the truth' ibid.

p. 56 'Only revealed injustice can be answered; for man to do anything intelligent he has to know what's actually going on' IQ.org, 31 December 2006.

p. 59 'Every person is the ultimate arbiter of justice in their own conscience' Internal WikiLeaks emails published by Cryptome, op. cit.

CHAPTER 4

p. 62 he was 'haunted by demons' which revealed themselves by the fact he had 'massive trouble sleeping' Lisa, author interview, September 2010.

p. 65 Freedom of Information requests they carried out later unearthed a trail of decisions made by 'radical feminists' Christine Assange, author interview, January 2011.

p. 66 [Assange's] 'technical advice' and support assisted in the 'prosecution of persons suspected of publishing and distributing child pornography on the Internet' Age, 'Assange Helped Our Police Catch Child Pornographers', 12 February 2011.

p. 66 according to Christine, her son also put his technical expertise to use helping Victorian police 'remove a book on the Internet about how to build a bomb' Christine Assange, author interview, February 2011.

p. 66 he thought the idea of leaking government documents 'to the entire world' was a 'ridiculous concept' Crikey, 'Daniel Assange: I Never Thought WikiLeaks Would Succeed', 17 September 2010.

p. 67 'I support similarly minded people, not because they are moral agents, but because they have common cause with my own feelings and dreams' Cryptome, http://cryptome.org/

p. 67 'He gets easily frustrated with people who aren't capable of working up to his level' *Crikey*, op. cit.

p. 73 [Elmer] said he had witnessed 'practices used by the Julius Bäer bank to evade or reduce its own tax payments' *Der Spiegel*, 3 March 2008.

p. 78 'The identification, exposure, or termination of employment of or legal actions against current or former insiders, leakers or whistleblowers' WikiLeaks, 'US Intelligence Planned to Destroy WikiLeaks', 15 March 2010.

p. 79 According to a 'Manual of Justice', purportedly written by Scientology founder L Ron Hubbard The Register, http://www.theregister.co.uk/

p. 80 It was unlawful to 'reproduce or distribute someone else's copyrighted work without that person's authorisation' ibid.

p. 85 'These acts were ordered, directed or coordinated by the top leadership of the Kenya police acting jointly with a common purpose' The Kenyan National Commission on Human Rights, 'Cry of Blood', September 2008.

CHAPTER 5

p. 90 The message was simply relayed to Hrafnsson: 'We were supposedly breaching bank secrecy laws' Kristinn Hrafnsson, author interview, May 2010.

p. 90 'Those very few that dare to question this insanity, they will be just basically character assassinated' Birgitta Jonsdottir, author interview, November 2010.

p. 92 'Legal obstacles, which cannot be identified … proceedings, which cannot be mentioned …' *Guardian*, 'Guardian Gagged from Reporting Parliament', 12 October 2009.

p. 92 It can also encourage what Geoffrey Robertson called 'libel tourism' *University Observer*, February 2010.

p. 93 The *Guardian* revealed to its readers it had been forbidden from telling them *Guardian*, op. cit.

p. 93 Assange argued that the secret gag order against the Trafigura report, 'remains in effect' WikiLeaks, '*Guardian* Still Under Secret Toxic Waste Gag', 14 October 2009.

p. 94 'A number of news organisations have got the facts wrong' Transforming Freedom, www.transformingfreedom.org

p. 96 As we chat in a Reykjavik café she remembers how well Assange and Domscheit-Berg performed Birgitta Jonsdottir, author interview, November 2010.

p. 97 Domscheit-Berg told me he'd been approached by a friend who 'had genuine interest in changing the world for something better' Daniel Domscheit-Berg, author interview, November 2010.

p. 97 '… we have to do the same thing in order to protect our sources [from] malicious, vexatious lawsuits affecting our ability to continue' Julian Assange, author interview, May 2010.

p. 99 'They were saying, "Yes, let's do this"' Birgitta Jonsdottir, author interview, November 2010.

p. 99 'Why don't one of you come there with me' ibid.

p. 100 Watson noted that the Icelandic delegation believed that if the Icesave issue wasn't resolved soon and Iceland defaulted on its loans it would 'set Iceland back thirty years' Wikileaks, 'Classified cable from US Embassy Reykjavik on Icesave', 13 January 2010.

CHAPTER 6

p. 105 Jonsdottir asked: "Can you help us do some video editing?" Gudmundur Ragnar Gudmundsson, author interview, November 2010.

p. 106 'I am in the helicopter, I am the member of the crew' ibid.

p. 106 'We originally thought this was a video about Afghanistan' interview transcript, Julian Assange, interview with Rhonda Pence, Press TV, *A World Beyond Borders*, 4 November 2010.

p. 107 'I could easily identify with those children because they are a similar age as my own' ABC TV, *Foreign Correspondent*, May 2010.

p. 107 'I didn't give up my job under the premise that I would never earn any money' Daniel Domscheit-Berg, author interview, November 2010.

p. 107 Assange started to move against Domscheit-Berg 'because his presence was causing problems' Julian Assange, author interview, December 2010.

p. 108 Assange admits that he 'engineered' a way that Domscheit-Berg 'would be kept away from more delicate things that we were doing' ibid.

p. 108 'It was just too tense, and it just became more aggressive and aggressive every day' Daniel Domscheit-Berg, author interview, November 2010.

p. 108 'It was very difficult; I walked out three times' Birgitta Jonsdottir, author interview, November 2010.

p. 109 Julian can deal with incredibly little sleep and a hell of a lot of chaos, but even he has his limits and I could see that he was stretching himself' Khatchadourian, Raffi, 'No Secrets', *New Yorker*, 7 June 2010.

p. 110 'Julian, there is something not right here' Birgitta Jonsdottir, author interview, November 2010.

p. 110 'I know for sure that there are no tapped phone conversations' ibid.

p. 111 'How can that be cool, you know that a 17-year-old kid has accumulated through shady dealings, with shady companies, three cars?' ibid.

p. 111 sending tweets worldwide and a letter 'to the Icelandic press about the Icelandic authorities collaborating with the CIA' ibid.

p. 111 Jonsdottir was blunt: the allegation was 'a load of bollocks' ibid.

p. 112 'Icelandic journalists have been unable to substantiate his claims' *Columbia Journalism Review*, 'Thin Ice', 1 April 2010.

p. 112 'Julian was getting ready to go on stage in the United States in front of the firing squad' Gudmundur Ragnar Gudmundsson, author interview, November 2010.

p. 112 'At the same time, we are displaying them as monsters,' one of the editors said Khatchadourian, Raffi, op. cit.

p. 113 'Are you crying? ibid.

p. 113 'Julian didn't want at that time to be practical, his mind was already in the States, he was already there preparing' ibid.

p. 113 'I actually didn't want him to take any computers along with him' Gudmundur Ragnar Gudmundsson, author interview, November 2010.

p. 114 'When you're dealing with a big bureaucratic state they just cannot respond that quickly' Julian Assange, author interview, December 2010.

p. 114 'The promise that we make to our sources' *Colbert Report*, 13 April 2010.

p. 115 He admitted to being 'a little bit worried' Julian Assange, author interview, December 2010.

p. 115 Assange took the floor, telling the assembled media that what they were about to see was 'a very rich story' Michael Collins, Democratic Underground.com, 5 April, 2010.

p. 117 'They are still traumatised and still suffer from the pain of their wounds' Interview (not broadcast) for *Foreign Correspondent*, ABC TV, April 2010.

p. 118 war as seen 'through a soda straw' *Los Angeles Times*, 'Gates Says Video of US Helicopter Attack in Iraq Out of Context', 14 April 2010.

p. 118 'When you have unarmed people including a wounded prostrate man on the ground ...' Julian Assange, author interview, May 2010.

p. 119 'We think the safest way to cover these operations is to be embedded with US forces' *Washington Post*, 'Military's Killing of Two Journalists in Iraq Detailed in New Book', 15 September 2009.

p. 119 Asked if he could say when he saw the video Finkel said, 'I can't' ABC TV, *Foreign Correspondent*, May 2010.

p. 119 'I assume they had the video, you know, close back to 2007 when these events happened' Julian Assange, author interview, December 2010.

p. 120 'They didn't show the actual shooting of the people' ABC TV, *Foreign Correspondent*, May 2010.

p. 120 the correspondent said they were doing that 'out of respect for the relatives' ibid.

p. 122 'I don't feel that the attack on the van was warranted' ABC TV, *Lateline*, April 2010.

CHAPTER 7

p. 127 'Should there be a centralised, automated, national censorship system between every newspaper and its reader ...?' Julian Assange, author interview, May 2010.

p. 128 'Ah journalists,' he smiled. 'Can't do an interview without a drink!' author's note, May 2010.

p. 130 He was also sent to a chaplain after officers noticed what was called 'odd behaviors' ABC News America, 29 November 2010.

p. 131 'Take me for who I am, or face the consequences!' Bradley Manning's Facebook page.

p. 131 Lamo said it was a sure way of discovering whether someone was a fake Adrian Lamo, author interview, June 2010.

p. 134 'I want people to see the truth, regardless of who they are ...' *Wired* magazine, Lamo chatlogs.

p. 134 'The American military said in a statement late Thursday that eleven people had been killed' *New York Times*, 'Two Iraqi Journalists Killed as US Forces Clash with Militia', 13 July 2007.

p. 137 He has also asserted that Assange 'groomed' Manning, Adrian Lamo, author interview, June 2010.

p. 137 'I have encouraged people to donate and I still do' ibid.

p. 136 he was grabbing what he could and 'firing bullets into the air without thought to the consequences of where they might land or who they might hit' Adrian Lamo, author interview, June 2010.

p. 136 the first contact from Manning came 'out of the blue' ibid.

p. 136 Manning contacted him via Twitter *Salon.com*, http://www.salon.com/news/opinion/glenn_greenwald/2010/06/18/wikileaks

p. 137 given access to a 'special servers' reserved for those who submitted the most sensitive documents Adrian Lamo, author interview, June 2010.

p. 139 'None of us knew that Bradley Manning was under arrest' Birgitta Jonsdottir, author interview, November 2010.

p. 140 'Leaking is inherently an anti-authoritarian act, it is inherently an anarchist act' ABC TV, *Foreign Correspondent*, June 2010.

p. 140 something Ellsberg jokingly put down to 'the Australian accent' Daniel Ellsberg, author interview, January 2011.

p. 141 'The Pentagon was of the belief that I was carrying two-hundred–and-sixty thousand classified US cables in my pocket and a whole bunch of other things' Julian Assange, author interview, December 2010.

p. 141 'We started hearing the reports that they were hunting for me' ibid.

p. 142 'He was genuinely concerned about being killed by the Americans' author note, August 2010.

p. 142 It would cause an 'uproar' Julian Assange, author interview, December 2010.

p. 143 'While I was on the train going under the Channel, I had tried to work out what I would say to him' *Columbia Journalism Review*, 28 July 2010.

p. 144 'He taught us we couldn't trust him' Nick Davies, author interview, February 2011.

NOTES

CHAPTER 8

p. 146 Schmitt had covered the military for many years and Keller saw him as a journalist with 'excellent judgment and an unflappable demeanor' *New York Times*, 'Dealing with Assange and the WikiLeaks Secrets', 26 January 2011.

p. 148 'He smelled as if he hadn't bathed in days' ibid.

p. 149 'Open a second spreadsheet' ibid.

p. 149 he was 'running around like he had like a shop … selling cigarettes' Daniel Domscheit-Berg, author interview, November 2010.

p. 149 Domscheit-Berg said that Assange had shown the New York Times some of the other cables he had Domscheit-Berg, Daniel, *Inside WikiLeaks*, Scribe, Melbourne, 2011.

p. 151 For Davies it was an experience to see a group of journalists working so closely together *Columbia Journalism Review*, 'The Story Behind the Publication of WikiLeaks' Afghanistan Logs', 28 July 2010.

p. 151 Assange was still 'spooked' by reports from the US the previous month that the Pentagon had launched a manhunt for him Interview with anonymous author source, August 2010.

p. 151 some of the reporters had the impression that Assange was ready to publish the documents on the WikiLeaks site immediately *Columbia Journalism Review*, op. cit.

p. 152 'We were starting from: "Here's a document. How much of it shall we print?" Ellison, Sarah, *Vanity Fair*, 'The Man Who Spilled the Secrets', February 2011.

p. 152 'Five days before publication the Spiegel guys asked me how far we are with the redaction' Daniel Domscheit-Berg, author interview, November 2010.

p. 152 'I asked the people that were processing the material making it ready for publication, and they said "we don't know anything about this"' ibid.

p. 153 'Man we're talking about ninety thousand documents here' ibid.

p. 153 recommendations made … 'on the identification of innocents for this material if it is willing to provide reviewers' *News.com*, 'Accused WikiLeaks Source Had Help, Says Hacker', 2 August 2010

p. 153 'I certainly didn't consider this a serious and realistic offer to the White House to vet any of the documents before they were to be posted' ibid.

p. 154 'If you think you have a hot phone, you charge the battery up fully, and then you post it overseas' SBS, *Dateline*, August 2010.

p. 154 He was 'pretty much doing something that his family did when they were involved in theatre and movie business' ibid.

p. 156 'I'm untouchable now in this country' ibid.

p. 157 WikiLeaks had 'tried hard to make sure that this material does not put innocents at harm' Frontline Club press conference, July 2010.

p. 157 Assange dismissed the group as 'people who prefer to do nothing but cover their asses' *Wall Street Journal*, 'Rights Groups Join Criticism of WikiLeaks, 9 August 2010.

p. 158 Assange said WikiLeaks had taken his advice and done a 'much bigger job of redaction' on the next tranche of documents they were about to release Daniel Ellsberg, author interview, January 2011.

p. 158 He had also gained a reputation, as Bill Keller pointed out, as someone who was 'smart and well educated, extremely adept technologically but arrogant, thin-skinned, conspiratorial and oddly credulous' *New York Times*, op. cit.

p. 158 'That's why I do what I do and the way that I do it' Julian Assange, author interview, May 2010.

p. 158 Yet despite his criticisms, he spoke of working on the Afghan War Logs 'in a collaborative basement' and identified the three outlets ... 'media partners' NPR.org, 'Leaked Reports Paint "An Unvarnished and Grim Look at the Afghan War"', 26 July 2010.

p. 159 'I've seen Julian Assange in the last couple of days kind of flouncing around talking about this collaboration like the four of us were working all this together' *Columbia Journalism Review*, op. cit.

p. 159 'He's making it sound like this was some sort of journalistic enterprise between WikiLeaks, the *New York Times*, the *Guardian*, and *Der Spiegel*' ibid.

p. 159 'Did it come from Bradley Manning?' ibid.

p. 160 'The battlefield consequences of the release of these documents are potentially severe and dangerous for our troops ...' *Military Veterans and Foreign Affairs Journal*, 29 July 2010.

p. 160 '... the truth is they might already have on their hands the blood of some young soldier or that of an Afghan family' ibid.

p. 160 The *New York Times* reported ... lawyers 'are exploring whether Mr Assange and WikiLeaks could be charged with inducing or conspiring in violations of the Espionage Act' *New York Times*, 'US Military Scrutinizes Leaks for Risks to Afghans,' 28 July 2010.

p. 161 Keller reported that Assange was 'openly contemptuous of the American government' *New York Times*, op. cit.

p. 161 When he was asked specifically if he had ever directly contacted Bradley Manning, Assange replied 'No' Julian Assange, author interview, December 2010.

p. 162 'So if they're trying to say I conspired with Bradley Manning ...' ibid.

p. 162 He understood that the *New York Times* may 'need to be not truthful because of threats' ibid.

p. 162 'We reject collaboration or revelation ... protected by us, he wrote' *WikiLeaks: Inside Julian Assange's War on Secrecy*, Guardian Books, 2011

p. 166 'We aren't involved in that,' one of the FBI agents said CNET.com, 'Researcher Detained at US Border, Questioned about WikiLeaks', 31 July 2010.

p. 163 'There's no doubt about that' *Walkley Foundation* magazine, January 2011

p. 166 Assange says he only posted the file so he could have confidence in WikiLeaks' ability to withstand what he called 'even a massive multi-continental roundup' Julian Assange, author interview, December 2010.

p. 167 'limiting his travels across international borders' *Daily Beast*, 'US Urges Allies to Crack Down on WikiLeaks', 10 August 2010.

p. 167 WikiLeaks could have 'committed serious criminal offence' *Age*, 'WikiLeaks Head Attacked by ADA', 28 July 2010.

CHAPTER 9

p. 168 she'd been connected with 'US-financed anti-Castro and anti-communist groups in Cuba' *Counterpunch*, September 2010.

p. 176 Assange said that as WikiLeaks, grew Domscheit-Berg's 'stature' and power grew more and more 'unstable' Julian Assange, author interview, December 2010.

p. 176 'because they were comfortable about women' Christine Assange, author interview, February 2011.

p. 176 Assange had come up against what she called the 'Scandinavian female' Birgitta Jonsdottir, author interview, November 2010.

p. 176 'If a guy acts in a certain way to a Scandinavian female, he is going to encounter big trouble, particularly when it comes to sexuality, and the boundaries' ibid.

p. 177 Birgitta described Assange as a 'wild child' ibid.

p. 177 'I don't want to get into that, it's too personal' ibid.

p. 177 He added that it hadn't 'backfired too many times' Julian Assange, author interview, December 2010.

p. 178 Assange had also given him some advice when he met his wife that he should 'get as much dirt' on her as he could Daniel Domscheit-Berg, author interview, November 2010.

p. 178 Jonsdottir says she has 'seen guys that were critical of him' meet Assange and be turned around in a few minutes Birgitta Jonsdottir, author interview, November 2010.

p. 178 'If your actions result in the terminating, incarceration or execution of my sources I will kill you' Julian Assange, author interview, December 2010.

p. 178 Assange said he had 'warned him on numerous occasions previously [about not] taking care of some security procedures or sources' Daniel Domscheit-Berg, author interview, December 2010.

p. 179 'At the time I meant it, yes. At the time that was the feeling' Julian Assange, author interview, December 2010.

p. 179 'It might be a good precedent to set for all our staff' ibid.

p. 179 He said that Assange thought of him as 'like a dog' that he needed to be 'contained' Daniel Domscheit-Berg, author interview, November 2010.

p. 179 Domscheit-Berg wrote that anyone who offered too much criticism was punished by having his rights suspended Domscheit-Berg, Daniel, *Inside Wikileaks*, Scribe, Melbourne, 2011.

p. 180 'We have certain responsibilities for this money, and we are taking this seriously' *Wired* magazine, December 2010.

p. 181 The demands for financial scrutiny came not only from those who opposed WikiLeaks activities in principle Cryptome, http://cryptome.org/

p. 182 The Wau Holland foundation would reveal it had paid more than '€100,000 in salaries for 2010, including about €66,000 to Mr Assange' *Wall Street Journal*, 'WikiLeaks Spending Ballooned, Data Show', 24 December 2010.

p. 184 He said WikiLeaks needed a 'charter', a 'strategy' and an end game Ken Day, author interview, May 2010.

p. 185 'disclosing classified information concerning "national defense" with reason to believe that the information could cause 'injury to the United States' US Military charge sheet.

p. 187 'I got a flurry of urgent phone calls and texts saying "you've got to meet him, he wants to meet you"' Iain Overton, author interview, December 2010.

p. 187 'I kind of kept on disappearing out' ibid.

p. 189 Overton said he was sure Leigh was 'pissed off' about it ibid.

p. 189 'The *Guardian* doesn't care that the government know' Julian Assange, author interview, December 2010.

CHAPTER 10

p. 192 'erratic and imperious behavior and a nearly delusional grandeur' *New York Times*, 'WikiLeaks Founder on the Run, Chased by Turmoil', 23 October 2010.

p. 193 'I am the heart and soul of this organisation' *Wired* magazine, September 2010.

p. 193 'I said I thought he was absolutely right in being mad at John Burns' Daniel Ellsberg, author interview, January 2011.

p. 194 At Der Spiegel, there was a growing sense of discomfort Interview with anonymous author source, February 2011.

p. 195 'Does the *New York Times* have a copy?' *Der Spiegel*, 'An Inside Look at Difficult Negotiations with Julian Assange', 28 January 2011.

p. 195 'What's the point in making an agreement if people will dishonour it?' Julian Assange, author interview, December 2010.

p. 196 Understandably nervous that it might be shut out of Cablegate again, it asked the *Guardian* for a copy Interview with anonymous author source, February 2011.

p. 197 'We're good at working together, we like each other' Leigh, David, and Luke Harding *WikiLeaks: Inside Julian Assange's War on Secrecy*, Guardian Books, UK, 2011.

p. 197 'He is genuinely interested in the journalism that he does, that is a big tick from me' Julian Assange, author interview, December 2010.

p. 198 with 'too many cables coming out too quickly' this would 'saturate the market' Julian Assange, author interview, December 2010.

p. 198 'We would have the *Guardian* and the *New York Times* campaigning against us' ibid.

p. 200 the 'hard drives were empty [and] there was nothing there' ibid.

p. 200 'What access codes?' Daniel Domscheit-Berg, author interview, November 2010.

p. 202 'It appears that the State Department thought we had a lot more than we did' Julian Assange, author interview, December 2010.

p. 203 After they passed through security, they were shown into a 'windowless room' *New York Times*, 'Dealing with Assange and the WikiLeaks Secrets', 26 January 2011.

p. 203 It was 'fair to say the mood was tense' according to Keller ibid.

p. 204 'I am criticising those who stole this material' *Der Spiegel*, op. cit.

p. 205 *Der Spiegel*'s headline followed the *Guardian*'s global perspective *Der Spiegel*, 'The US Diplomatic Leaks: A Superpower's View of the World', 28 November 2010.

p. 207 It would allow the US to 'prepare their own spin' now that it knew the identity of the cables, and thus the material they contained Julian Assange, author interview, December 2010.

p. 208 If the US military computer logs line up with 'every goddamn record of what we release that's very strong evidence,' he said. ibid.

p. 209 'There is nothing laudable about endangering innocent people' Hillary Clinton, NPR news, December 2010.

p. 209 He called on 'any other company or organisation that is hosting WikiLeaks to immediately terminate its relationship with them' *Guardian*, 'WikiLeaks Website Pulled by Amazon after US Political Pressure', 2 December 2010.

p. 210 if Amazon was 'so uncomfortable with the First Amendment, they should get out of the business of selling books' WikiLeaks, Twitter, 2 December 2010.

p. 210 'They've put American lives at risk' Politico.com, 'Mike Huckabee: Leaker Should Be Executed', 30 November 2010.

p. 210 'He is an anti-American operative with blood on his hands' Sarah Palin, Facebook.

p. 210 'Well I think Assange should be assassinated actually' *Age*, 'The Noose Tightens around Assange', 3 December 2010.

p. 212 he 'had nowhere to go', 'was instantly recognisable' Mark Stephens in author's notes, 7 December 2010.

p. 212 'Many people believe Mr Assange to be innocent, myself included' ibid.

p. 213 'We now know that Visa, MasterCard and PayPal are instruments of US foreign policy' *Telegraph*, 'WikiLeaks: Julian Assange Says Visa and MasterCard are "Instruments of US Foreign Policy"', 14 December 2010.

p. 214 Assange left a spirited message on Ellsberg's phone, saying he was 'calling from a Norman Basement Slammer' Julian Assange in author's note, December 2010.

p. 214 'He's not interested in advice' Seymour Hersh, author interview, December 2010.

p. 215 ' ... the administration felt compelled to say publicly that the revelations had seriously damaged American interests' Reuters, 'US Officials Privately Say WikiLeaks Damage Limited', 18 January 2011.

p. 215 internal US Government reviews of Cablegate had determined that the leaks had caused only 'limited damage to US interests abroad' ibid.

p. 216 his identity should be guarded as a 'protected' source *Sydney Morning Herald*, 'Arbib Revealed as Secret US Source', 9 December 2010.

p. 216 'To aggressively attempt … fearless press' Walkley Foundation magazine, December 2010.

p. 218 'During my time in solitary confinement in the bottom of a Victorian prison I had time to reflect' Julian Assange in author's note, December 2010.

CHAPTER 11

p. 222 'I have not done anything that can be considered criminal' ABC radio, *PM*, January 2011.

p. 222 'an outrageous attack by the Obama administration on the privacy and free speech rights of Twitter's customers' *Sydney Morning Herald*, 'US Court to Hear Twitter-WikiLeaks case', 15 February, 2011.

p. 222 the public's ability to 'participate meaningfully in this ongoing debate' Electronic Frontiers Foundation, https://www.eff.org/files/filenode/dorders_twitter/Motiontounseal.FILEDversion.pdf

p. 223 WikiLeaks described the hearing as 'the first round in the US Government's legal battle against Julian Assange' *Daily Telegraph*, 'Julian Assange Blasts US Bid for WikiLeaks–Twitter Information', 15 February 2011.

p. 224 'It was as if for the first time someone told the Tunisians "You are not insane. You are right to hate him"' Florence Beaugé, author interview, February 2011.

p. 224 Even Bill Keller from the *New York Times* was fulsome in his praise *New York Times*, 'Dealing with Assange and the WikiLeaks secrets', 26 January 2011.

NOTES

p. 225 police brutality was 'routine and pervasive' WikiLeaks, http://wikileaks.ch/cable/2009/01/09CAIRO79.html

p. 225 Secretary of State Hillary Clinton made special mention of Tunisia and Egypt, naming them as countries where the 'free flow of information' was threatened Newseum, http://www.newseum.org/news/2010/01/clinton-urges-global-internet-freedom.html

p. 226 Assange was buoyed by her comments Julian Assange, author interview, May 2010.

p. 226 'They're annoyed by people publishing; they're annoyed by a free press' ibid.

p. 226 According to US author Jonathan Alter, Obama was 'fearsome' on the subject Politico.com, 'Justice Dept. Cracks Down on Leaks', 25 May 2010

p. 227 'They're going after this at every opportunity and with unmatched vigor,' Politico.com, ibid.

p. 228 the media in Sweden had "turned very hostile" towards Assange *Age*, 'Assange appeal gets under way', 8 February 2011.

p. 228 one of the women who accused Assange of rape had let him carry on having sex with her when she woke up even though he wasn't wearing a condom ibid.

p. 228 The Swedes wanted Assange for questioning and possible prosecution for 'unlawful coercion' *New Statesman*, 'Why Assange Lost', 28 February 2011.

p. 229 'It is hyperbolic and irrational to suggest there was wickedness involved' *Age*, op. cit.

p. 229 Judge Riddle pointed out ... "alien as far as our system is concerned" *Guardian*, 24 February, 2011.

NOTES

p. 230 'He denies the allegations which is fairly ambiguous' Daniel Ellsberg, author interview, January 2011.

p. 232 'He has grown up being the cleverest person in the room' Nick Davies, author interview, February 2011.

p. 232 Julian 'always wins because he is smarter, and he's right' 'Lisa', author interview, September 2010.

p. 232 'I am somewhere on the autistic side' Nick Davies, author interview, January 2011.

p. 233 Ellsberg is not optimistic that WikiLeaks will win the battle against secrecy and force organisations to be more open Daniel Ellsberg, author interview, January 2011.

INDEX

INDEX

INDEX

INDEX

INDEX